Transforming Universities

Higher Education Policy Series
Edited by Maurice Kogan

Higher education is now the subject of far reaching and rapid policy change. This series will be of value to those who have to manage that change, as well as to consumers and evaluators of higher education in the UK and elsewhere. It offers information and analysis of new developments in a concise and usable form. It also provides reflective accounts of the impacts of higher education policy. Higher education administrators, governors and policy makers will use it, as well as students and specialists in education policy.

Maurice Kogan is Professor of Government and Social Administration at Brunel University and Joint Director of the Centre for the Evaluation of Public Policy and Practice.

Higher Education Policy Series 48

Transforming Universities

Changing Patterns of Governance, Structure and Learning in Swedish Higher Education

Marianne Bauer, Berit Askling,
Susan Gerard Marton and Ference Marton

Jessica Kingsley Publishers
London and Philadelphia

The right of Marianne Bauer, Berit Askling, Susan Gerard Marton and Ference Marton to be identified as authors of this work has been asserted by them in accordance with the Copyright, Designs and Patents Act 1988.

First published in the United Kingdom in 1999 by
Jessica Kingsley Publishers Ltd,
116 Pentonville Road,
London N1 9JB, England

and

325 Chestnut Street,
Philadelphia
PA 19106, USA

www.jkp.com

© Copyright 1999 Jessica Kingsley Publishers

Library of Congress Cataloging in Publication Data

A CIP catalog record for this book is available from the Library of Congress

British Library Cataloguing in Publication Data

Transforming universities : changing patterns of governance, structure and learning in Swedish higher education. – (Higher education policy ; 48)
1. Education, Higher – Sweden 2. Education, Higher – I. Bauer, Marianne
378.4'85

ISBN 1 85302 675 1

Printed and Bound in Great Britain by
Athenaeum Press, Gateshead, Tyne and Wear

Contents

Part IV: Academe in a Context of Policy and System Changes

Part V: The State, Higher Education and Knowledge Formation

Epilogue

Appendices

List of Figures

List of Tables

Preface and Acknowledgments

This book covers change and continuity in the higher education system in Sweden during the 1990s in an environment of new patterns of social demands and accelerating international competition, and against a background of tradition, policy and system characteristics of Swedish higher education during previous decades. In a setting where European universities are struggling with the implications of such an environment, our project can be seen as a study of the Swedish case of transforming higher education and its institutions to meet new challenges. This project is also a part of the research program 'International Study of Higher Education Reform', the remit of which is to make a comparative study of the processes and impact of higher education reforms in England, Norway and Sweden.

The Swedish case will later be compared with the corresponding cases of the other two countries. Our approach to the comparative study is to identify key phenomena and to develop and use theories and concepts to illuminate and explain reform in these countries while preserving each country's context. Therefore, the system and context of each of the three countries will be presented in separate books before the comparative analysis will be reported. Thus, this book constitutes the first part of the contribution from the Swedish research team.

The original idea of such a comparative study emanated from a discussion between some English researchers and some Swedish higher education leaders in a conference in 1993. The discussion focused on the obviously different directions in which the higher education systems in the two countries appeared to be moving – the British system having been affected by the Thatcher Government's encroachment on higher education and the Swedish system having experienced continuous decentralization for more than a decade.

This idea was intriguing enough to be further developed by the English researchers, and in the Spring of 1994, Maurice Kogan and Mary Henkel at the Centre for the Evaluation of Public Policy and

Practice at Brunel University presented a proposal for an Anglo-Swedish study on 'The Impacts of Reform of Higher Education'. They contacted and started a discussion with Marianne Bauer and Ference Marton at Göteborg University in Sweden, both engaged in the university's new-established committee for quality assurance and development. Since the Swedish higher education reform of 1993, then recently launched under the slogan 'Freedom for Quality', had quality of higher education in focus, a comparative study of reforms appeared most relevant and challenging for theoretical and methodological reasons as well as for practical application within the university.

Due to the far-reaching nature of the project, from policy-making at state level to values and conditions among academic staff at basic level, our Swedish research team, so far having represented mainly psychological-pedagogical research areas, needed completion by researchers within policy science and system research. In the summer of 1994, Susan Gerard Marton, assistant researcher at the Department of Political Science at Göteborg University, became a member of the project. In 1995, Berit Askling, then professor in Education at Linköping University, joined the project and later in 1997 she received a chair at Göteborg University and also is responsible for the university's quality program.

In the meantime the international program became reinforced by the association of a Norwegian research team under the leadership of Ivar Bleiklie at the LOS-Centre and the Department of Administration and Organization Theory at Bergen University in Norway.

Our book has been given the rather grandiose title of *Transforming Universities* with the subtitle *Patterns of Governance, Structure and Learning in Swedish Higher Education*. With this title we allude to change in visions and undertakings at all levels of the system, as the universities attempt to fulfill the rising expectations and demands placed on them in order to remain major centers for advanced knowledge in the new millennium.

This book has been produced in collaborative effort by the authors, with Chapters 1, 2 and 11 in particular reflecting this. A different main author has been responsible for Parts II-IV, although each Part has been thoroughly discussed in the group. Thus, Part II, covering the macro level, has been written by Susan Gerard Marton, Part III, containing the meso level, has been written by Berit Askling, and Part IV, treating the micro level, has been written by Marianne Bauer.

Berit Askling, furthermore, is the author of the historical background presented in Chapter 3. The idea and formation of the Epilogue has been a topic for discussion by the entire Swedish research team, although it is written by Ference Marton and Susan Gerard Marton. For the book as a whole, we share responsibility together.

Without the deep knowledge in the field of higher education of our English colleagues, Mary Henkel – the leader of our comparative research program – and Maurice Kogan, and their initiative for a comparative project, this study would not have come to exist. During all its phases we have profited from their good advice and generous support, for which we are deeply grateful. We have also appreciated the stimulating cooperation with the other members of the English team, Steve Hanney and Sandra Jones.

When the Norwegian team joined our program they brought further perspectives on our own study through the similarities and differences of these two Nordic higher education systems. The opportunities to cooperate and discuss with Ivar Bleiklie and his research colleagues, Roar Høstaker and Agnet Vabø, have been greatly appreciated and very much enjoyed.

We have also profited from various kinds of support from many people at the Department of Education and Educational Research and the Department of Political Science, both at Göteborg University. We received many helpful comments from the participants in the Graduate Seminar on Public Policy and would especially like to acknowledge them.

The carrying through of this study was dependent on the access to and interaction with the universities and colleges which were sampled for study. We thank the rectors of these six institutions for their welcoming attitude and for their openness in our interviews with them. We are also most grateful to all the other respondents – deans, heads of departments, administrative leaders and the academic staff – who, in spite of clearly arduous working situations, took time to answer our questions. In addition, our study benefited from knowledge gained in interviews with persons working at the Ministry of Education and at the Higher Education Agency as well as persons associated with the Swedish Parliament. We thank them for their time and for their very insightful comments.

In the quite demanding work of carrying through, transcribing and categorizing interviews, we were lucky to receive most competent assistance by Ragnhild Nitzler and Christina Segerholm at Umeå University. We thank them for their assistance.

At later stages of our work we have engaged further professional competence. We thank Andreas Hermansson for his assistance with the study of the external funding situation in two departments. Emi Hijino has scrutinized the language and made admirable attempts to join and amalgamate our different writing styles.

The comparative research program has been sponsored by a three-and-a-half-year grant from the Swedish Council for Studies in Higher Education. This basic grant was later reinforced by further support from Göteborg University and Brunel University. The Swedish part of the project between 1994 and 1996 was also sponsored by the Government's Committee on Follow-up of the 1993 Higher Education Reform (RUT-93). We are grateful to our sponsors for this financial support.

Part I

A Study of Swedish Higher Education Reform
Setting the Stage

Introduction

Throughout the centuries, universities have survived by transforming themselves under the impact of extrinsic pressures and intrinsic virtues, and thereby succeeded in keeping their position as the major higher education institutions and the center for developing and transmitting advanced knowledge. Today universities are extending and flourishing as never before, but at the same time their uniqueness and integrity are increasingly being questioned. Sheldon Rothblatt writes about 'the disappearing boundaries of the universities' and argues that the European universities during the past 20 to 30 years have gone through a period of great uncertainty in which the uniqueness of the universities has been questioned and challenged by trends and circumstances that may influence the functions of the universities and their relationship to society:

> it appears that universities are no longer being thought of as particularly special, except where favored by history and architecture. Their functions can be taken over and performed by others, by private research institutes and think tanks, by industrial and government laboratories, by ad hoc teaching and corporate classrooms, by continuing education, extension and Open University lecturing, or they can be internally transformed, so that in ethos and style they really are merely simulations of other types of institutions. (Rothblatt 1995, p.33)

However, the university as a special place with its own identity has long been a cherished idea among academics. The various ideas about the university, over time and between countries, gave rise to different traditions of higher education (see, for example, Rothblatt 1994). Wyatt in his overview of *Seven West European Thinkers on the Essence of the University* (1990) depicts different contexts and thoughts that have had impact on university traditions in various countries.

But the common foundation of the academic value structure – academic freedom and autonomy for the universities – was laid down to protect knowledge formation, or more solemnly 'the search for truth', against extrinsic pressure and dependence on various external authorities. For centuries it has conveyed an idealized picture of the academic, driven by passion for truth and without any other motive but curiosity. There is further an implicit, idealistic presumption that a proper attitude to scientific knowledge also implies an ethical and moral standpoint (Olausson 1995). Clark (1995c, p.241) expresses it like this: 'Universities make a particular wager with knowledge within which a scientific or rational pursuit of truth develops its own morality, one that leads some participants and constituent groups to a particular sense of responsibility embedded in the scientific ethic and the academic calling.'

Humboldt's ideal for the universities with 'Lehr- und Lernfreiheit', which warranted professors and academic teachers the right to lecture on whatever theme they wished to, and the students full freedom to choose discipline, university and teachers, are still part of the basic values in spite of doubts that these principles were ever fully realized (Ben-David 1991), and furthermore the greatly changed circumstances at today's universities (Rau 1993). Humboldt's ideal of knowledge – 'Bildung' – implied that the studies were to involve an emotional active outlook in a wider context; not just knowledge should be imparted but also insights in how knowledge could be reached. Research, teaching and 'Bildung' were, thus, brought together in a communicative process (Blomqvist 1992, 1994).

The strong emphasis on individual academic autonomy that Humboldt's ideal seems to imply is put into the context of 'collective pursuit of truth' by Polanyi (1962), claiming that the independence and academic freedom of the individual scientist can only function within the authority of the network of scientists, 'the Republic of Science'.

> The Republic of Science is a Society of Explorers... It appears that a society bent on discovery must advance by supporting independent initiatives, co-ordinating themselves mutually to each other. Such adjustment may induce rivalries and opposing responses... Even so, all these independent initiatives must accept for their guidance a traditional authority, enforcing its own

self-renewal by cultivating originality among its followers. (Polanyi 1962, p.72)

'The Republic of Science', according to Polanyi, in spite of increasing specialization and fragmentation, is held together because there is 'a considerable degree of overlapping between the areas over which a scientist can exercise a sound critical judgement...This network is the seat of scientific opinions' (Polanyi 1962, p.59). But the accelerating process of increasing specialization of scientific knowledge has challenged thoughts on forces uniting the university in spite of its growing plurality. Karl Jaspers, for instance, a critic and a defender of the German university tradition after both world wars, according to Wyatt (1990), was contemptuous of the idea of a university that passively accepted fragmentation glossed over with something called 'allgemeine Bildung'. Jaspers, according to Wittrock (1993, p.351) argued that 'within each scholarly pursuit it was possible to reflect about the foundations of these activities and to reach out to other fields, thus preserving some aspects of the unity of a university'. Open communication is an essential value in Jasper's justification of the liberal university, an idea further developed by Habermas in 'the communicative process, inherent in all discourse and teaching, in its ideal form, unaffected by strategic consideration of power and professional interest' (Wittrock 1993, p.352).

The university must overcome, not only the plurality and accelerating fragmentation of scientific knowledge, but furthermore, according to Blau (1964, p.273), any organized community, like a university, in order to survive the total turnover of its membership must institutionalize its principles governing social relations and patterns of conduct. Few organizations, if any, apply such extended and comprehensive induction as the universities do for the novice to undergo before becoming a full member of the academic community. Blau maintains, however, that such strong value formation, also contains a counterinstitutional component, namely those basic values and ideals that have not been realized, which are the ultimate source of social change.

That remnants from past periods continue to play an active role in the system despite the fact that the ideology itself is dead is discussed by Liedman and Olausson (1988, pp.20–21) who name this phenomenon 'frozen ideology'. Although idealistic views of the scientific endeavor have been questioned and criticized by representatives of philosophy, epistemology, sociology of science and others (for example, Toulmin 1972; Merton 1973; Elzinga 1994), they have shown a strong resilience, probably a sign of their usefulness, not only for the purpose of safeguarding the knowledge formation processes, but also for the academic community itself.

The various 'classic' ideas of a university are necessarily based on the perception and experience of universities as elite institutions, whether for 'Bildung' or for professional education. In present times of 'mass higher education' (Trow 1974) and demands for 'new production of knowledge' (Gibbons *et al.* 1994), the limitations of these ideas become apparent.

Wittrock (1993, p.361) in his historical analysis of the 'three transformations of the modern university' concludes that, 'although there is no reason to expect the demands for higher education and scientific knowledge to decline – quite the opposite – such may well occur in a fashion that makes any discussion about 'the idea' of a university appear to be hopelessly antiquated.'

Although the *idea* of the university is antiquated, there are many competing ideas about the purpose of universities today that are well assembled and formulated in the antithesis of a 'multiversity'. This multiversity, according to Rothblatt, is more comparable with a 'metropolis continuously stretching its borders and inviting its inhabitants to consider a wide variety of possibilities' (1994, p.9).

In a paper on the changing role of the university in the approaching 'knowledge society', Peter Scott points to the apparent paradox of:

> on the one hand intellectual confusion, on the other flourishing universities. Today the signs of intellectual dissolution are everywhere. All semblance of a shared academic culture rooted in supposedly universal cognitive values, unified subjects that transcend the particularities of disciplinary traditions and transient market exchanges, has disappeared... Higher education, once marginal, has become socially pervasive at the very time when traditional intellectual structures have been dismantled or allowed to decay. (Scott 1997, pp.7–8)

So, more than ever, the universities of today seem to be confronted with challenges both by demands from the surrounding society in the form of mass higher education and strategic research, and by internal intellectual dissolution and institutional disintegration. Our study of Swedish universities should be seen in this perspective.

Chapter 1

Transforming Universities
Issues and Conceptual Framework

Research issues

In this study we investigate some aspects of change in the Swedish higher education system that are crucial for the transformation of the Swedish universities in these times of uncertainty and increasing global competition. The topic is broad and so is our approach. We cover issues of higher education policy making and central governance, institutional leadership and management, and beliefs and reactions among academic leaders and staff.

This study has two major poles:

1. The values and prerequisites for the academic tasks of knowledge formation and maintenance through learning, teaching and researching (analyzed in Chapters 9 and 10).

2. The policy formation processes and the reform decisions by state authorities concerning the higher education system, its conditions, goals, governance and relations to society (developed in Chapters 4 and 5).

Our intention is to investigate change and variables influencing change by approaching them from these two points of departure, i.e. both from a bottom-up and from a top-down perspective. Our aim is to contribute to the understanding of the dynamics at these two poles and of their interaction as well as mutual impact. Our ambition is to build bridges between policy formation processes at the state level and conditions for knowledge formation processes at the basic level by incorporating the institutional level (Chapters 6–8).

The object of the study is reform, as a frequently used and yet little understood instrument for change of higher education. Even though a major central reform must be seen only as a link in a more comprehensive process of social and political change, it signifies a particular effort to assemble and analyze the existing conditions, trends and challenges and suggests measures for the direction of future development. The major focus of the study is the Swedish higher education reform of 1993 (H-93 reform) (Government Proposition (Gov. Prop.) 1992/93:1) and the processes of change preceding and following it. The previous major reform in Sweden took place in 1977 (H-77 reform) (Gov. Prop. 1976/77:59) and forms a point of reference for the study. There are some specific reasons for studying the H-93 reform in Sweden. It breaks the trend of earlier central reforms in the country in that it is setting goals in more academic terms than before, and makes a radical shift in model of governance by changing the distribution of power, devolving authority for decision making and action from the state to the higher education institutions: 'Freedom' – and responsibility – 'for Quality'. Another aspect of H-93 is that, proposed by a Conservative coalition government, to a great extent the reform can be seen as a codification of continual system changes and adjustments of central regulation that have taken place during the 1980s – under a period of Social Democratic governments, again returning in 1994 – thus constituting an important link in the ongoing political process of change and continuity in policies.

It should be emphasized here that our study is *not* an evaluation of the H-93 reform. It is not limited to comparing how government reform policy and goals correspond with the reform outcome. It is not asking the question whether the reform has been successful or not.

Neither is this study primarily an investigation of reform implementation. It is not limited to analyzing 'what happens' on the way down in the system from reform decision to its realization or counteraction in institutions and departments. It is not asking the question why the reform has been successful or not.

As already declared, our investigation has a wider perspective of change. It is a study of change and continuity in values, conditions and policy at all levels of the system – state and society (macro), institution (meso), individual and academic community (micro) – and of the dynamics through which they occur at and between these levels.

In spite of successful university adaptation over centuries, history shows that developed systems of higher education are also full of constraints upon change. Such systems have become 'deeply institutionalized... which means in effect that the constraints upon change and imperatives for change are increasingly located in the system' (Clark 1983, p.183). Both constraints upon and imperatives for change appear to depend largely on the way the system operates. Therefore, a central reform, aiming to change the way the higher education system operates, constitutes an opportunity to catch sight of some of the change processes, otherwise hidden within the complexities and ambiguities of the higher education system.

Swedish state authorities have often resorted to reform initiatives without patiently abiding action and reactions from the university. This type of comprehensive central policy making has been typical for Sweden. Lindensjö and Lundgren (1986) talk about two generations of reform cycles of the whole educational system in Sweden, starting in a centralist manner with primary education in the 1940s. The background of tradition and development of the Swedish higher education system is outlined in Chapter 3 with particular attention to the centralistic reform strategy during the 1960s and 1970s and the following continuous process of decentralization (Niklasson 1996; Askling and Almén 1997).

Bleiklie (1996a) mentions two different perspectives on reforms. One is the usual definition within political science of reform as a complex of goals with adherent means. The other, and later developed perspective, is reform as a link or a part in a more comprehensive social and political process of change. In our investigation we shall use both perspectives for different purposes: the latter to relate the reform issues to the context of other concurrent or preceding change, and the former perspective to study the specific reform and its internal coherence and compatibility with intrinsic values in the field of higher education.

Since the H-93 reform is primarily aimed at issues of education (while research issues have been treated in other government propositions) this study, consequently, will have the same focus, leaving research aspects only to peripheral consideration.

We shall look at and attempt to explain change and continuity:

- in content and values of reform policy and in the policy formation processes at national level

- in the instruments of the reform concerning the structure of the system and the models of governance

- through the impact of the reform, and of other concomitant change, on higher education institutions and their responsibility, obligations and internal distribution of authority, as well as on the response and action by the institutional leadership

- through the demands on basic units, affecting academic working conditions and professional roles and status, and

- in academic values and professional identities influencing reception of and reactions to the reform by faculty.

As a special 'case' within our extensive research-field we have chosen to highlight at each level a limited but essential theme of the H-93 reform – the quality issue. Not only does this concept provide the catch phrase of the Swedish reform 'Freedom for Quality', it also involves a rich field for international comparison, since quality control and enhancement have been a concern within higher education policy in practically all parts of the world during the past few years (see, for example, Westerheijden, Brennan and Maassen 1994; Bauer and Kogan 1997), a trend termed the development of 'The Evaluative State' (Neave 1988; Henkel 1991). Another reason for the relevance of the quality issue is that, more than many other specific reform themes, it involves and reflects the change in values, distribution of responsibility and challenges of an expanding higher education system. Furthermore, quality in higher education and research should be related to processes of knowledge formation (Bowden and Marton 1998).

Conceptual framework for the study object

We need a systematic framework to study and interpret change in higher education, but 'systematic approaches are hardly at hand. Change remains the most recalcitrant subject in the social sciences' (Clark 1983, p.182). Considering the protean character of the concept of change it is hardly surprising that there exists no comprehensive theory to cover the processes of change and resistance to change in higher education (or elsewhere). Our framework is built on the basic structure of the higher education system and uses two major aspects of its dynamics to illuminate change: purpose and authority.

The higher education system

System is a diffuse concept. Analyzing patterns of the higher education system Teichler (1988), had structural aspects in view, primarily diversification versus integration of the system, ensuing in particular as a consequence of growing student numbers and heterogeneity of the student body, which was leading to different strategies of access. On the other hand, according to Clark (1983), a system approach in research on higher education includes both how higher education is organized and governed. In comparison, Teichler mentions changes in governance, like reduced government control and devolved authority, mainly as a tool for stimulating institutional initiatives and thereby promoting diversity. Comparing higher education systems in different countries, Becher and Kogan (1992) identified differences in two aspects: the first, similar to Teichler's analysis, is related to access (and the structure of institutions) and the second is related to governance and control.

The model of a higher education system as conceptualized by Becher and Kogan (1992) has four levels of the system (individual, basic unit, institution and central authority) and two modes or components of the everyday life of the academic world (the normative and the operational). This model has guided the building of our own framework for the task of investigating change at both state, institutional and individual levels. Furthermore, with its pronunciation of internal and external aspects of change, both purposive and accidental, this model is appropriate for a study of a major external reform.

Clark (1983) bases his account of the organization of higher education as a social system on three elements, in which the handling of knowledge is the crucial activity. The first element includes tasks and how they are conceived and arranged. The second element is belief, that is, primary norms and values. The third element is that of authority or the distribution of legitimate power. In Clark's own words: 'As the system develops, it builds [its] own sources of continuity and change... it acquires structures of work, belief and authority' (p.183).

These elements agree well with the two aspects of higher education that we shall focus on, purpose and authority, where the purpose aspect can be said to include the combined elements of tasks and beliefs.

Furthermore, Clark underlines that such 'existing structures have response sets that shape what follows' (p.184). To ensure that enough attention is given to this principle of existing response sets in our investigation of change Chapter 3 contains an overview of the development of the Swedish higher education system during the past forty years.

All four higher education researchers referred to above also consider the change in structures to have an important impact on the change in the conditions for basic activities, a crucial issue in our study of reform. 'Changes that proceed by altering the structure alter the fundamental biases of a system, changing the source of opinion and power expressed in the agendas of decision and in the procedures of daily operations' (Clark 1983, p.236).

Concepts and models of change

Change is hardly a less diffuse concept. Although there exists no comprehensive theory of change in higher education, there is a multitude of studies of various aspects of change.

Several types of subdivision of the basic phenomenon of change have been suggested. Dill and Friedman (1979, p.412), for instance, point to the difference between organizational and individual change and between purposive and accidental change. Becher and Kogan (1992, pp.131–132) also mention differences in scope and time-scale of changes as well as the essential difference between internalist and externalist sources of change. In their model of a higher education system the change process is defined in relation to a concept of dynamic equilibrium between the internal normative and the internal operational modes. Research on change in higher education has often been directed towards innovation and improvement (e.g. Berg and Östergren 1977; Levine 1980; van Vught 1989) – a process that can be looked upon as nested within a broader change process.

Various frameworks for the study of change in higher education have also been suggested. Chin and Benne (1969), for instance, differentiate between three types of social change: rational-empirical, normative-re-educative and power-coercive. Dill and Friedman (1979), in their analysis of frameworks for research on change in higher education, compare the models of 'complex organization', 'conflict', 'diffusion' and 'planned change'. Through an analysis of the four frameworks by means of causal flow-graphs and emphasis on the variables that influence change, they conclude that study of change needs a combination of frameworks which should regard the types of change, organization and levels within them.

With the comprehensive aim to knit together analyses of political reforms and processes of change as they manifest themselves on the different levels, we have, as already mentioned, chosen to focus on two principal aspects of policy change: the change in purpose and the change in distribution of authority. In the following sections we will illustrate some of the major ideas within these branches of research on change in higher education.

Change in purpose of higher education

There are many different conceptions of higher education and its purposes. Most of them are partial descriptions, reflecting only certain kinds of interests. Ronald Barnett (1992, pp.18–19) gives the following as examples of dominant concepts of higher education:

- the production of qualified manpower
- a training for a research career
- the efficient management of teaching provision
- a matter of extending life chances.

Further, he recommends to ask what set of interests is being defended or what form of partiality is being promoted by a particular approach.

In any case, the purpose and tasks of higher education institutions relate to the formation and exchange of knowledge – teaching, learning and researching. The purpose of higher education reform, therefore, must necessarily have something to do with either change in, for example, the type, amount and purpose of knowledge, or the effectiveness by which the knowledge activities are carried out. Although reforms may have far-reaching political, social and economic goals their consequences on the conditions of knowledge formation are crucial. However, Teichler (1988, p.99) points out that debates as well as research on structural change of higher education 'seldom focus on the major issue of controversy... i.e. to what extent learning in higher education is most successfully promoted' by one model or another.

In order to enhance and develop the conditions for the formation and exchange of knowledge, a reform consequently must contain a conception of knowledge and its use. Although such conception is seldom explicitly formulated in reform propositions, it can be construed or interpreted from values expressed in these documents and from the policy process. Barnett points to 'the changing forms that knowledge takes according to the evaluations that society places on those different forms of knowledge... What counts as knowledge is not just social but societal. Accordingly, knowledge is not given: it is

socially sustained and invested with interests and backed by power'
(Barnett 1997, p.5).

As we shall discuss in Chapter 4, there has been a shift in Swedish
government policy towards educating for the knowledge society. This
'knowledge society' is a comprehensive and diffuse term. Peter Scott
has pointed to the paradox that 'the closer we approach to a
"knowledge society", the more diffuse become our notions of what
counts as "knowledge", and the more problematic, even precarious,
becomes the status of traditional "knowledge" institutions, pre-
eminent among which is the university' (Scott 1997, p.5). After
having gone through attributes of the knowledge society and changes
in the nature of knowledge in the late twentieth century, Scott
indicates serious challenges to the traditional university. He
anticipates a mass university that will be a transgressive institution. It
will transgress 'once-fixed institutional boundaries, ... higher
education's former social base, ... traditional organisational forms, ...
the old academic culture with its inflexible approach to alternative
knowledge traditions and to truth-seeking. And it will have to do all
these things in order to survive in the "knowledge society"' (Scott
1997, p.13).

These movements indicate extensive change in the purpose of
higher education.

Change in distribution of authority

The growing scale, complexity and importance of higher education
during the past decades, together with the economic conditions and
increasing market dependence, challenged the higher education
institutions. Consequently the prevailing forms of regulation,
planning and state control became unsatisfactory and new models of
governance were called for in which patterns of authority and
legitimacy could be restructured.

In a study on governmental strategies and innovation, van Vught
(1989) contrasts two extreme cases of governmental strategy that
differ in their fundamental assumptions about decision-making. The
two strategies are named 'the strategy of rational planning and
control' and 'the strategy of self-regulation'. Maassen (1996, p.62;
also Maassen and van Vught 1994) claims that while literature offers a
wealth of governance models it can be argued that, when the
underlying assumptions of these models are carefully analyzed, only
two basic models remain, namely the model of rational planning and

control and the model of self-regulation. The former is based on rational decision while the latter bases decision-making on cybernetic principles.

Decision theory has been questioned because of its unrealistic assumptions on decision-makers. They are expected to consider the values and probabilities, i.e. the likely outcomes, of all alternatives before making a decision. Furthermore, there exist even more unrealistic assumptions about collective decision-making. Braybrooke and Lindblom (1970), for example, after radical criticism of these assumptions, concluded that the rational perspective is fruitless and unhelpful for decision-makers in 'the real world' who are unable to handle all the information necessary to make a rational decision. Similarly, Lane (1993, p.74) criticized the model of rational planning and control for its lack of realism.

The cybernetic perspective, on the other hand, is based on the assumption of the necessity to reduce variety by focusing only on a few, critical variables and on the principle of feedback from these variables. For collective decision-making, opinions and preferences of different units need not be integrated. Instead multiple actors in loosely coupled units are assumed, each one operating according to cybernetic principles (Cyert and March 1963).

With a growing awareness of the uncertainty of conditions, goals and the very meaning of progress, governments' demands and expectations on the higher education institutions have heightened (Bauer 1994). A strategy is needed that 'acknowledges the limitations of acquiring knowledge and exercising control over an object of planning which, in itself, already consists of a complex set of mechanisms of decision-making', and tries to 'incorporate the benefits of this complex set of mechanisms by limiting itself to setting broad frameworks and by providing facilities for the behaviour of decentralised units' (van Vught 1989, p.39). Such change in governance has occurred in several European countries lately and has been termed a shift from 'Model of State Control' to 'Model of State Supervision' (van Vught 1989; Neave and van Vught 1991; Maassen 1996). The former model is demanding docile institutions and the latter, self-regulating institutions. The model of state supervision thus implies that state authorities let the institutions take over responsibilities and do not mingle with the management of the institutions. This calls for the latter to develop the necessary steering and regulating on their own, something that requires a stronger leadership function than before. At the same time, such self-regulation within an institution should follow the same principle to benefit from the existing complex set of decision-making mechanisms.

A two-dimensional typology of higher education

We have given above salient examples of reflection on and studies of the purpose of higher education on one hand, and on the other, the distribution of authority and governance strategies. Although higher education policy and reforms usually contain elements of both these aspects there are few research attempts to cover both simultaneously, perhaps because they tend to fall under different disciplinary interests.

Bleiklie (1994a, p.4) points to the scarce supply of 'analyses that deal critically with the relationship between organizational principles like institutional autonomy and individual freedom and the scientific activity itself'. He does, however, examine three alternatives of university policy norms based on German idealism, American functionalism and radical rationalism and their relations to autonomy and heteronomy (Bleiklie 1996a, pp.26–35).

For our purpose of tracking the change through the whole system of higher education from state policy to conditions and reactions of the academe, we are going to combine these two major aspects of higher education reform and change: purpose and authority distribution.

We define the purpose 'dimension' in terms of relative emphasis of intrinsic academic values and extrinsic values in the formation of purpose for higher education. In relation to quality concepts, intrinsic aspects have been characterized by van Vught (1997, pp.80–81) as referring to 'the basic values and ideals which form the very heart of higher education', while 'the extrinsic qualities refer to the capacities of higher education to respond to the changing needs of the societies of which they are a part'. Under the surface of these coarse categories there exist exceedingly complicated relationships between 'the very heart' and responses 'to the changing needs of societies'. Barnett, in his challenging new ideas on critical thinking in higher education (1997), talks about three dominant conceptions of 'academic' that depends on who makes the value judgment. They are

(1) a fading academicism, where value is judged by the knowledge producers themselves; (2) an ever-stronger instrumentalism,

where value is judged by the external community; and (3) a newer operationalism, where value is produced by the producers acting directly in the world, subject to criteria of the wider world. (Barnett 1997, p.150)

These conceptions are indicative of the kinds of change that is occurring in the purpose of and conditions for knowledge formation.

The second aspect has to do with responsibility for how the mission is carried through and the goals are obtained. It is, therefore, related to how authority is distributed over the levels of the system in order to attain optimal effect. Change in this dimension is usually expressed in terms of centralization and decentralization, that is, in patterns of the devolution of responsibilities.

A basic scheme for the analysis of change in purpose and authority accordingly looks like the diagram in Figure 1.1.

A reform, seen as a summing up of tendencies and aims at a particular time, according to this scheme, can be characterized with respect to its purpose and its distribution of authority as compared, for instance, with earlier government policy or with other countries. It can also be compared with how they agree with prevailing values and views among academic staff.

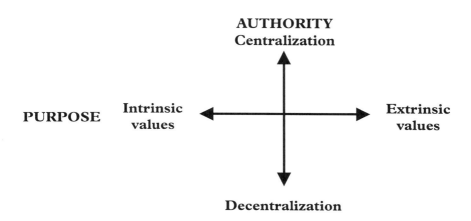

Figure 1.1 Two dimensions of change in higher education

The basic scheme presented in Figure 1.1 is further developed and applied for the macro level by Susan Marton (1997) to characterize different types of higher education systems. In this case the authority dimension entails the distribution between the state and higher education institutions. The resulting four quadrants represent four prototypes of higher education systems characterized by different emphases on the two dimensions. This typology and its relationship with concepts of autonomy is further developed in Chapter 4 and Figure 4.1.

Issue of 'Quality' as a case

As described in Chapter 4, quality is a central constituent in the H-93 reform conception of the purpose of higher education. The knowledge-goal of the reform is far-reaching; it is formulated in terms of the need to strengthen Sweden as a 'nation of knowledge' (Gov. Prop. 1992/93:1). To increase knowledge by raising both student numbers and the quality of higher education and research is considered to be decisive for the development of the country as a whole.

'Higher quality' is, of course, not explicitly defined in the government proposition, but this goal is said to be directly connected to the means – a widened freedom for the institutions and decentralized responsibility. However, the goal of higher quality is combined with a new performance-based resource allocation system and with demands for quality assurance and accountability. Apparently, the umbrella-concept of quality, in Sweden as in several other countries, has been used to cover various reform intentions such as the increasing need for effectiveness, innovation and accountability.

The redistribution of responsibility for quality can be seen as part of the above mentioned transition of governance to state supervision and devolution of authority, in which the principle of feedback of relevant information is essential for the steering function (van Vught 1989, 1995). The model of state supervision/self-regulation will be used as a frame of reference also to analyze how actors responsible at the different levels – state, institution, individual – fulfill their respective obligations and roles concerning assurance and enhancement of quality (Askling and Bauer 1997).

Our dimension of purpose is connected to different views of higher education and consequently to different approaches to quality. Barnett, in his analysis of concepts of quality of higher education

(1992), points to the fact that the modern debate about quality has mostly taken place in a conceptual void. But 'what we take higher education to be will have implications for how we conceive of quality, how we attain it, how we evaluate our success in achieving it, and how we improve it' (Barnett 1992, p.16). To be able to enhance or assure quality there must be a reasonably clear conception of it. With the acceptance of a relativistic quality concept arises the problem of how to form normative recommendations for reaching higher quality. In a relativistic elucidation of quality in the university world, Bohlin (1998) concludes, however, that a normative ambition does not contravene a relativistic conceptualization. All underlying 'theories' for judgment of quality are not equally well-based and acceptable, which means that relativism does not have to lead to arbitrary compromise. On the contrary, the deeper an understanding a relativistic perspective provides, he claims, the further it can be used to correct unsatisfactory states of conditions.

The approach to quality will thus vary depending on who is making the judgment. Different stakeholders or interest groups represent different values and apply different criteria. For instance, the three major categories with influence on higher education that Clark (1983) has paid attention to – the state, the academic oligarchy and the market – carry different roles and also vary in their preferential system for quality control. The quality judgment in these three cases is formed by, respectively, the commissioners, the producers and the users of knowledge.

Rolf, Ekstedt and Barnett (1993) defined a related threefold categorization of quality systems as follows (to which we have added the categories of the primary evaluators):

1. Administrative systems, which are given the resources and authority to steer others by rules or goals (bureaucrats).

2. Professional systems, in which the same category of actors (in this case academics) combine the functions of producing work and supervising the quality of one another's work (scientists/teachers).

3. Market systems, in which results are dependent on transactions where supply and demands meet (customers/students).

Examples of the first type are evaluations and quality audits designed and carried through by higher education agencies. (For a detailed description of the types of evaluations carried through by the Swedish Higher Education Agency see Askling and Bauer 1997.)

Judgment of research quality by means of peer review is the prototype for supervision of quality in the professional system. Another example is the definition of quality in higher education as 'better learning', recently elaborated by Bowden and Marton (1998).

Examples of market system judgments depend on who is looked upon as the 'customer'. In the H-93 reform the students were meant to be such a market force through their free choice of education and institution, though this intention was hindered by the limits of the higher education system. Other forms for student influence on quality, like course evaluations, are currently being developed.

Scott (1997, p.10) offers another example, referring to the much debated 'Mode 2' research which is claimed to require a new definition of quality in which 'peer review is superseded by new ways of defining "good" science that are both more political and more commercial'.

A broad approach

In this chapter we have introduced our study object and its two poles of policy formulation and knowledge formation. In order to build bridges between them, however, the intermediate institutional level, constitutes a central part of our empirical study. Given our conceptual framework, presented in this chapter, we therefore operate on three levels – state level, institutional level and individual level.

Chapter 2

Theoretical Perspectives, Design and Methods

Theoretical perspectives

Within the general system approach, introduced earlier, we shall apply an actor/structure perspective for the interpretation of our results. In order to identify crucial structural elements in the system, we will use a few particular metaphors which have been developed by Swedish researchers in the Swedish context of extensive structural reforms.

The first metaphor is 'frames' as a straightforward characteristic of such factors which are often found to have significant effects on reform decisions and their implementations by restricting or widening the factual maneuverability of the actors. The second metaphor is 'arenas for formulation and realization of policy', which emphasizes that reform decisions and their implementation are enacted on different scenes with different players, rules and visions. The third metaphor is 'space of action', that is, the remaining available space within which the actors can act after the structural framing factors have been considered.

The frame/process model

The 'frame/process model' was originally prepared by Urban Dahllöf as a tool for empirical studies on reforms and change processes in an educational system such as that in Sweden with its traditionally heavy reliance on the state (Dahllöf 1967, 1971, 1999).

From the assumption that the mechanisms of the educational processes must be explained both at the micro level and at the macro level, Dahllöf searched for a historical and contextual understanding of the implications of a policy when it is to be implemented in an educational system. He took the view that educational processes and educational outcomes are often influenced by, and sometimes also determined by, circumstances and preconditions on various levels in an educational system. Such 'framing' factors are not always taken into account or paid attention to when reform goals are formulated, desirable processes are outlined and outcomes are assessed and interpreted. Therefore, the actual space of action of the major actors in an educational system (politicians, institutional leaders and academics), according to Dahllöf, is not just defined by goals and intentions but also by a series of such framing factors. On various levels in the system, these framing factors have impact on how the actors perceive, define and eventually use their own space of action.

> The main issue of the so-called frame factor approach is not only to recognize the existence of a certain set of constraining conditions, but also to trace in more detail their influence on the chain of events forming the educational process, and in that way to assess their importance for a variety of different outcomes, according to the general sequence of Goals – Frames – Process – Outcomes. (Dahllöf 1991, p.183)

The frame factor approach does not in itself provide a direct explanation for the variety of possible processes and their respective outcomes. It is, however, according to Dahllöf, a helpful tool in classifying the most significant, but often not the most obvious, aspects of a situation and in tracing the most probable relationships in a chain of events. The frames do not determine, but do restrict, how the actors may respond and what they may do.

Originally, the concept of frames focused on physically constraining and directing conditions in the teaching process, external to it and thus also out of control of teachers and students. In empirical studies Dahllöf demonstrated the powerful framing effect of structural characteristics. Sometimes these were so much taken for granted as parts of the system that their actual framing effect was totally overlooked. Under influence from Bernstein (1971; 1977) and Bourdieu (1977), Lundgren (1977) broadened the frame factor model. Significant current and historical structures on various system levels were identified and related to actors' own interpretation of their meaning.

The frame factor model can be looked upon as a map, generating questions and hypotheses about the interplay between policy, structures, organization and actors (Lundgren 1996). It is a tool of particular usefulness in an educational system like the Swedish one, with its tradition of heavy reliance on all-encompassing structural changes as a major reform strategy.

Arenas of 'Policy Formulation' and of 'Policy Realization'

Different approaches have been used to illuminate the policy formation and implementation processes respectively, but they have rarely been combined or related to each other. To illuminate the policy formulation process Bleiklie, Marton and Hanney (1997) are developing the policy network approach by focusing on both the actors and the structural relationships in the network (Atkinson and Coleman 1992; Raab 1992; Dowding 1995). The policy network is conceptualized broadly, allowing for relationships between the state and any kind of organized actor who tries to affect public policies.

An important insight gained from implementation research (despite its numerous problems) is that essential obstacles for the realization of centrally formulated intentions are often concealed within the activities to be reformed. Rothstein (1998) discusses to what extent those who are involved in implementing public policy actually have influence. The existence of complicated hierarchies may lead to a situation where 'what appears on one level to be a decisive factor in a program is embedded in larger social structures, and is therefore influenced by factors operating on deeper levels' (Rothstein 1998, p.70). This may, not in the least, be the case in universities with their specific ideological, social and organizational features due to their task of knowledge formation and exchange.

Lindensjö and Lundgren (1986), in an attempt to relate the two processes to each other, apply and develop the frame factor model in order to illuminate the different frame factors influencing the context of policy formulation and the context of policy realization respectively. With the metaphor of 'arenas of policy formulation and policy realization' the authors indicate that the surroundings of political decision-making and of implementation affect decisions and realization. That is, the reality where goals are formulated and the reality where goals are to be realized or implemented are being steered by different conditions, causing a rift between them that cannot simply be rationally arched. It is said to be two entirely different games, sometimes with incompatible rules, formulated on the basis of totally different conditions on each arena.

The arena-metaphor was first used to study how government policy and directives were transformed into the realities of a local school in the beginning of the 1980s (Lindensjö and Lundgren 1986). It may not appear to be equally well suited in the 1990s for a decentralized higher education system. Bleiklie (1996b), however, illustrated the incompatibility between the two arenas in an analysis of reactions by academe to three different central reforms. Three typical patterns of implementation were revealed: ritual implementation, adaptation of the activity in order to exploit extra resources and adaptation of the reform to established practices. It may be interpreted that a redefinition of a policy is taking place in the 'arena of realization' as a result of the discretion of the local units, that follow entirely different norms than those of the policy formulation arena. The question that Lindensjö and Lundgren are actually asking is whether there is a qualitative difference between the context of policy formulation and the context of realization. This may still be a valid question.

Although the 'Arena Model' may appear too static to be useful in a perspective of dynamic change, it provides a point of view that turns attention to the 'two contexts' with their different rules, conditions and priorities. Another benefit with looking at these 'arenas' as two separate contexts is that the functions of intermediary bodies – frequently interspersed between governments and the academic society (Neave 1994) as a kind of coupling station – may become more visible (Askling and Bauer 1997).

Space of action and realized autonomy

Our third metaphor, space of action, is more dynamic than the two earlier mentioned ones, since it takes into account more explicitly the point of view of the actors after the restricting impact of various frame factors has been considered. Focus is on the space then available as room for manoeuvres which can be used by the actors depending on their capacity.

This metaphor is based on a discussion in the social sciences, the actor/structure relationship (Etzioni 1968; Lundqvist 1987). It concerns 'To what degree can societal actors decide their course of action, and to what degree are they compelled to follow a course not chosen by them?' (Etzioni 1968, p.251, cited in Lundqvist 1984, p.1). In addressing this issue, Lundqvist (1987) has built a model of 'actor autonomy'. By slightly modifying Lundqvist's model, we are able to depict 'realized autonomy' in terms of two attributes: the space of action and the actor's capacity for action.

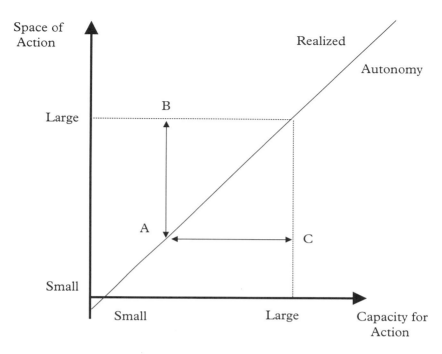

Figure 2.1 Actor's realized autonomy

The key point in the above model is that the actor's autonomy is dependent upon the extent to which he succeeds in exploiting his space of action and his capacity for action in order to realize his own preferences. In the term capacity of action, we include not just the actor's ability based on his knowledge and skill, but also his awareness and motivation to act.

If the actor is located at point A, but the space of action is large as indicated by point B, then the actor has not realized as much autonomy as he is entitled. However, if the actor is again located at point A, and his own capacity for action is large as indicated by point C, then the actor is not able to utilize his full capacity for action because his space of action has been restricted. It is interesting to note that both situations result in the same realized autonomy, represented by point A. Thus, realized autonomy is not identical with the space of action that an actor is allowed under certain structural arrangements, but it is also an issue of what capacity actors have to use the space of action given to them. This distinction in conceptualizing autonomy is substantial for all levels of our study as we discuss the space of action given in relation to the capacity for action on the state institutional and individual levels.

Design

A central theme in our study of the two poles of policy and knowledge formation is the interplay between actors and structures in a changing higher education system. We identify three major levels where such interaction can be documented and the consequences of it can be empirically identified and analyzed. These include the state (macro), the higher education institutions (meso) and the individual and the academic community (micro). These three levels form the basis for our empirical studies. They have also formed the main structure of our book.

On each level, we analyze our main findings in relation to the two dimensions of purpose and distribution of authority. Furthermore, on each level, we use the quality issue as a special case. Quality is a useful concept with which changes at the macro level of policy and system can be linked with changes at the micro level concerning goals, teaching and assessment. Many of the reform intentions are 'operationalized' in measures which are referred to as 'quality work'. These measures challenge the internal power structure and call for considerations concerning purpose and mission.

Following Teichler's map of higher education research (1996a, p.441), we move within all four 'spheres of knowledge in higher education' that he mentions:

- quantitative-structural aspects
- knowledge- and subject-related aspects
- person-related as well as teaching- and research-related aspects
- aspects of organization and governance.

Issues at the macro level (reported in Part II) include changes in the Swedish state and in the creation and execution of higher education policy in the context of generic structural development. Research issues to be covered in the macro level study are, for example, how political actors' shifting values in regards to the purpose of higher education have been reflected in the H-93 reform, and whether changes in the governance of the higher education system are related to these shifting values. What changes have taken place in this policy formation process when one compares the major policy movements between 1977 and 1993? To answer this question, the policy formation process at the state level is analyzed with regard to the interplay between, and the exercise of power by, the political parties, the bureaucracy, interest groups and various academic and business elites. By using a network approach to understand power shifts, we also illuminate how higher education reforms emerge, develop, culminate and are caught up by new social, structural and political change.

The meso level (Part III) bridges the national level of policy-making to academic work and values at basic level and is essential for the understanding of changes in working conditions and professional identity among academics. In our meso level study we consider the institutional level as a mediator between policy and practice. System changes (concerning governance and structure) are looked upon as manifestations of political intentions which are used as political instruments for implementing far-reaching changes in the educational system (and also in a wider social context). Such system changes directly affect the institutions and their leaders and in turn also academic staff and students. They form the preconditions and define the space of action for the academics at the basic level.

An important research issue regarding the meso level is to examine how the new expectations on expansion and renewal have been met by the institutions and what kind of changes in structure the institutions have undertaken by themselves. The institutional leaders have the twofold task of fulfilling the expectations from the government for institutional management and the expectations from the staff for academic and collegial leadership. A number of questions arise: What are the reactions of the leaders to various aspects of the reform and other recent changes? How do the institutional leaders define and perceive the traditional and new tasks of the academic leaders? How do the institutions handle their institutional autonomy and their new role with regard to internal governance and devolution of authority? To what extent and to whom is the increased authority further devolved within the institution? What models of institutional governance are emerging?

The issues at micro level (Part IV) concern the academics in the higher education institutions, who carry out and accomplish the higher education mission of teaching/learning and research under changing conditions and requirements. They base their activities on values and reasons contingent to the nature of academic work, but must also respond to the multifarious demands from society. How goals and means of the reform coincide with or are adverse to prevalent academic values, identities and traditions is discussed. How this encounter will affect the academics is, as mentioned above, primarily dependent on how the reform is received and acted on by the institutional leadership.

The major question at the micro level study is how the degree and the type of devolution within the institution will affect working conditions and professional roles. The explicit reform issues must further be seen in the context of other concurrent change in structure, demands and attitudes. These changes will have impact on working conditions and on the perceived significance of the reform. A special focus will be on how the traditional academic views on quality in research, teaching and learning – usually strongly associated with the academic discipline and with the idea of academic autonomy – are being challenged by strengthened institutional autonomy and new demands for accountability.

Our studies of these three levels form the basic data for the general conclusions presented in Part V. With this design, issues are analyzed concerning the relationships between the two poles: the demands of the state, as made explicit through policy and reforms of higher education, and terms laid down as conditions for knowledge formation through learning and research. The interpretations of change and continuity in the two major aspects of purpose and distribution of authority at the three levels of the higher education system during past and present periods lead, finally, to a discussion of conditions for development of higher education.

This design and our empirical data also allow us to make a normative turn and reflect on the direction of the future transformation of universities – an exploration presented in our epilogue.

Methods and material

Case method

The method used in our international project (see Preface), is a comparative case study over time. In the Swedish case we focus primarily on the recent period of higher education reform (H-93), in light of the previous major reform from 1977. The case study method applied in each country (Sweden, England and Norway) is a single, holistic case study which provides 'a paradigm of investigation which permits us to comprehend the purposes for which and the strategies by which policy is elaborated' (Castles 1989, p.8). By adopting the 'disciplined-configurative' mode of analysis as outlined by George (1979, p.50) we intend to use general variables for purposes of description and explanation. This method is often criticized for its limited ability in generalizing from a single case. Yet we believe that the uniqueness of a single case can be overcome by describing it 'in more general terms, that is, as a particular value of a general variable that is part of a theoretical framework of independent, intervening, and dependent variables' (George 1979, p.47). Heclo further supports this approach and states: 'Such a study is intended to monitor or explicate some larger phenomenon and thus is to be planned under the impetus of theory rather than the excrescent accumulation of whatever data happen to turn up' (Heclo 1972 in George 1979, p.179).

Thus, the phenomenon under study in our Swedish research project is change in higher education systems. Our study is driven by theories of policy formation and policy realization, connected by the frame factor theory and a space of action model. For further elaboration on our project's international comparative methods see Kogan (1996c).

Material and data

The data from which this book draws conclusions are derived from documents, statistics and semi-structured interviews. This includes Parliament and Government reform documents and material from central agencies. Reports and descriptions of organization and the distribution of authority and responsibility as well as accounts of their systems for quality assurance and development, have been collected from the institutions in the study. When relevant, documented information from other Swedish higher education institutions has also been employed. The statistics used have been obtained from Statistics Sweden, the National Higher Education Agency and from individual institutions and departments.

Since the focus of our international comparative project is on the universities, we have, for the Swedish study, selected four universities as study objects – two large and two smaller ones of varying age.

However, in order to cover the institutional variance of the Swedish comprehensive higher education system, we have also included one large and one smaller college[1] in our study.

At the basic level, six disciplines were selected for the study to cover the range from the humanistic and social sciences to the natural sciences: history, modern languages, sociology, economics, physics and biochemistry. The study thus concentrates on the more academic fields of knowledge and excludes, for example, the more professionally oriented faculties of law, medicine and engineering. This limitation was due to the hypothesis that reform demands and possible change or non-change in values and attitudes among academic staff would be better observable within the chosen disciplinary fields. Another weighty reason for the selection of disciplines was the design of the comparative study, i.e. consideration of reform characteristics and conditions in British higher education.

These six major disciplinary areas are represented in the study by various subfields, like economics and business studies and different modern languages. They also differ in what concerns types of departments or units in which they are based. Since the respondents in the interviews have been guaranteed anonymity we do not identify the individual institutions and basic units in the study.

Table 2.1 Sources of Empirical Data			
	1975–1998		1994–1996
	Government and Agency documents	*Institutions' reports*	*Interviews*
Macro	X		12
			Universities	Colleges
Meso	X	X	14	5
Micro		X	61	16
			Total: 108	

---

1 In this book we use the term 'college' for a type of institution with a limited provision of undergraduate education but without the right to award doctoral degrees and without permanent funding for research. In Swedish these institutions have commonly been referred to as 'mindre och mellanstora högskolor'.

Interviews

The interviews with institutional leaders and faculty were carried out during the spring term of 1995, thus, two years after the launching of the reform. At the meso level, interviews were made with the rectors,[2] other institutional leaders, deans and top administrators (two to five persons at each institution). At the micro level, seven to fourteen academics (including the head of department) from each of the six disciplines were interviewed (see Table 2.1). The interviews were approximately one and a half hours in length.

For the selection of academic staff to be interviewed we asked the heads of departments to suggest some more experienced and some newer faculty among whom we could sample respondents. This procedure implies a risk of obtaining a biased sample depending on preferences of the head. Yet, taking into account the limitation in numbers of interviews possible to undertake, we considered it more important to reach academic staff in the 'center' of the higher education activities. In spite of efforts to get a more even age distribution, our sample is probably quite representative of the present population of faculty at the higher education institutions. The group is strongly dominated by men born in the 1940s and socialized into the higher education system during the late 1960s and 1970s. (See Appendix 1.)

The rectors of the six institutions all gave very positive responses to our request to let their institutions take part in the study. All persons being approached for an interview immediately agreed (only one person found it impossible to find a suitable time for the interview). Several persons expressed appreciation about the opportunity to talk about these matters.

Our interviews with the academic teachers/researchers were structured in three groups of themes. The first group started with questions concerning the respondents themselves – their professional position, activities, priorities and roles as well as their academic careers and who/what had influenced them most. Finally, they were asked if anything occurring during the past few years had been a

---

2   'Rektor' is the Swedish term corresponding to the British 'Vice-Chancellor' or the American 'President' for the universities but also for the head of other types of higher education institutions. In this book we use the term 'rector' throughout.

reason for change in these matters, or if their answers would have been practically the same three years ago.

The second category of questions was about which ideals and missions of the university, according to them, ought to be the leading principles for its operations. In connection to this we also asked for their conceptions or notions of quality in higher education and research and how they thought one could go about in order to assure and enhance this kind of quality. Finally, they were asked about their view concerning the preconditions and possibilities to keep up the quality of teaching and research at their own university and department in the near future.

The third and final group of questions concerned the H-93 reform. Questioning started with a more neutral question about which had been the most important changes at their university during the past two to three years, and what implications these had had for themselves and for their university. The responses to these questions were then used as a starting-point for investigating their knowledge about and attitudes towards the H-93 reform. Finally, they were asked about which elements in the reform they considered to be of greatest significance for the future development of higher education and its institutions.

At the macro level, the purpose of conducting the interviews has been to shed light on and confirm the information obtained from official government documents. This is quite different from the micro and meso level where the interviews comprise a large part of the primary empirical material. As a result, both the time frame for conducting the interviews and the amount of interviews necessary for empirical reasons differed substantially at this level. A total of twelve interviews were conducted (approximately two and a half hours in length) during the time period of February 1996 to March 1998 with the majority taking place during 1996.

At all levels of our investigation, the interviews were recorded on tape and transcripts were produced soon afterwards. Given the somewhat sensitive nature of the topics discussed, we guaranteed that the participants would remain anonymous. Thus, the quotes which appear in this book are not identified by name, but rather by type of organization and position which the respondents hold or held. In situations where quotes are publicly available (for example, published debate articles in newspapers or official statements from politicians) references are of course complete. However, these are used in conjunction with other anonymous quotes in an attempt to provide full context and texture to the book. We alone are responsible for the translations from Swedish to English.

We have handled the vast amount of interview data by using a computer software called QSR NUD*IST which stands for 'Non-numerical Unstructured Data Indexing Searching and Theorizing'. This program allowed us to develop our own coding system for the project, according to which the interview data were then classified and stored. Interview data could then be retrieved under a variety of different themes, and the relevance of it for our theoretical framework could also be recorded using this type of software.

Chapter 3

Higher Education Policy and System Changes in Retrospect

Background

For many centuries, Sweden has been ethnically, linguistically and religiously, a very homogeneous nation. This is no longer true, since approximately one million of its 8.7 million population are immigrants, including citizens from other Nordic countries, or have at least one immigrant parent. The national language is Swedish, except in the very north where there are both Finnish-speaking people and the Sami. (Facts about the current structure of the Swedish higher education system are presented in Appendix 2.)

Parliament is the country's highest decision-making authority. With the exception of six years of non-socialist rule from 1976 to 1982, the Social Democrats were in power from 1932 to 1991, either alone or in coalition with other parties. In 1991, the non-socialist parties collectively won a majority and ruled for three years. However, after the 1994 election the Social Democrats were again in power and formed, as several times previously, a minority government. A characteristic feature of the Swedish administrative system is the division of tasks between the ministries and the central administrative agencies.

Framework and themes

Many comparative studies have convincingly shown that educational systems are deeply embedded in the very formation of nations. Thus, they also reflect the fundamental steps taken in each nation to create its modern state. Crucial changes in purpose, governance, and overall structure often seem to be surprisingly similar in Western countries.

However, a closer examination often indicates that when changes have been undertaken, they reflect conditions that are characteristic for their own national context (Clark 1983; Dahllöf 1984, 1999; Scott 1995, Teichler 1996a).

Today, when more initiatives are expected to be taken by the higher education institutions themselves, there is necessity for in-depth knowledge of the very nature and function of the system. Still, changes in purpose, conditions, and governance in a particular system must be seen in relation to the background factors which not only form the frames of reference of the actors but also of the researchers in that particular system. Therefore, in this chapter we will give an overview of some characteristic features of the Swedish higher education system, mainly with regard to its overall structure and governance. The perspective chosen is that of the system as a mediator between policy and practice, functioning as an instrument for expressing policy by framing the conditions and the activities of the institutions and the actors.

Towards a modern higher education system in Sweden (pre-1960)

Since the 15th century, Swedish universities have been responsible for training almost all kinds of higher civil servants in accordance with a fairly strict degree system, which reflected the demands of the national state and its schools, church, and judicial system (Liedman and Olausson 1988; Blomqvist 1992). The universities were subordinate to the state in recruiting and appointing professors and teachers. The academic corps was closely allied with the state administration (Svensson 1987). This long tradition of close relations between the state (and the church and the public) and the schools evidently formed a particular readiness for certain measures to be taken when the first period of expansion was to be met. Besides, with such a tradition of state governance, Swedish universities and colleges have never had a legally autonomous status as those of Anglo-Saxon universities (Lane 1992).

In the beginning of the 20th century, Swedish universities attracted just about one percent of 20-year-old individuals (Blomqvist 1992). Then, during the first half of the century, the number of students at the universities and specialized institutions gradually increased. The institutions were state governed, and the rules and regulations were often laid down after long and respectful negotiations between the government and the professors. Although most studies were, in one sense, professionally oriented and prepared for state positions, the academic world was closed, restricted and dominated by the academic professoriate. They looked upon themselves mainly as civil servants (Svensson 1987). At the time, the open admission to the so-called free faculties (humanities, natural and social sciences) and the following increase in student numbers were not identified as problems. On the contrary, the expansion of comprehensive and upper secondary schooling at that time brought about a demand for subject teachers for the schools, and, thus, the gradual expansion of the number of university students was welcomed.

The goals of the universities were rather diffuse and not explicitly formulated. There was, however, one exception: the universities were expected to carry out research under the protection of the state. Researchers were looked upon as 'motors' in the development of society (Westling, Angsmark and Blomqvist 1997). Within the overall framework of professional preparation for the public sector, goals and content of undergraduate education were self-evidently set by the academics themselves.

Funding was not regarded as a problem either. In 1958, for example, the resources allocated to undergraduate education were dependent on the actual number of students entering undergraduate education. This was called the 'automation', and was a generous funding mechanism, particularly for the faculties of humanities and social sciences to which access was not restricted. As pointed out by Westling *et al.* (1997), the fact that the state did not control the volume of funding gives an indication of the strong and independent position of the universities at that time. The institutions received funding in relation to the number of students who started programs and courses, independently of how many of these students actually completed their programs and courses. This funding model was suggested by a governmental commission chaired by the Rector of Uppsala University in what is known as the 1955 University Commission (Statens Offentliga Utredningar (SOU) 1959:45; 1963:9). A large administration on the national level was created for allocating the funds in accordance with the rules that had been set up.

While funding was not considered a problem, the recruitment of qualified university teachers was. A new position called the university lectorate was established, entirely for teaching. The lecturer had his/her main teaching duties in undergraduate education, thus allowing the professors to do research and take part in graduate education. The introduction of this 'university lecturer position' was also recommended by the 1955 University Commission and was established in 1959. This position introduced an uneven and unfamiliar division between research and teaching and, as will be evident later on in this chapter, has since caused constant problems and discussions about how to overcome this separation. At that time, quality was not a particular issue in the way it is today, but using today's language, the creation of the lecturer position was a measure to improve the quality in teaching.

The political governance of higher education was guided by a belief in human capital theory and a trust in the academics to plan the curricula. The system was extended and enlarged in many dimensions and variables at the same time: more students, more student places in the form of open access, more resources, more institutions, more lecturers and more scheduled lectures. In the reform process of growing expansion, the academics of the universities were well represented. Relations between the academic oligarchy and leading politicians were cordial as they appeared to work hand in hand towards a common goal (Elzinga 1993). The internal governance was in the hands of the rector and a number of internal decision-making bodies, all with a solid academic representation.

The access to research facilities and the right to award PhD degrees formed a demarcation between the two old universities (Uppsala and Lund), a few specialized institutions and two modern city colleges (Stockholm and Göteborg) on the one hand, and vocationally-oriented colleges on the other hand. (A major category in the latter group was teacher colleges.) Thus, the system was mainly structured as a binary system.

The higher education system today enrolls more than one-third of the cohorts of young people aged around 20. Even so, this is still a low percentage compared to many other western countries. The development towards a mass higher education system has also meant successive redefinition of what is actually to be classified by 'higher education'. As a result, making comparisons over time is somewhat troublesome. From the middle of this century, successive periods of expansion (see Figure 3.1) have been marked by broader access, greater diversity both of students and studies, and a wider range of goals and obligations.

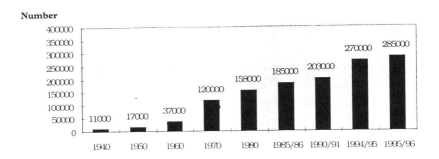

Figure 3.1 Number of higher education students 1940–1995
Source: SOU 1997:7; Högskoleverket 1996d

Expansion in the sixties: paving the way for a structural reform (1960–1977)

In the 1960s, a period of rapid expansion took place. The number of students increased from 37,000 in 1960 to 120,000 in 1970 (see Figure 3.1), mainly in the faculty of humanities and the new faculty of social sciences (where it was easy to expand). Of course, many of the students in these faculties were first generation students. However, many of them did not intend to prepare for a teaching profession, which was the main task of the faculty of humanities, but they combined courses organized in half-or one-year long discipline-based studies which did not fit to the structure of the labor market and its prescribed requirements. The course offerings were sensitive to student demands, and the 'automation' made it rewarding for the institutions to be sensitive to these demands. However, neither the students nor the institutions were sensitive to the labor market.

The expansion in student numbers, in combination with the automatic resource allocation system and the new senior lecturer position, became very expensive. In most subjects the amount of teaching increased from about 5 hours a week to 20–25 hours, with the professional schools as a model. Consequently, senior lecturers among undergraduate staff increased enormously (Dahllöf 1984).

A new commission was appointed, the 1963 University and College Commission, also chaired by the Rector of Uppsala University (SOU 1965:11–12). The task was to prepare a proposition for a further expansion of the higher education system. The Commission suggested the establishment of branches to the universities. As these institutions were restricted to undergraduate education, the expansion was met by a continuation of the binary system.

'Throughput' became a buzzword in the argumentation for a renewal of the undergraduate education structure, while 'planning' became a buzzword in the debate on how to cope with identified problems in society. In order to increase the fairly low examination rate in the faculties of humanities and social sciences, the Commission also suggested a system of fixed study plans.

In 1964, Parliament decided on a restructuring of the universities' internal governance. The decision-making power was allocated to the university board (the Konsistorium – the assembly of deans), and the rector and registrar, which was a new position, formed the Rector's Office (rektorsämbetet). The registrar was the head of the central administration and was also a formal member of the Konsistorium, with a right to vote. The central administration got several accountability obligations and in the following twenty years these obligations increased extensively.

In 1966, the government commissioned an expert group with the sole task of structuring all undergraduate education in a comprehensive system of national study lines.[1] All members of this expert group (called the Universitetskanslers-ämbetets arbetsgrupp för fasta studiegångar, UKAS) were civil servants, which meant a break from earlier procedures. Working groups of representatives for various disciplines were annexed to this group. The so-called UKAS system of firmly regulated study lines was presented in 1968. It was met with surprise and criticism from the professors, mainly from the faculties of humanities and social sciences. The study line system in these faculties meant a significant break from the traditional discipline-dominated structure. It also met with heavy opposition from the students, who used the proposed system as a target for their

---

1   The model was taken from the so-called professional training programs (such as medical education) and was now applied to all kinds of undergraduate education that led to university degrees.

attacks on the political steering and the growing bureaucratization of education.

In the following year, 1969, a slightly modified system was presented by a working group (called PUKAS, where P stood for (Olof) Palme who was the Minister of Education at that time). General study plans were laid down for each line. The lines were to be divided into courses and the courses to be expressed in points (expected study time), aiming at giving the students a better overview of their studies and, at the same time, giving the institutions (and the government) a better overview of the students' progress. The so-called point-production was also directly linked to the students' study loans and grants. This link called for a close, continuous examination of the point-production.

Although this system was not greeted with any enthusiasm by the academics, it was accepted, since the students were calmed down and the academics felt saved from feared student revolts. Student representatives were also invited to take seats in the faculty boards, a measure which contributed to calming down the students' opposition. This invitation, in 1968/69, formed the start of the so-called FNYS-project,[1] which was introduced as a trial period of broader student participation and teacher-student cooperation, but without the fixation of a time period. In retrospect, however, the professors lost much of their historical authority in this trans-formation process (Elzinga 1993).

The extensive national restructuring of undergraduate education changed the role of the national intermediary body. Up to this point, the university chancellor had mainly acted as a spokesman of the rectors, and was elected by the Academia, in accordance with the tradition from medieval times. Now, this tradition was terminated. In 1964, a new intermediate board was established as a national authority and was now called the University Chancellor's Office, UKÄ. The chancellor was appointed by the government. According to its instruction from the government, the new Office was expected to elaborate plans for the future development of higher education in accordance with societal demands. The office was also expected to undertake investigations of its own. The office was truly an

1   FNYS is the acronym for Försöksverksamhet med nya former för samarbete mellan lärare, studerande m fl. (Experiment with new forms of student and staff cooperation).

intermediate body, and played an active role between the government and the institutions by aggregating national data on student numbers and student progress as a base for further governmental decisions (Lane and Fredriksson 1983).

During this period of rapid expansion, the pedagogical aspects of the expansion were also paid attention to, especially with regards to teaching quality. In 1965, the University Chancellor's Office initiated an investigation to review academic teaching and examination (Universitetspedagogiska utredningen, known as UPU). The Rector of Uppsala University was again the chairman of the investigating commission and the members were senior academics and students. The commission published several reports. In its final report, the commission suggested several measures to be undertaken in order to support teachers in improving their teaching methods (Universitetskanslersämbetet 1970). For example, as a direct consequence, staff development centers were established at the large universities and topics such as students' examinations and assessments were highlighted in development projects and research work. It was also recommended, but not stipulated, that teachers ought to be offered courses in pedagogy. Furthermore, a Research and Development unit was established at the National Board.

So far, we have described the development of undergraduate education. With regard to research, the shift from a close reliance on regulated and earmarked funding to direct funding to the institutions, which became the major trend in the 1990s, was initiated much earlier. Already in the 1940s and 1950s, national research councils were established, and a substantial amount of resources were designated to these new national bodies, governed by representatives of researchers that were elected by university faculty members. The research councils formed a kind of interinstitutional national faculty board. They also formed a national market for researchers and their departments, and made the researchers more independent relative to the resources of their own institutions. In the 1960s, sectorial research boards were established. These boards funded socially relevant applied research, which in fact implied a reduction in the researchers' autonomy (Elzinga 1993; Nybom 1997). In addition, through such arrangements, the separation of undergraduate education from research was further emphasized.

An extensive reform in 1977

All the efforts during the 1960s to manage the expansion by establishing institutions and by introducing fixed plans and study points can be seen as a series of preparations for the H-77 reform. What follows is a description of the H-77 reform and its effect on the educational system.

In 1968, the government established a commission preparing a proposition for an extensive reform of the entire higher education system (the so-called U-68 Commission). The commission was chaired by the Under-secretary at the Ministry of Education while the other members of this commission were high-level civil servants in charge of the national boards that would be mostly affected by the reform. This composition raised a lot of objections from the universities. As was the case in UKAS a few years earlier, the academics were excluded from having influence on the political reform work.

The higher education system was now explicitly looked upon by the commission as a tool for reforming society, not just for coping with the expansion of student numbers. The influence of Keynesian principles and the ideas of full employment and planned growth were evident. After five years of investigations, the results of the Commission's task were published in an 800-page report (SOU 1973:2). Following an extensive preparation phase (by the so-called U68-beredningen), including a circulation of the report for comments, a proposition was to be presented to the Parliament in May of 1975. At about that very time, however, the ruling Social Democrats lost the election. After some political confusion, the proposition was somewhat adjusted and the new non-socialist coalition government presented it as its own. In 1977, almost ten years after the first measures were taken by the U-68 Commission, the Parliament decided to set the reform into work the very same year.

The 1970s represented a period of large-scale political programs, and the H-77 reform reflects this trend. The reform did not just aim at educational improvements, but also at radical social and political ones. The reform covered such areas as the structure of under-graduate education, the content of the studies, and a totally restricted admissions system. The expansion was met with a manifestation of the principle of equality, by the use of centralized planning and a uniformity in structure. Following the suggestions of the PUKAS working group, all undergraduate education was now to fall within five main vocational sectors with the normal study plan to be determined by the National Board in Stockholm and implemented equally throughout Sweden. The five sectors were: technology; administration, economics, and social work; medicine; teaching; and cultural work and information.

Key goals of the reform were to reduce the social stratification in students' enrollment for further education and the differences in status and prestige among the study lines. Also important was the goal to achieve a more equal geographical distribution of educational opportunities. The main means to reach these goals was through the creation of a system in which all post-secondary education was integrated in the 'Högskolan' and subordinated to a common higher education ordinance. Former teacher education colleges were used as the base for the creation of regional colleges. The uniformity of the system at large aimed at reducing the differences in status and prestige of higher education institutions.

With such a structured system, it was assumed that the national standards of the degrees could still be taken for granted despite the expansion of the system. As a consequence, accountability was still mainly seen as observance of the regulations and the teachers still held the main responsibility for examining their own students (a practice which gave strong autonomy to the individual teacher). In contrast to this, the tradition of external examiners and peer reviews have been kept and actively protected in research and graduate education (Askling and Bauer 1997).

Funding for undergraduate studies was earmarked to lines and courses and based on fixed numbers of study places. Thus, this was the end of the 'automation' system of funding. The total number of study places in every line and at every institution was decided by Parliament (the *numerus clausus* principle), which meant that admission was restricted – and still is. Access to the higher education system was centrally regulated and administrated, and a new access rule (the 25:4 rule) was introduced. This so called 25:4 rule allowed for persons of at least 25 years of age with four years of work experience and equivalent high school competence in English and Swedish to qualify for admission. The centralized admissions meant that the institutions and their faculties had no influence on the selection of their own prospective students.

However, with regard to research resources, the division between teaching and research (which began with the creation of the senior lecturer position in the late 1950s) was solidified by the Parliament's decision to provide funding to the institutions based on separate categories for research and for undergraduate education.

Thus, from one point of view, the reform just meant a relabeling of those institutions which prior to 1977 did not belong to the higher education sector. From another point of view, the H-77 reform meant a substantial increase in aspirations, as all institutions within the sector were subordinated to one and the same Higher Education Law and Ordinance and it was declared that all undergraduate education must be based on scientific knowledge. However, this declaration was not accompanied by a corresponding increase in resources for realizing these aspirations. As will be evident later in this chapter, this postulate had implications for the interpretation of quality twenty years later.

In the new parts of the system, the regional colleges, this aspect of the reform was not only considered a challenge, but also a qualitative problem. It evoked an intense debate among teachers in teacher education concerning what was to be considered the scientific knowledge base for their vocational lines. Concepts such as 'professional knowledge', 'scientific knowledge versus practical knowledge', and 'tacit knowledge' were brought to the fore, as were the pedagogical and methodological consequences (Bergendal 1990).

In the H-77 reform, the importance of the planning and coordinating role of the intermediary body with regard to the national system was further emphasized. In order to manage such a unified system, with long-term planning and resource allocation needs, the government established a new National Board for Universities and Colleges (UHÄ), thus dismantling the University Chancellor's Office (UKÄ). The exclusion of the word 'Chancellor' in the renaming of the board announced further breakage of its link to the academic heritage. The new name pointed out its main role to be that of a national authority. The board was expected to take necessary initiatives in the creation of new study lines and courses. Thus, initiatives were expected to be taken on the national level, where one got the best overview of the system at large. National study plans were prepared by the Board and were directed to local study line committees. Elzinga (1993) calls this formation the creation of the 'University of Sweden', composed of local campuses. Every university should in principle be considered the equal of all other universities (Liedman 1992).

The reform also aimed at a decentralization of decision-making power for matters concerning undergraduate education. In order to support innovation and flexibility on curriculum matters, a new kind of decision-making body, the so-called study line committees, was constructed for the more detailed preparation of the lines and their courses. The National Board (UHÄ) also commissioned a series of investigations on innovation and innovation processes in higher education and on the role of local planning for renewal (Berg and Östergren 1977).

The very composition of these study line committees reflected innovation. Representatives of non-academic staff were invited to take part, as were representatives of students and of the corresponding vocational fields. The demands of the students, the labor market, and society were brought into the higher education context as new legitimate points of reference for curriculum decisions. In this matrix organization of disciplines and lines, the lines were meant to be the predominant ones. However, the widened space of action for local initiatives by the committees to renew the lines within the framework set by the national study plans was seldom utilized as much as it was intended. One major reason was that, often, the three groups of representatives blocked each other, since no group could prove that its own standpoint was 'better' than anyone else's (Askling 1983; Eklund 1986). Nevertheless, the matrix organization brought about a heavy bureaucracy (Lane 1989; 1990).

The composition of these committees, with representatives from all categories of academic teachers, students, and vocational fields, also meant a further step away from the authority of the professoriate on undergraduate issues. The formal influence of the professors was thus reduced simultaneously from two directions (students and staff). As all these measures were launched by the government as steps towards democratization of society in general and of work places in particular, it was almost impossible for the professors to argue against such a dispersion of influence. Even so, as civil servants and respected chair holders, the professors felt that they still held the academic responsibility of their disciplines. Furthermore, it was congruent with the growth of corporatism in Sweden at that time (Ruin 1979; 1991).

Thus, the reform in 1977 created a higher education system marked by several contradictory characteristics: It was first of all, a strange combination of restricted admissions and mass education. Second, it created a new organization of centrally-designed vocational study lines in the faculties of humanities, social sciences and natural sciences (within the other faculties the traditional professional line structure remained) in combination with decentralization measures aimed at supporting local innovation and change within this uniform system. Further, there was a plea to remain true to Humboldtian ideals of research connected to undergraduate education while most institutions were denied permanent funding for research and, additionally, deliberately developing towards sectorial and mainly applied research. The vocational orientation reflected the old tradition where the higher educational system was sensitive to the needs of the state and the state apparatus, including the urgent needs of the politicians at that time, to establish an extensive public sector rather than to the needs of the private sector to get qualified personnel. However, in the faculties of humanities, social sciences, and natural sciences the strong vocational orientation was an unfamiliar element – but not to the universities in general.

The reform left a 'heritage' which has been brought to the fore in the recent concern for quality. From the point of view of most academics, stipulations in the Ordinance in the 1970s concerning research connections formed a powerful and demanding definition of quality. The uniformity in structure and in Ordinance, in combination with the heterogeneity with regard to research facilities and staff duties, formed a conceptual framework through which the issue of quality was later interpreted.

Tinkering with decentralization

In the beginning of the 1980s, some senior academics belonging to the Social Democratic party questioned the firm structure of the so-called 'free' faculties and the introduction of a knowledge structure which was mainly based on social relevance (Myrdal 1982; Gustavsson 1982; af Trolle 1990).

From 1978, a division within UHÄ had the task to carry through a 'Reform Follow-Up Program' ('Reformuppföljningsprogrammet') in which problems and difficulties with the H-77 reform were identified. In 1983, adjustments to the access system took place in order to provide more study places for the growing age groups from secondary schools. Also, the institutional organization was questioned, as was the system of study lines for its lack of freedom for student preferences and choices.

During the 1980s, the Social Democratic party gradually retreated from its earlier centralist policy. By taking several steps towards further decentralization and deregulation of the state apparatus, the government expressed a belief in local responsibility as an important means for supporting flexibility and efficiency. As a consequence of the desire to improve flexibility in the system, the role of UHÄ was questioned. Although the planning role was still predominant, a new instruction to the Board in 1988 added both evaluative and assessment functions. An entire restructuring of the Board took place in 1990. However, this reorganization lasted for just one year.

In the 1980s, the number of students was kept almost at the same level, with a total of about 180,000–188,000 enrolled students, and between 40,000 and 45,000 new entrants per year, despite the considerable increase in the number of applications for places. By the end of the 1980s, a gradual decrease in the government's strong confidence in the public sector became apparent. A new steering system for the entire Swedish public sector based on goal-oriented regulation, extensive autonomy on internal matters, and accountability was introduced (Gov. Prop. 1987/88:150, 1988/89:65). This reorganization of the Swedish bureaucracy appears to be in line with similar trends in the other Nordic countries towards new public management (Bleiklie 1996a, Hölttä 1995).

With regard to higher education, successive steps of modification from the firm structure of undergraduate education were taken during this period and a radical restructuring of the funding system was proposed to be set into action in 1993. At about the same time, the Social Democratic government commenced an increase in the number of study places and a breakup of the lines in undergraduate education.

In 1989, Bengt Göransson, the Social Democratic Minister of Education responded to criticism from students regarding poor teaching and called upon a commission to scrutinize the state of the art of teaching in undergraduate education and to suggest measures for its improvement. Their point of departure was not political visions, but was to identify shortcomings (UPU, twenty years earlier, had a similar point of departure).

The work of the commission, similar to the UPU at the end of the 1960s, was led by a rector and its members were senior academics and one student ('Högskoleutredningen', SOU 1992:1). The final report from the commission was entitled 'Freedom, Responsibility, Competence', and was met with positive reactions from both academics and students. Many academics were almost flattered by the many references to Humboldtian ideals, and to the declared need for a connection between research and undergraduate education as major criteria for increased quality in higher education. Following its directives, the commission simply kept to issues in teaching and learning and took the current structure and organization of the system for granted. The recommendations were also similar to the ones launched by the UPU twenty years earlier:

- pedagogical/methodological training for teachers
- an awareness of the steering power of examination
- experimentation with new kinds of examinations
- course evaluations
- the use of external examiners.

As proposed by the Commission, a National Council for Under-graduate Education was established by the government. It may be noted that when the commission report was to be presented to the minister, a Conservative government had succeeded the Social Democrats.

The 'freedom for quality' reform in 1993

In 1992 and 1993, Per Unckel, the incoming Conservative Minister of Education and Science, published the government's ideas on the direction of higher education and research in a series of propositions and bills, using many of the key concepts from the Commission's report, such as 'quality', 'freedom', 'academic autonomy', and 'academic competence'. However, for Unckel, the ideas referred mainly to phenomena on the system level, which was not the case in the Commission's report (Ministry of Education and Science 1993; Unckel 1994).

The propositions gave a broad presentation of the policy. In many respects, it also formed a criticism of the policy of state regulation which was considered a main factor of the Social Democratic model of governance of the 1970s (and at the same time at least partly ignoring the fact that the Social Democrats themselves retreated from that kind of governance in the late 1980s). The new government used its political sphere of action for implementing substantial changes in the resource allocation system and in the representation in the boards, thus in two fundamental ways changing the preconditions for governance and management of the institutions. In contrast to the H-77 reform, the H-93 reform was prepared and supervised by the Ministry of Education, who, in turn, invited the rectors to informal meetings.

Government influence over higher education institutions was to be radically reduced, it was argued, in order to create more favorable conditions for fulfilling higher education's dual role as an institution for education as well as centers for critical thought. In contrast to the rhetoric of the H-77 reform, the new reform saw higher education not just as a tool for political goals but rather for supporting national interests in an international and competitive marketplace. Thus, a more profound decentralization was announced.

The main – and radical – change in the H-93 reform was the shift from state governance through regulation and input control to governance through control of outcomes and through external forces acting upon the universities and colleges. The influence from current British higher education policy was evident as were references to positive experiences from the market-orientation and competitiveness of the American university systems.

In the new Higher Education Ordinance in 1993, the dual leadership at the universities shared by the rector and the registrar was abandoned, and the rector became instead both the academic *and* the administrative leader of the university. The autonomy in the internal organization and in the internal allocation of resources for under-graduate education increased. Further, the universities obtained the right to appoint their own professors. On the other hand, in the university boards, the external representatives, who made up the majority of the board, were appointed by the government.[3] In addition, the centrally determined permanent study line system was abolished, except for the professionally oriented lines, which still

---

3　Since January 1998, the rector is no longer the chairman of the university board. The chairman is now one of the external representatives.

represent about 40 percent of all undergraduate education (Statistiska Centralbyrån 1996b). The academics regained their influence on curriculum matters, through the abandonment of external representation on study line committees.

Also introduced in 1993 was a new resource allocation system for undergraduate education. This was done by replacing the former input-based system by an output-based system, in which the institutions are given an educational assignment before the commencement of each three-year period. Resources are to be based on estimated examination rates in the lines, and not only by fixed price tags per enrolled student. These estimates are made by the institutions (formally by the university boards) and allow for a certain amount of risk-taking by the institutions. The resource allocation system is based on performance, but not, as initially intended by the government, linked to quality assurance and dependent on national quality indicators.

The funding of research and post-graduate education at the universities and the specialized institutions has not been changed. This funding is still predesignated to each faculty area, which means that the government still exerts influence on the relative proportions of research funding to the faculties and, thus, the volume of postgraduate education. However, there also exist other forms of state funding for research. In addition to the earlier-mentioned research councils, there are available to researchers today a number of foundations for strategic research. These research foundations were established in 1994 by the Conservative government after having dismantled the large wage earners' funds. This radical measure has considerably raised the total amount of state funding for research, despite reduction in the state funding that goes directly to the institutions for research. Conservatives have thus contributed to a shift in the proportions between direct and indirect state funding of research. Today, the universities rely much more on external funding of their research. Since this funding is directly dependent on and, more precisely, is the result of actions of individual researchers or research groups, it strengthens the economic autonomy at the departmental level relative to the institutional level (Askling, Almén and Karlsson 1995).

A key concept in the reform is quality. The use of this concept implied a quite new view regarding quality matters. The increased institutional autonomy in decision-making was to be counterbalanced by an increase in external control. Competition between institutions was expected to encourage both efficiency and quality. National assessments and quality indicators directly linked to funding were expected to exert external *ex post facto* control as well as informing students.

Despite the overall impression of deregulation and loosening of the central structure, the total number of study places at a given institution was still restricted by national budget considerations. Student grants and loans were still to be centrally administered, separate from the university system, and many degrees in vocationally-oriented programs were still expected to adhere to a national standard.

As a consequence of this new way of looking at the relationship between the state and the institutions, the role of UHÄ was once again reconsidered. In 1991, new instructions were set into action, followed by a new reorganization. It was said that evaluation and follow-up studies were to be the main tasks of the Board in the development towards further deregulation of the higher education sector and a further increase in autonomy of the institutions. However, in 1992, UHÄ was closed down, and its remaining functions were split up among new bodies. The admission system formed one service body, the investigation- and research-oriented functions were concentrated in one very small body and the evaluative functions formed the basis of the new Secretariat of Assessment and Evaluation (later renamed 'the University Chancellor's Office').

Further expansion and partial return to a more centralist policy

Propositions, governmental decisions, and parliamentary bills are important documents when scrutinizing formal changes within a particular field. At the same time, their importance must not be overestimated. The political will in a government proposition or the 'power' of a bill can be radically reduced by circumstances that already occurred early in the implementation phase of a reform.

The Higher Education Reform of 1993 is no exception to such a statement. Soon after the bill came into effect, the Conservative government faced new and unforeseen conditions which modified the whole idea of the institutions competing with each other for positive quality assessments by students, government, and the market.

In order to cope with increasing unemployment and a budget deficit, the government had to cut public expenditures and, thus, partly retreat from its own policy on higher education reform. Due to rapid changes in society, which were out of reach of government control, the government was forced to break its own rules of deregulation and intervene in its own planning cycles and waver between long-sighted, policy-oriented changes and short-term ad hoc adjustments (Askling 1997b). For example, the institutions were given a number of additional assignments, such as summer university courses. These assignments were more regulated and prescribed than the assignments in the regular three-year contracts.

The shift towards a supervising model of governmental steering has been slow. The University Chancellor was successful in turning the demands for formalized public and external control into more humble and modest pleas for quality development programs to be examined by audit teams.

Since 1994, the Social Democratic party forms the government and a return to the ideals of centralism is evident in many of the measures taken (Högskoleverket 1997c). For example, the government has increased its control of the large strategic research foundations and of the university boards by appointing external representatives as chairs. However, when it comes to how to control quality in higher education, the new government has so far kept a low profile.

In 1995, a new National Agency for Higher Education was established and the University Chancellor's Office was integrated into this agency. The agency is responsible for exerting *ex post facto* control over institutions by using national assessments and audits. The agency also received responsibility for accrediting institutions with the right to award degrees and for establishing professorships at institutions not having permanent research funds (some of the colleges have now (1998) been successful in their applications for university status).

System changes in a forty-year perspective

When Sweden entered into the first period of expansion, there were, as in many other European countries, strong elements in the higher education system of the so-called professional model that reflected the needs of the state and the state professions (Bleiklie 1996a). These elements formed a basis for the social engineering policy of the 1960s and 1970s and the strong vocationalisation of higher education. Over the years, influence from the Humboldt ideals have had impact, not in the least by the work of the Higher Education Commission at the end of the 1980s. Through intense interaction with Anglo-American higher education institutions, the Swedish higher education system has gained increasing influence of the so-called personality model, reflecting the Oxford and Cambridge ideals of civilizing the gentlemen (Bleiklie 1993; Kerr 1994a; Scott 1995). These influences form, then, a mixture of norms and expectations.

Ruin (1991), in an overview of political preferences and institutional reforms in the Swedish higher education system, identified six developmental trends, which have all been used since the 1970s:

- planning
- democratization
- corporativism
- decentralization
- re-professionalization
- marketization.

In each one of the two major reforms in Sweden (1977 and 1993), all six elements can be identified. Although the two reforms, in many respects, can be looked upon as the opposite of each other, both of them are parts of a larger development: the expansion of the higher education system as an 'agent' in the modernization of the Swedish society. Each one of the reforms reflects the 'spirit of the time' with regard to reform intentions and reform strategies. The H-77 reform was a reaction to an uncontrolled and costly expansion of the number of students, which started in the early 1960s. The H-93 reform was meant to support a necessary further expansion of higher education, albeit within a more controlled economic framework. The H-77 reform aimed at rational planning of the higher education system through a uniform structure of the entire system. At the same time it also aimed at innovation and change through a decentralization of responsibilities on curriculum issues, which was still to be accomplished within the framework of nationwide equality of standard. The extensive H-93 reform aimed at facilitating change and creating flexibility through an extensive decentralization of responsibilities for 'heavy' issues to the institutions, counterbalanced by ex-post control of efficiency and quality of the outcomes.

Thus, from the 1960s to the 1990s, a fundamental shift has taken place with regard to the government's trust in central planning. From having had the total initiative of the development of the basic structure of higher education in the 1970s, the government today has left much of its former space for initiatives in creating programs and courses and in staffing to the institutions themselves. In the rhetoric of the H-77 reform, the well-consolidated binary structure of the higher education system was almost denied, although it was quite evident that there were major differences between the old and the new parts of higher education with regard to stratification of students, composition of staff, and access to research resources. In the H-93 reform, these ingrained superficial notions of uniformity on the national system level were questioned. The variation among the institutions with regard to size, content and resources is no longer concealed. The institutions are encouraged to create a distinctive image of themselves, perhaps thereby opening up for a more explicit stratification of the system.

With reference to the current concern for quality, the quality control of undergraduate education was, earlier, mainly exerted by use of administrative measures. Within this framework, the autonomy of the individual teacher was fairly extensive, compared to university teachers in many other countries where there is a long tradition of external examination, national assessments, and peer reviews as collegially accomplished quality control.

Thus, since the 1980s, a deliberate movement to devolve power over the academic internal affairs of the higher education institutions is evident. Although, it is not until the 1990s that this devolved power (from the point of view of the government) is expected to be used by the institutions for their own coping with the extensive expansion of student enrollment and increased demands on effectiveness and market orientation. The point of reference in curriculum planning is nowadays more in the hands of the academics, but the academics are more in the hands of the institutions, and these, in turn, are more dependent on the markets.

Thus, successive system changes have created a higher education system which, behind a facade of uniformity in structure on the national system level by integration of different institutions and different programs, still maintains a great variation of institutions, staff compositions and student recruitment and, of course, also in teaching and in student learning. The institutional uniformity was earlier insured by use of the model of central rational planning. However, now, institutional pluralism in design and function is expected to develop by decentralization and self-regulation.

Teichler wrote:

> Thus, it remains an open question as to what extent policies regarding decision-making in higher education which emerged during the 1980s in various Western European countries will develop a clear profile regarding structural implications. Also, one might examine in the future whether such policies have substantial effects on institutional patterns of higher education systems. (Teichler 1988, p.103)

The H-93 reform together with our empirical data can provide some evidence when examining what kind of effects on institutional patterns the governmental policy might have had.

Part II

The State and Higher Education

Introduction

We shall now characterize and explain the policy formulation arena and the reform decisions made by the state authorities concerning the higher education system, its conditions, goals, governance and relation to society. As we stated in Chapter 1, our study of change (and non-change) focuses on the purpose of higher education institutions and the way in which authority is distributed over the higher education system. Thus, at the macro level we concentrate on how the state envisions this mission for the higher education institutions, and how the state uses its authority to manage the higher education institutions. We are well aware from previous literature (Ashby and Anderson 1966; Berdahl 1990; Björklund 1996; Niklasson 1996; Gumport 1997) that the relationship between government and higher education institutions is a tenuous one, with claims for institutional autonomy by the academics and claims for accountability by the governments. Yet we believe the terms institutional autonomy and accountability are often conceptually fuzzy and therefore difficult to operationalize. Thus an effort is made at the beginning of Chapter 4 to further clarify institutional autonomy (and the way in which it relates to accountability). This is followed by an empirical analysis of the policy changes in Sweden (1970s to 1990s) along two dimensions (purpose and authority), dimensions which we find crucial to the concept of institutional autonomy.

In order to alleviate some of this tension between higher education institutions and the state, it has been emphasized that higher education policy-making should be based on some form of consensus between the two – a consensus which could thus allow for the chance of policy success (Trow 1993a). Informed by these ideas of tension and the need for consensus, the task of Chapter 5 is to analyze the extent to which 'negotiation' in the higher education policy arena occurs and is consensual. Clark discussed this negotiation process in terms of the 'triangle of coordination' with the three points consisting of the state authority, the academic oligarchy, and the market (1983, p.143) Becher and Kogan added a fourth point, thus expanding the various negotiating interests to represent a quadrilateral composed of professional, governmental, market, and public/social utility interests (1992, p.177). Emphasizing the possibility of change in this process of negotiation, Kogan states that the 'extent to which the institutional and central norms are in conflict, or are in accord, varies with the beliefs of politicians of the time and of the academics whom they sponsor' (1984, p.67). Our empirical analysis of this negotiating process will be aided by a 'dynamic network approach' for understanding and explaining policy change. This network approach, further described in Chapter 5, allows us to study the usage of power by the various interest groups during the Swedish reforms of 1977 and 1993.

Political and economic background

Before we begin with Chapters 4 and 5, we should recognize that the changes that have occurred in Swedish higher education policy are indirectly affected by changes in the political and economic conditions in the country. In Chapter 2, we referred to such changes as frame factors (frames which do not determine, but may restrict what can happen). For our policy area, we have identified the most important macro-structural 'frames' as:

1. The movement from corporatism to pluralism primarily in the 1980s.

2. The increasingly difficult economic challenges which have brought changes to the model welfare state, with a movement away from full-employment policies.

We will not attempt to make causal links between the actors in our study and these structural conditions with which they are confronted (since this remains one of the most challenging and often impossible tasks for social scientists; see Rothstein 1988). However, in our study of the policy formation process, we will pay attention to how the actors reason about these structural variables in their own policy statements and justifications of policy actions, thus providing a better understanding to the context in which policy was formed.

From corporatism to pluralism?

In the past, Sweden has often provided social scientists with their nation-state example of social corporatism for empirical case study. In his 1990 book, *The Welfare State in Capitalist Society*, Mishra demonstrates that Sweden provides one of the most successful examples of social corporatism with policies supporting full employment, universal social services, and the maintenance of basic minimum living standards. The main features of Swedish social corporatism are the concerted actions involving major economic interests and the state, based on a broad consensus on the need for a mixed economy and the preservation of the welfare state.

The goal of maintaining full employment was achieved in Sweden between the 1970s up to the late 1980s based on a combination of anti-cyclical investment policy and an active labor-market policy. The Swedish Labor Market Board (AMS), consisting of representatives of the government, the Swedish Employer's Confederation (SAF) and the largest trade unions – consisting of the Swedish Trade Union Confederation (LO) with largely blue-collar members; the central Organization of Salaried Employees (TCO) with largely middle management white-collar workers; and the Swedish Confederation of Professionals Association (SACO) – worked together to arrange extensive training programs and relocation programs for workers. The objective was to try to combine higher productivity and full employment with that of wage solidarity. Wage bargaining was centralized at the national level with the goal of reducing social and economic divisions in society. Thus, the state in Sweden played a dominant role in the relationship of capital to labor and, furthermore, the success of social corporatism was also reflected in the commitment to universal social services.

However, macro-level socioeconomic developments have called into question the model of social corporatism which supported the Swedish welfare state. In 1983, the tradition of tripartite negotiation (government, labor and business) underwent extreme pressure as the employers' organization (SAF) withdrew from centralized wage negotiations (Lewin 1994). Lewin attributes much of this breakdown to the position of LO in regards to the wage earners' funds policy starting in the early 1970's. At this time, the Social Democrats yielded to pressure from LO and introduced a policy whereby a percentage of the profits earned by businesses would be placed in large 'funds' owned by the trade unions. The ultimate goal of these funds was for the trade unions to acquire (at some undetermined time in the future) the businesses from the capitalists. The funds were to be managed and controlled jointly by union officials, representatives of the employer's associations and government officials. The ensuing debate over these funds was heated and controversial, with the final legislation representing a much weaker version than LO originally intended and which would be connected to the system of general government pensions (known as 'ATP') which was put in place in 1983 (Lindbeck 1997). In 1994, the Conservative coalition government dismantled these wage-earners' funds and distributed the money by creating brand-new research foundations (see Chapter 3).

By the early 1980s, SAF's frustration was mounting. The whole basis of the social contract (established at Saltsjöbaden in 1938) seemed to be at risk as LO adopted a more 'Marxist' posture (reflected in the wage earners' funds goal of industry ownership). In addition, the passage in 1976 of the democracy at work laws (*medbestämmandelagen*) which LO very actively supported, was a break in the old understanding about the rights of employers and the rights of the employees. Thus in 1992, SAF finally chose to 'bid farewell to the whole corporative set-up' by breaking contact with LO and marching 'out of the board rooms of the central government agencies' (Lewin 1994, p.73).

As corporatism in Sweden has declined over the past decade, many social scientists have pondered the question of what is replacing/will replace the corporatist system. In the study entitled *Democracy and Power in Sweden*, evidence is presented that Sweden in the 1990s is quite different than the days of the 'Swedish model' – due to factors such as deregulation and internationalization of the capital markets, increased cooperation with the EU (resulting in membership in 1994) and restructuring of the public sector (SOU 1990:44). But a clear conclusion as to what these changes mean for the future was not possible. The authors of the study did highlight particular tendencies in the Swedish state which can be interpreted as a movement towards pluralism. These include the decreasing importance of the Public

Investigative Commissions[1] in forming policy proposals, the expansion of lobbying and opinion building by various societal actors, the growth in direct forms of influence/contacts (with big businesses for example), and the increased diversity in the demands of the interest groups.

Economic pressures on the welfare state

In the late 1980s and early 1990s, Sweden faced a difficult macroeconomic situation which certainly put pressure on the 'Swedish model'. In 1988, Marklund reported on economic recession and resulting welfare stagnation in his book *Paradise Lost? The Nordic Welfare States and the Recession 1975–1985*. The situation had not improved much by the mid to late 1990s. Economic performance, measured by GDP per capita, had fallen significantly in comparison to 25 other OECD nations (from fourth in 1970, to ninth in 1990, and down to sixteenth in 1995; see Appendix 3). Productivity growth since the 1970s had been sluggish, with reports stating that public sector productivity growth was in fact negative between the period 1970–1992 (Murray 1996; Lindbeck 1997, referring to Ds. 1994:24). The significance of such a lack of productivity is further compounded by the fact that public sector expenditures had risen from approximately 42 percent of GDP in 1970 to 63 percent in 1995 (Lindbeck 1997).[2] The difficult economic times took their toll on employment, as Sweden for the first time in decades reported unemployment statistics of more than 10 percent (see Appendix 4). Managing the country's budget became the prime task for the politicians in the late 1980s and early 1990s as the budget deficit sky-rocketed to 14.5 percent of GDP in 1993 (see Appendix 5).

---

1 Known as *Statens Offentliga Utredningar* (SOU), these public investigations are a major component of the Swedish policy-making process. The commissions are often established at the request of the Parliament, however, the Government has the final right to call for these investigative commissions. The Government also has several possibilities to influence the work of the SOU, two of the most important being the right to appoint the members of the SOU and the right to form the instructions which the commission is to follow during the investigation. In addition, the Government determines the amount of money and the length of time which the commission has at its disposal during the investigation. (See Larsson 1993.)

2 *Source:* OECD Economic Outlook 57, 1995 and National Institute of Economic Research (KI).

Extensive cuts in welfare programs resulted, but the payment of
unemployment benefits and social costs resulting from unemployment continued to place a heavy strain on the budget. (See Appendix
6 for budget expenditures in higher education.) The political debate
was very much connected to the famous 1993 report of the Lindbeck
Commission (SOU 1993:16) entitled *New Conditions for the Economy
and Politics* (this Commission was appointed by the State to suggest
policy for the future, and was led by the prominent economist Assar
Lindbeck).

Most likely in response to the increasingly difficult economic
situation, public administration in Sweden in the 1980s was
particularly characterized by desectorization and decentralization,
accompanied by a 'management by objectives' philosophy
(Mellbourn 1986; Bladh 1987; Söderlind and Petersson 1992; Pierre
1995). The Conservative coalition government of 1991–1994 pushed
further the transformation of the public sector, stating that those
areas of public service which could function in a competitive market
should do so. Thus, state ownership in service entities was
significantly reduced as conversions into company status and sell-offs
by privatizations took place (Ringqvist 1996).

In particular, significant changes in the social services (for example
in child care, elderly care, and the elementary and secondary school
systems occurred (Stenelo 1988; Möller 1996). New steering
mechanisms, such as the decentralization of authority from the
national to the municipal level and the encouragement of flexibility
rather than strict planning and regulation, were introduced. Since the
early 1990s, detailed steering of the state bureaucracy has basically
been abandoned, an initiative launched by the Social Democratic
governments. Instead of explicit yearly budgets, new economic
frameworks with a three-year time period were implemented, which
allowed the public bureaucrats more freedom to decide how best to
use resources to achieve the best results (Ringqvist 1996).

Chapter 4

The 1993 Reform
A Shift in Purpose and Authority with 'Freedom for Quality'

Building an analytical framework

With Figure 1.1, (p.27) we introduced two dimensions of change in higher education systems (purpose and authority) which are useful in characterizing the tendencies and aims of a reform. Within these two dimensions, we can typify four kinds of state governance for the higher education system, which are depicted below (Figure 4.1)[1]. The vertical axis reflects the distribution of 'Authority' between the state and the higher education institutions, centralized and decentralized. (Note the terms governing and governance used here in Part II describe the relationship between the central government level and the higher education institutions, they are not used in the sense of university internal governance unless specified as such.) The horizontal axis represents the state's view on the 'Purpose' of higher education, along a dimension of cultural to utilitarian. Cultural values would emphasize the disinterested pursuit of knowledge, given the understanding that in such pursuit, the goals of society are best met in the long run. Utilitarian values would on the other hand, emphasize that knowledge should be pursued/created in the process of meeting socially determined goals. It is important to recognize that although these four types are based on concepts of higher education systems as observed in locations such as Europe, Scandinavia and the United States, they are however theoretical models.[2] The range of

---

1   Figure 4.1 is based on work in Marton (forthcoming) *The Mind of the State: The Politics of University Autonomy in Sweden, 1968–1998*, Göteborg Studies in Politics, Göteborg University. The terms 'cultural' and 'utilitarian' are further explained there.

2   In a similar endeavor, however, at the level of internal university governance, McNay (1995) uses two dimensions (policy definition and control of implementation) to capture a range of models of universities: 'collegium', 'bureaucracy', 'corporation' and 'enterprise'.

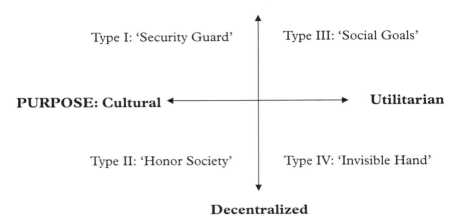

Figure 4.1 A model of four types of state governance of higher education

theoretically possible choices has been narrowed down however to exemplify and epitomize different logics favored by different systems – but not absolutely or essentially exclusive logics. We recognize that within the same state governing system, mixtures of these governance types may exist at the same time.

With these four types of state governance, one can also analyze the concept of 'institutional autonomy'. In so doing, it becomes evident that the degree of institutional autonomy will vary between the four different types of governance. These four types thus add depth to the institutional autonomy debate, moving it beyond the common conception of institutional autonomy as just related to the vertical shift of authority from centralized state authority to decentralized state authority (van Vught 1988), or the conception of institutional autonomy as being related only to the purpose of the university (Tasker and Packham 1990). Rather, these four types demonstrate that institutional autonomy is intricately tied to understandings of both the purpose of higher education and the way in which the state exercises authority. As Neave has pointed out:

What influences one's perception of State control is the degree of intervention, the intensity of the intervention and whether, as a result of that intervention, one's collective or personal interests are forwarded or blocked. It is theoretically well within the bounds of possibility to have a higher education system subject to formal state control and yet to have minimal interference or to have a degree of intervention which, if not negligible, is nevertheless perceived by those it affects as part of the natural order of things. In short, it is not State control *per se* which is the source of disquiet so much as what is perceived as *reinforcing* State control beyond established bounds. One is never so conscious of State control as when it assumes a dynamic which obliges central authority to take initiatives and, like Captain Kirk, to boldly go where it has never gone before. (Neave 1997b, p.6)

But before discussing institutional autonomy in each governing model, it is helpful to clarify how one can define the criteria for evaluating institutional autonomy. It is important to note that institutional autonomy is often confused with academic freedom, and that further clarification is necessary. Berdahl's definition is quite helpful in this regard, where: 'Academic freedom is that freedom of the individual scholar in his/her teaching and research to pursue truth wherever it seems to lead without fear of punishment or termination of employment for having offended some political, religious or social orthodoxy' (1990, pp.171–172). Institutional autonomy is the degree of freedom the university has to steer itself. But this does not necessarily make the task of defining the term any easier. As Eric Ashby once stated, 'the question as to what constitutes autonomy in universities is anything but unambiguous, and the patterns of autonomy which satisfy academics are very diverse' (Berdahl 1990, p.169).

In an effort to clarify the autonomy issue, Berdahl discusses two types of autonomy – procedural and substantive:

> Substantive autonomy is the power of the university or college in its corporate form to determine its own goals and programmes – if you will, the what of academe. Procedural autonomy is the power of the university or college in its corporate form to determine the means by which its goals and programmes will be pursued – the how of academe. (Berdahl 1990, p.172)

It is Berdahl's opinion that in the area of procedural autonomy (such as audits, financial controls, personnel policies) the government should have a low profile, since 'procedural controls are probably counter-productive and certainly irritating' (Berdahl 1990, p.173). But in regards to substantive autonomy, Berdahl suggests that a 'constructive partnership' be formed between the state and the higher education institutions, with 'sensitive mechanisms for bringing together state concerns with accountability and academic concerns with autonomy' (Berdahl 1990, p.173).

However, Berdahl's distinction between procedural and substantive is very difficult to operationalize for empirical study.[3] We would like to suggest that in Figure 4.1 it is helpful to think of substantive autonomy in terms of a dimension labeled 'purpose', i.e. what the role of higher education in society is/should be along a continuum based on either cultural or utilitarian values. As previously mentioned, cultural values emphasize the disinterested pursuit of knowledge and utilitarian values emphasize that knowledge should meet socially determined goals.

We would further like to suggest that Ashby and Anderson's (1966) components of institutional autonomy can be classified as components of Berdahl's 'procedural' autonomy, and we cite them here as freedom:

- from non academic interference in the *internal* governance of the institution
- to allocate funds as the institution sees fit
- over the recruitment of employees, and in determining their conditions of work
- over the selection of students
- to design and deliver the curriculum
- to set standards and determine method of assessment. (Ashby and Anderson 1966 in Tight 1992, p.1384)

For some unexplainable reason, the list does not include the term 'research', but only mentions 'curriculum' – a term which is most commonly thought of in regards to teaching. Nonetheless, in our analysis, the concept of institutional autonomy will also entail freedom to design and deliver research.

---

3   See Gumport (1997, p.19) where further conceptual complexity is suggested from two separate uses of procedural autonomy; first, procedural autonomy on the 'technical side' (e.g., personnel, purchasing, and accounting polices), and second, 'procedural autonomy on the academic side' (e.g., redeploying faculty resources to undergraduate instruction, cutting programs, and establishing performance/productivity measures for faculty work).

We recognize now that the above list relates to the distribution of authority from the national government to the institutions, which we will call the 'authority dimension', running along a continuum from 'centralized to decentralized'. In our discussion of the four types of state governance which follows, we will use both dimensions of authority (procedural autonomy) and purpose (substantive autonomy) to better understand variation in institutional autonomy.

The first typology which results from such a combination, here labeled *'security guard'*, strongly emphasizes academic freedom and a very wide degree of substantial autonomy, with the unity of science and teaching as the key elements for the university. Referred to often as the Humboldtian ideal, this tradition has the nation-state playing an important role, but a role which limits the nation-state's interference in university affairs. Accordingly, knowledge is to be pursued for the sake of knowledge itself, thus the role of the state is only to safeguard and guarantee university autonomy so as to protect the university from both forces on the outside of the university (religious powers for example), and threats from within, such as internal power struggles (Bleiklie 1994a). This typology is not very restrictive of institutional autonomy, since the 'state recognizes and accepts the university's own authority on the basis of its scientific contributions' (Mayer 1997, p.1). However, the state can retain some control over the universities in the appropriation of funds and in the area of faculty appointments, where the appointment of senior professors for example was seen as a 'civil service' issue.

The second typology, which we here call *'honor society'*, is most closely associated with the example of the British autonomous institution. In similarity with the 'security guard' model, the primary goals are based on cultural values, emphasizing the disinterested pursuit of knowledge. In addition, there is a high awareness of the universities' role in the 'forming of student character' (Clark 1995c, p.58) as evidenced by the traditions of Oxford and Cambridge. Academics have a large zone of substantive autonomy and they 'set their own objectives, evaluate each other by processes of peer review and accord maximum autonomy to both individuals and the basic units in which they work' (Kogan 1992, p.1929). The role of central government is minimal, with no role assumed as 'protector' of the institutions from outside (and inside) forces as with the 'security guard' model, but instead, there is a deliberate decision on the part of central government not to get involved. Thus a type of 'trust', an 'honoring' of one's words, exists between the central government and the universities, which is here alluded to by labeling this model the 'honor society'. This model is the least restrictive on all criteria for institutional autonomy given the minimal role of government.

The third typology, labeled *'social goals'*, is located on the other side of the purpose dimension, where utilitarian requirements are dominant. Often referred to as the 'command/managerialist' model in the higher education literature, this type assumes a more limited degree of substantive autonomy where 'academic objectives are subsets of social objectives which can be laid down by systems and university managers' (Kogan 1992, p.1929). Here we also place the traditional 'welfare state model', with socially defined goals for higher education and research. Bleiklie's (1994a) description of the university as 'public agency' also falls into this category. As 'public agency', the university is part of the national civil service and is required to implement national public policy, and should do so loyally. The state, as the financial and political authority, exercises its power through legislation and budgetary policy. Yet the state also exercises power in areas that are viewed as traditionally 'academic', i.e., admission policies, type of curriculum, research agendas and assessment methods, areas which we have defined as procedural. Given both the authority of the state as well as the predominance of state goals, rather than the internal goals of the academics, this model strongly restricts the extent of institutional autonomy.

Our fourth typology, *'invisible hand'*, reflects the theoretical possibility of academics functioning in an open market as providers of services to clients who are willing to purchase them. Students will be buying courses, and research will be supported by external sponsors and commissioned projects (Kogan 1992; Gustavsson 1997). However, the state may act as a provider of subsidies in this model, thus helping to set the terms of the market. Based on the ideas of new public management, Bleiklie has outlined a model of the university as 'producer of educational and research services'. Under this ideal, which he calls the university as 'corporate enterprise', the university 'consists of a leadership and different functional (academic, technical and administrative) staff groups servicing different user groups in need of the services the enterprise offers' (Bleiklie 1994a, p.11). Efficiency in delivering useful products, i.e., research and graduates, is a predominant goal, and all 'affected' groups are entitled to input in university affairs (For empirical examples of this type, see Cerych

1985; Walford 1988). Thus, the extent of substantive autonomy is restricted by a variety of 'affected' groups, not just by the central government as is the case in the 'social goals' category. This 'invisible hand' typology, with its emphasis on meeting external demands from the 'markets', 'clients' and 'customers', also puts procedural autonomy somewhat at risk as traditional criteria such as the content of the curriculum and the agenda for research, as well as methods of assessment, are in need of approval/support from markets and customers. This need for approval and/or support can also be understood as having a slightly restrictive effect on the institutions' freedom over internal governance, distribution of funds, employee decisions, and even assessment methods to some degree. Yet given that the institution operates in a market, it can itself totally determine the conditions of admission, thus choosing to admit any type of student it so desires.

Certainly, the models of state governance depicted above can be understood as 'snapshots' of systems which can be changing frequently in response to the political conflicts in society. We recognize that governments may attempt to increase their control over some areas, such as funding, while providing more freedom in areas like curriculum development. But we hope that by defining institutional autonomy in terms of these criteria of procedural autonomy, and locating them within the four types of state governance mentioned above, the complexity of the concept can be grasped. We now see that there is a relationship between 'substantive autonomy' and 'procedural autonomy' so that changes in Berdahl's 'substantive autonomy' (here called 'purpose') entail changes in the components of 'procedural autonomy' (here called 'authority'). Thus any discussion of institutional autonomy should also include a description of what is the purpose of the higher education institutions. To assist in this undertaking, we present an heuristic tool in the form of Table 4.1 below. Here, procedural autonomy is evaluated by taking into account the different forms of substantive autonomy in order to get a more complete picture of the restrictions upon institutional autonomy in each governing model.

Table 4.1 Degrees of restriction on procedural autonomy under four types of state governance

	Types:			
	Security Guard	*Honor Society*	*Social Goals*	*Invisible Hand*
Procedural Autonomy Concerns:				
a. Internal Governance	Medium	Very Low	Very High	Low
b. Funds	Medium	Very Low	Very High	Low
c. Employees	Medium	Very Low	High	Low
d. Admissions	Very Low	Very Low	Very High	Very Low
e. Curriculum	Very Low	Very Low	Very High	Medium
f. Research	Very Low	Very Low	Very High	Medium
g. Assessment	Very Low	Very Low	High	Medium

With the help of Table 4.1 above, we can now rank the four types of state governance in terms of the degree to which they restrict institutional autonomy, both substantive and procedural, which is depicted in Figure 4.2.

We will now review the empirical evidence from the Swedish case and report the view of the state (represented by the Minister of Education and the Parliament's Education Committee) on our two dimensions – starting with the purpose of higher education (cultural or utilitarian) and followed by the distribution of authority (centralization or decentralization). After the presentation of the empirical data, we will analyze at the end of this chapter the changes in Swedish higher education policy in relation to our model of state governance (Figure 4.1). The analysis of the political power shifts which we believe lay behind some of the changes in the two dimensions is presented in Chapter 5.

AUTHORITY
Centralized

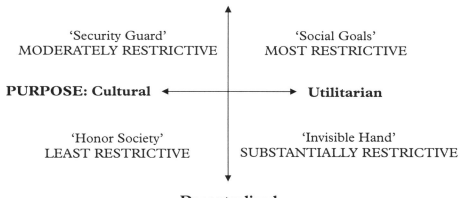

'Security Guard'
MODERATELY RESTRICTIVE

'Social Goals'
MOST RESTRICTIVE

PURPOSE: Cultural ◄————————► **Utilitarian**

'Honor Society'
LEAST RESTRICTIVE

'Invisible Hand'
SUBSTANTIALLY RESTRICTIVE

Decentralized

Figure 4.2 Four types of state governance resulting in different degrees of institutional autonomy

Shifting purpose

As mentioned in Chapter 3, politics in Sweden in the late 1960s and early 1970s reflected the dominance of a 'spirit of rational planning and central management', which for higher education led to a transformation of the system (Lane 1990; Ruin 1991; Bauer and Henkel 1997; SOU 1997:7). In this section, we will analyze the shift which has transpired between the 1970s and the 1990s in view of the purpose of higher education as exemplified by the Swedish politicians in power at the time. This shift in purpose is analyzed in terms of three subcategories: first, dealing with the role of education/knowledge in society; second, with the role of higher education in the nation; and third, with the view towards quality.

From educating for work to educating for the knowledge society

In terms of providing education, the higher education system was totally reorganized in the late 1970s with all education now to be categorized by five main sectors connected to the job market (see Chapter 3, p.53). The idea that education was for the purpose of attaining a job – thereby contributing beneficially to the Swedish work force and to the functioning of the public sector – influenced most political action at this time. In explaining the H-77 reform, the Minister of Education declared one of the reform's main tasks was 'to widen and differentiate the total educational offering, especially in consideration of the relationship to the job market and the renewal of *'arbetslivet'* [4] (Gov. Prop. 1975:9, p.406). Higher education planning at the Minister level included such details as structure and curriculum of the general study lines. For example, the Minister with the Parliament, made decisions regarding whether the study line for social work should belong to the section for health care or to the section for study lines dealing with administration, economy and societal work (Gov. Prop. 1975:9, p.430). The faculties of humanities, social sciences and natural sciences were mentioned as having 'many students... following [study] lines which lacked a more obvious connection to the job market' (Gov. Prop. 1975:9, p.437). The Minister added that 'all of the study lines in these faculties will contain elements of work preparation' and that it was even 'necessary that the plans for student capacity under different study lines be better adjusted to the opportunities on the job market which are predictable for a particular education' (p.437).

In order to ensure that educational offerings matched the needs of the job market, representatives of different occupations were to become members of the study line committees (refer to Chapter 3, p.55). As the Minister justified his position to Parliament, he stated, 'The contributions from *arbetslivet* provide a meaningful connection to the area in which the students expect to be participating' (Gov. Prop. 1975:9, p.518). In addition, emphasis was placed on the need for reform in the educational offerings, with the Minister declaring, 'I see it [the contributions from *arbetslivet*] as essential for the continued renewal of the higher education institutions' study lines and also as a valuable inspiration source for research and for research education' (p.503).

By the late 1980s, various countries were adopting 'new public management' techniques in the administration of the public sector,

---

4   *'Arbetsliv'* and *'arbetslivet'* literally translate into 'working life', however this is a somewhat strange translation. Thus, we will prefer to use the Swedish word to capture a multitude of English understandings – such as the work environment, working world, working situation, career satisfaction, and job/occupational satisfaction.

with efficiency and flexibility as key concepts and Sweden was no exception (Osborne and Gaebler 1992; Ringqvist 1996; Bleiklie 1997). This was later manifested in Sweden with a new budget and planning system for the entire public sector, with three-year budget 'frameworks' which granted the authorities in the bureaucracy more freedom in deciding how best to use the resources to achieve the best results (Department Series 1995:73; Gustavsson 1995). When introducing some of the new public management techniques to higher education, the Minister of Education stated:

> As with other public service sectors, it is important that planning, steering and the follow-up of the higher education institutions are regularly tested. Only through this can a suitable guarantee be created for the effective and authoritative decision-making in questions of strategic importance for research and higher education. Before the 1990s, the higher education institutions must be prepared to meet different types of societal changes, which we today can only barely predict. The meaning of this is that the institutions will need to prioritize more and more. Not only technical development, but changes in the structure of the job market and changes in the age distribution of different working groups, are putting pressure on the higher education institutions for changes in the educational offerings. The investment which other countries are making in higher education and research will come to mean sharp demands on the activities within the Swedish higher education institutions if we want to keep up with international standards in the future. (Gov. Prop. 1988/89:65, p.3)

However, even with this discussion of societal changes and the related difficulty of future forecasts, we see at the same time, in the same government proposition, that the legacy of the emphasis on education for work remains as the Minister states that the structure of dividing education into five work-related sectors is: 'a natural, basic structure for planning the tasks of the higher education institutions even with the new resource system' [three-year budget frameworks] (Gov. Prop. 1988/89:65, p.6).

By the spring of 1991, the importance of these centrally-planned, work related study lines seemed to fade. The same Minister of Education proposed, and the Parliament approved, the abolition of the centrally determined, permanent study lines and declared that the curriculum and study line planning work at the national level was no longer needed. The organization of education would therefore be an issue only for the higher education institutions. The study lines would be replaced by a system of 'degrees' (*examen* in Swedish) and the right of a higher education institution to award a degree would be based on the evaluation it received during the National Board of Universities and Colleges' (UHÄ) quality review. However the government and Parliament reserved the right of final determination on awarding degrees in cases of high cost degrees involving expensive equipment/ training or degrees which were seen as necessary to preserve the best interests of the nation (Gov. Prop. 1990/91:150). This ground-breaking document even mentioned that yearly planning of the total size of the higher education system should also be further decentralized, taking consideration of the overarching needs of the central state authorities rather than in terms of absolute job market predictions. Yet no specific policy change in this matter took place until later in 1994.

As the 1990s began, the politicians' view of the purpose of education certainly shifted. So did the composition of the ruling government, with a switch to a Conservative coalition government. By 1992, a vision of society as a knowledge society was prevalent in all government propositions dealing with higher education. Presenting his reasons for a new purpose for higher education, the Minister of Education stated:

> A change in the growth for the need for knowledge by the individual, in his/her role as worker as well as his/her role as a citizen, has occurred during the last years. Industrial production is all the more technical. In private and public services, there are demands for more theoretical knowledge. (Gov. Prop. 1992/93:169, p.5)

This was also supported by a belief that modern society is 'a knowledge society' – a society where 'the old division between knowledge and occupational skills will be all the more untimely, irrelevant and out of fashion' (Gov. Prop. 1992/93:170, p.1).

In comparison, the purpose of knowledge certainly came to embody a broader meaning for the politicians ruling in the early 1990s than those of the 1970s. Both the inability of rationality to solve societal problems as well as the speed of knowledge developments and knowledge transfers were cornerstones for the policy ideas in the 1990s. For example, the Minister of Education explained in February of 1993 that:

> it is the unique combinations based on basic knowledge from which advances are made. Education in the humanities and the social sciences as well as the natural sciences, and the ability to

handle unknown quantities of information are presently of importance. The humanities provide us depth/anchorage in our culture, language, and history. They help us to understand when narrow rationality does not suffice. (Gov. Prop. 1992/93:170, p.1)

In discussing the tremendous pace at which new knowledge is acquired, the Minister later emphasized:

In the future information and knowledge society, the education and research system [of a nation] will have a strategic role. These new conditions are also changing the role and form of education. The importance is on learning to learn. This will be a condition in order to perform in an all the more changing society. It will be important to be able to sort, select and work-through, but also to learn more and to learn again. (Gov. Prop. 1993/94:177, pp.20–21)

Reflecting on the system of undergraduate education in the past, the Education Minister in 1992 stated that:

The now abolished study-line system was built on an unreal belief that through the central planning of everything it was possible to predict societies' and the individuals' need of education for the future *arbetsliv*... Central planning of the contents and breadth of higher education can work against future generations of students' chances to develop and renew their knowledge in stride with societal changes. Deeper knowledge within areas which are chosen freely by the students is the best preparation for the future. (Gov. Prop. 1992/93:169, p.8)

Thus, according to the reasoning of this Minister, it seemed appropriate for a 'modern society' to abolish the study line system. The new 'degree' system matched the requirements of this changing society. As the Education Minister further explained, 'The degree system is internationally comparative. The selection of educational possibilities will be more flexible and diverse in the future and will be more suitable to the heterogeneous student population of the future' (Gov. Prop. 1992/93:169, p.7).

From democratizing higher education to meeting diverse market demands

The 1970s and 1980s can be characterized as a period where the goals for the higher education system were determined by the State to quite an extensive degree. One of the overarching goals, as pronounced in the principal proposition, was 'to democratize the organization of [higher] education and to adjust its ways of working for a more comprehensive recruitment of students' (Gov. Prop. 1975:9; p.406). The internal organization of the higher education institutions was to be 'democratized' as representatives for students, workers, and general society were given the right to representation on the various regional, university/college, faculty, and department boards. Such an arrangement seemed totally justifiable to the Minister, who stated:

> In the bodies which shall be responsible for, among other things, the balance between different types of education and between different higher education institution's and locations ... the reason is obvious for a strong representation of the general interest according to my understanding. With the connection to societal planning and the use of society's resources in general... it can not reasonably be a matter wholly, or even in the first place, for those who work in the educational institutions (Gov. Prop. 1975:9; p.502).

The Minister did not interpret the reform plans for the internal organization as a threat to academic freedom over research (although accused of this by the academics, see Chapter 5) and declared:

> representation for the employers and the employees within the occupational areas concerned on the boards which are responsible for planning...is an appropriate way to facilitate the relationship between the higher education institutions and *arbetslivet*, something which I see as important for the continuing renewal of the higher education institution's study lines and also as a desirable inspiration source for research and graduate education. (Gov. Prop. 1975:9, p.503)

Although a questioning of this representation in the internal organization of the higher education institutions surfaced again in 1983, only minor changes were made as the Minister stated, 'In my opinion, there is no reason to execute any sweeping organizational reform. The higher education institutions need peace and calm in order to concentrate on their main tasks' (Gov. Prop. 1983/84:52, p.7).

Unlike the emphasis during the 1970s on democratizing higher education to meet society's goals, the early 1990s focused on meeting the demands of various 'markets'. As could be expected, one of the largest 'players' in these markets was business. Blaming the previous national system of centrally planned curriculums and centrally controlled limits to the size of each higher education institution, the newly appointed Conservative Minister of Education claimed that this 'caused a lowering of the competencies of the Swedish work force', and that, as a result, 'Sweden now needed to increase education which had connections to the private sector and to business' (Gov. Prop. 1992/93:169, p.3). Sweden was seen as losing its competitive edge and needed to regain its position in the knowledge intensive industries. Problems cited included the low number of employees in business with academic degrees, the difficulty in transferring research results to the high-tech businesses, and the changing composition of the job market with less than 20 percent of the work force employed in industry while the service sector was dramatically increasing (Gov. Prop. 1993/94:177, p.18). These problems were also frequent topics on the debate pages, as business leaders and politicians sought new ways to solve the nation's economic problems. To foster more cooperation between the higher education institutions and the business community, the Minister of Education proposed that the higher education institutions be able to conduct research in the form of companies, receiving start-up capital from the government (Gov. Prop. 1992/93:170, p.29).

Another crucial player in the 'market' were the students. The Minister of Education was so interested about their views on how the higher education system should work that he commissioned the Swedish Central Statistics Bureau to conduct a representative survey of student opinions on higher education. According to the Education Ministry, the students were concerned about quality, about the connection of their education to research in the scientific community, and about their freedom to combine various courses together to make an acceptable degree (Gov. Prop. 1992/93:169, p.6). This was quite a change from the 1970s when the National Association of Student Unions, the SFS, was the major source for expressing policy concerns.

Further exemplifying the shift towards market demands was the newly developing policy towards the colleges. During the 1970s and 1980s, the colleges did not have permanent research resources, but were allocated funds for 'research supporting activities' from the university faculty to which they were connected. This appears to have been a very awkward solution, since the 'subsidiary' college had to request the funds from the 'head office' university. In 1993, the Conservative Minister of Education stated that in the division between the universities and the colleges, the colleges should concentrate on undergraduate education. However, advocating market solutions, the Minister also stated that the 'colleges should develop research in conjunction with the needs of business in their area' and that this could be a way in which 'the colleges could profile themselves' (Gov. Prop. 1993/94:177, p.49). Adding to the ongoing debate as to how equal and unified the Swedish higher education system really was and/or is, the Minister in 1993 stated:

> It is especially important that the smaller and middle-sized colleges, which can not have the universities' more complete coverage of educational offerings, form an optimal arrangement/offering of educational degrees which match their own conditions for the development of competency and can match the needs of the students and the surrounding work force in the community. (Gov. Prop. 1992/93:169, p.59)

From promoting social equality to creating academic excellence

In addition to the focus on democratization of the higher education institutions (measured in terms of which groups had input into decisions concerning higher education), the H-77 reform also concentrated on equality in terms of social class access and geographic access to higher education (Gov. Prop. 1975:9, p.406). As described in Chapter 3, the H-77 reform created a unitary higher education system to include all education after the high school level. With central planning and the study line system, it was assumed that high educational quality would be maintained on a equivalent basis throughout all higher education institutions in the country. Geographic access was increased by the large expansion in colleges, which was also seen as helping the effort to expand access for various social classes (Gov. Prop. 1976/77:59, p.21). Furthermore, continuing education programs were important 'to give new groups of students the same chance to have a college education' (Gov. Prop. 1976/77:59, p.44). (Acceptance of these new groups of students in order to reduce the gaps between social classes was particularly aided by the 25:4 rule: see Chapter 3, p.53.)

More than ten years after the major 1977 reform, these principles of social equality were still upheld by the ruling politicians. The quality of the educational system, not of each institution, had to be maintained on an equivalent basis – a characteristic which distinguished Sweden compared to many other countries. This was evident in statements such as: 'Quality of the education at the smaller and middle-sized higher education institutions should not be presumed to be different than the quality of the education which is given at the universities and colleges with permanent research funds' (Gov. Prop. 1987/88:100, p.30). This was further supported with the statement that, 'The first principle is high and equivalent quality within all higher education institutions. ... Their activities shall be equivalent, regardless of where they are conducted. The most important thing is not where one's studies have taken place, but what one has studied' (Gov. Prop. 1988/89:65, p.4). (This did not apply to the production of research however, which was seen as requiring a division between the universities and colleges so that research would meet international scientific quality standards.)

In order to achieve the goals of social equality, the government and the Parliament made decisions on how the resources were to be used in determining the size of each school and the various types of education to be taught there. As explained by the Minister, 'Through the range and concentration of educational investments, important preconditions for tomorrow's society are given. It is therefore necessary that the overall balance be decided by the government and the Parliament' (Gov. Prop. 1988/89:65, p.12). One of the first hints of a possible movement from the usage of the higher education system in achieving social equality to a greater emphasis on the internal tasks of the higher education institutions appeared in the early 1990s. The Minister stated at that time that:

> an increased focus on results and degrees, with more attention on how well the activities of the higher education institutions compare to international comparisons should take place, at the sacrifice of detailed steering through decisions on the number of study places. Instead of the previous emphasis on long-term, relatively detailed central planning, this means a change to thinking in terms of renewal and the development of ideas at the local level. The continuing, complete judgment of direction, variety and coverage, and the local placement of studies by the Government and Parliament will be an integrated part of a more overarching plan at the state level. (Gov. Prop. 1990/91:150, p.68)

However, the message was rather ambiguous since the evaluation was to be based on:

> how well the activities of the higher education institutions meet the needs of society in regards to the direction and variety of education, on its availability to different student groups, and on its productivity. Higher education institutions will also need to meet

the demands for work-related skills and to allow for one to achieve advances within different areas of education and research. (Gov. Prop. 1990/91:150, p.69)

By 1993, it appeared that competition, not equivalence, was the best way to achieve high quality, with the Minister of Education declaring that: 'The university or college which does not always put quality first will quickly lose the confidence of the students, the employers, and the State as well as its reputation in the international scientific community' (Gov. Prop. 1992/93:169, p.18). 'Freedom for Quality' was the new slogan, as rules and regulations were further abolished.[5] A political expert working for the Minister of Education at the time explained:

> How do you develop quality? How do you stimulate the development of knowledge? This reform was based on the assumption that quality must grow from underneath. How do you get it to grow from underneath, from the student, to the teacher, to the researcher – this can not be planned from above. It comes from their own initiative. In order to do this, the Conservative government was trying to create an institutional framework, with rules and responsibilities so that consequences could be seen. ... What the Conservative government was trying to do was establish freedom by establishing clear rules. Give private education a chance. ... What was important was choice, freedom within an institutional framework... (Interview, political advisor)

The above statement is further supported by the Minister's declaration to the Parliament that,

> Questions of qualifications, selection and acceptance should be solved within the 'framework' for the very general guidelines which are outlined in the 'Higher Education Ordinance'. These issues are central for high quality. For high quality, the institutions must be able to recruit students who are well-motivated, and well-prepared. There should also be an acceptable permanence in these rules. (Gov. Prop. 1992/93:169, p.7)

The theme of 'freedom for quality' also related to the conditions for and production of research. As was noted in Chapter 3 (p.60) and to be further discussed in Chapter 5, the conditions for and the

---

5   Björklund (1996, p.142) mentions how the Higher Education Ordinance was reduced from 130 pages (for the period before 1993) to 60 after the New Ordinance in July 1993.

resources available for research in Sweden dramatically changed during the early 1990s. Articulating the government's research policy, the Minister of Education stated that:

> research policy has as its purpose to create conditions for science to reach the front line of knowledge. The underlying point in this is that research results can not be demanded, but are created in the natural interplay between humans. (Gov. Prop. 1992/93:170, p.71)

The Minister's view of conditions for quality research was based on the role of the individual researchers, and in addition was a multifaceted view:

> Successful research has as its most important source the individual researchers' creativity and ability to develop. Curiosity and interest to ask new questions, to critically question established truths, to find solutions to old or new problems and to widen the horizons of knowledge are the most important driving forces of research... Research has many dimensions. Internally it shall support the creation of fundamentals upon which both basic and advanced education are based. Externally, research is an important precondition that our nation's welfare in the broadest sense can be insured. (Gov. Prop. 1992/93:170, p.2)

In order to foster and support front-line research in an ever-changing society, the government in the early 1990s believed in the need for new organizational forms for research. As stated in the 'Education and Research: Quality and Competitiveness' proposition:

> When the speed of knowledge production and the complexity in society increases, it is all the more important that the renewal of research develop and take into consideration society at large. When reality changes quickly, it is especially crucial that research contribute to interpreting and explaining the changes. ... Research develops in an international environment. Research discoveries transmit quickly between countries. This underscores that even within the research system, there is a need for increased ability for renewal. Solid structures and organizational forms need to be broken up in order to allow for the possibility of prioritizing and creating new thoughts. (Gov. Prop. 1993/94:177, pp.22–23)

Shifting authority

We have seen above that quite a significant shift in the purpose of higher education from the 1970s to the 1990s has taken place as the emphasis has shifted towards the needs of a knowledge society, the needs of diverse market demands, and the need to create academic excellence. In addition, we will also empirically investigate what changes, if any, occurred in the distribution of authority (centralization to decentralization). Was there a connection in the H-93 reform between the politicians' overall goals regarding purpose of the system (our first dimension) and their policy actions in terms of governance (our second dimension)? By studying the way in which authority was (or was not) distributed through all levels of the system – the bureaucracy, the university leadership, the individual academics, and even the students – we will be able to further analyze the movement (if any) towards a new governance model.

Creating competition in the higher education marketplace

As we have seen earlier, it appears that the theme for the early 1990s could have been freedom from planning in order to create competition to achieve quality. At least this seems to have been the logic behind many of the Minister's reforms during the period 1991 to 1994. Efforts were made to break with the previously dominant position of the State where the belief and practice was that:

> responsibility for the steering of the direction and composition of higher education and research must lie with the government and the Parliament. This is done through decisions on the goals of education which is in the Higher Education Law. This is carried out by decisions on the approval of general study lines and their placement at the various higher education institutions as well as decisions on the number of new study places for each study line – or a group of lines – at the concerned higher education institution. ... Not only how many, but also which students shall be accepted is of interest from a steering perspective. The government and Parliament have regulations for student qualifications and final selection/admittance. ... The government and the Parliament therefore are responsible for the overall decisions on higher education's principle structure, location and size – weighed against the needs of society, individual demand and available resources. (Gov. Prop. 1988/89:65, p.5)

In the early 1990s a change in policy was evident in the new resource allocation plan (described in Chapter 3) which was to bring competition into the system. The higher education institutions would be competing at the undergraduate level for students (within the boundaries of top limits still set by the government) and would be allocated money not just based on how many students they enrolled, but also on the semester-based study results of the students (known as 'student-money' which followed the student no matter which higher education institution he/she enrolled in). As for doctoral education, financial allocations would be partly based on how many Ph.Ds the higher education institution produced during a year. Thus, the new steering system meant that: 'the government and the Parliament were no longer going to say in detail how many students in each area would be educated at each location. Instead it would be the student and the institution, through their mutual choices, that would select each other' (Parliament Education Committee, UbU92/93:14, p.41). Yet this system of resource allocation was not seen as completely adequate by the government because it could lead to the higher education institutions' graduating or advancing students just in order to receive financing. Thus, a number of policy actions were discussed, beginning with a system of performance indicators which would rank quality at the higher education institutions. This task was assigned to the Secretariat of Assessment and Evaluation, led by the University Chancellor, who was to be assisted by leading academics and academic elite organizations. The government believed that the higher education institutions should compete primarily in some type of competitive market, and advocated making public the results of all the evaluations. In justifying such a belief, the Minister emphasized that: 'By showing differences in quality of the same type of education at different higher education institutions, those responsible for the education will work further to achieve the best possible results' (Parliament Education Committee, UbU91/92:18, p.6). However, the idea of performance indicators fizzled out as it was criticized by a variety of leading academics and organizations. Instead, an evaluation of the higher education institutions' quality development work was to be conducted, with 5 percent of the undergraduate budget allocated based on the results of this evaluation. In commenting on this legislation, the Minister stated:

> The principles which have been established by the Parliament mean that the higher education institution which has an undergraduate education of high quality will also be given more resources. The main reason is to provide incentives to the higher education institutions to improve their quality. In addition is the importance of a clear signal that resources are not just allocated

based on quantitative results. ... The major motivation for a connection between quality and the distribution of resources is ... the
belief that further measures are needed and that it must clearly be
understood that it pays to systematically work to improve quality
in undergraduate education. (Gov. Prop. 1993/94:177,
pp.75–76)

In addition to these competitive mechanisms regarding quality, the
Minister of Education also announced that the structure of the
system would change, allowing for both private universities and
private research foundations to be formed (these institutions to be
organized legally as private foundations, rather than as State entities)
with the help of financing from the wage earners' funds (see Chapter
3, pp.60–61). The need for various kinds of diversity in the system was
paramount for the Minister. In particular, there was a need for
renewal in research – in order to provide better possibilities for faculty
recruitment and flexibility, as well as intensified internationalization.
The need for this was evident in statements such as 'Without
sacrificing the necessary long-term emphasis, the research system
must, better than [it does] today, have the ability to handle new
problems and challenges' (Gov. Prop. 1992/93:170, p.8.).

Stronger leadership to guide more autonomous universities

The key tasks of the higher education institutions' highest decision-
making body, or board, has long been a subject of much detail, as well
as controversy, in Swedish higher education policy-making. After the
H-77 reform, changes already appeared in 1983 as the members of
the boards complained about their lack of influence over the financing
of research and doctoral education. (This responsibility for financial
planning for research and doctoral education had previously been
allocated to the faculty boards directly.) Thus in the early 1980s, the
Minister of Education suggested that the institutions' board would
have to approve these plans from the faculty boards (Gov. Prop.
1983/84:52).

By December of 1988, the tasks of the boards were further
expanded. The Minister cited a long process of decentralization from
the state level to the higher education institutions which was
justifiable given the special nature of the activities of the higher
education institutions and the many decisions on the local level which
were connected to the scientific community. The Minister explained
that the autonomy of the higher education institution is not only an

autonomy for the board and the rector's office, but to a large extent is self-determined on the various organizational levels within the higher education institution in questions regarding the inner workings of the higher education institution. In line with this reasoning, the Minister of Education stated:

> Thus, the board of the higher education institution is responsible as well for the functioning of the higher education institution, its form and the broader development of the higher education institution within the framework which the government and the Parliament have declared. At the same time, the board should bring forth proposals which benefit the development of the higher education institution in the long run. In this lies the idea that the board should initiate a continuous evaluation of the activities and take initiatives for renewal within the different sectors and faculty areas. (Gov. Prop. 1988/89:65, p.4)

This however was a radical change from the tasks of the boards in the 1970s when their primary task was to implement centrally determined goals and regulations and manage the allocation of resources to undergraduate education as prescribed by the central government.[6] With the passage of the government's extra spring budget in 1991, the responsibilities for the board were further expanded. This legislation declared that the higher education institutions' funding requests would go directly from the institutions' board to the central government, rather than to the central bureaucracy, the National Board of Universities and Colleges, where they had previously been reviewed and worked on and then sent to the government (Gov. Prop. 191990/91:150, p.6). In 1992, the importance of these reports was further emphasized, as the new Conservative Minister stated that these funding requests would provide a new and interesting basis for determining his own position on issues of resource allocation. To quote the Minister:

> In a higher education system where the resources are divided after quality and the results of graduation/completion rates, larger demands are placed on the accounting results and the analysis and extended evaluation in the annual reports... (Gov. Prop. 1992/93:169, p.58)

---

6   For discussions of decentralization in Swedish higher education, see also Lane and Murray 1985; Lane 1991; Askling and Almén 1997.

In addition, further leadership demands were placed on the boards as the H-93 reform emphasized that:

> It will be the responsibility of each board to decide how the allocated money from the government should be distributed and used internally to accomplish the tasks of the institution. Responsibility for quality must also weigh highly in the allocation principles used internally at the institutions. (Gov. Prop. 1992/93:169, p.17)

Increased local freedom to determine the administrative composition of the rector's office at each higher education institution was also stressed by the Minister of Education, making a break with the past centrally regulated administrative positions. The Minister declared:

> The decision to no longer have centrally arranged and hired administrative heads for the universities and colleges with permanent research facilities does not mean that there is no need for highly qualified administrative and economic competence at the side of the rector. It is important that the leadership be formed so that it is possible to have rectors who are not only bosses for large government authorities but who also are academic leaders. (Gov. Prop. 1992/93:169, p.95)

Thus a shift towards more autonomous universities and colleges began to emerge in the early 1990s. Leadership at the institutional level was to be strengthened as the state pulled back from its previously highly regulative posture. The higher education institutions were now viewed more as somewhat independent entities which were responsible for their own fate. A radical development in this process was the idea to connect resource allocations to quality evaluations – an idea which was most difficult to implement (see Chapter 3, p.60 and Chapter 5, p.126–7).

Institutional autonomy to ensure academic quality

In an international perspective, institutional autonomy in Sweden has, since the 1960s, been rather minimal (Clark 1983). The H-77 reform certainly did not alter the situation. Yet, ten years later, movements towards increased institutional autonomy first began to appear when the Social Democratic Minister of Education stated that 'educational quality is an issue which in my understanding can only be marginally affected by central decisions' (Gov. Prop. 1987/88:100, p.206) and thus explained that when everything is seen together, it is not external factors such as the regulation of the organization and the admissions which single-handedly lead to the motivation characterizing the work in the classrooms, seminars, laboratories, etc. Thus the Minister concluded that 'Attention needs to be paid increasingly to the whole complex of organizational and economic conditions which decide how much the student will achieve in striving towards knowledge, problem-solving ability and independent judgment' (Gov. Prop. 1987/88:100, p.206).

A questioning of the dominant position and interference of the state in areas often seen as crucial in protecting 'institutional autonomy' had begun. For example, by 1990, the government's right to appoint professors was questioned by the Minister of Education when he declared:

> By appointing the professors, the government and Parliament have decided on the subject-content basis of the permanent research organization and research education. In my opinion, it is no longer necessary for the state in such a detailed way to take a position on the use of resources which are available for research education and research. The state's priorities in this regard to research education and research at the higher education institutions shall include the balance between faculty areas and between the higher education institutions. (Gov. Prop. 1990/91:150, p.72)

By 1992, and in conjunction with a change in the ruling government, the political statements were clearly in favor of significant support for institutional autonomy. The higher education institutions were seen to have responsibilities which were to complement those of the state, described here as:

> The State must give the universities and colleges incentives for a desired development in conjunction with the demands from the world around them and the students' interests. National considerations and prioritizing must therefore sometimes be done and a framework for the organization should be given. Detailed regulation of the organization has therefore no role to play in the research and higher education [system] of the future. (Gov. Prop. 1992/93:169, pp.93–94)

Thus, in regard to the new distribution of authority to the higher education institutions, the Minister pronounced that the State was:

> not only bringing a right for the universities and colleges to decide on the educational selection but also brings a responsibility [for the universities and colleges] to renew and develop the education which is offered through a process of constant, continuing prioritizing. (Gov. Prop. 1992/93:169, p.58)

It was recognized by the politicians that meeting these new responsibilities would not be easy for the higher education institutions, but the restructuring of both the higher education institutions' boards and the office of the rector was to provide enhanced leadership capabilities (see above). As stated in the government's proposition *Higher Education for Increased Competence*:

> The rules up to now, which have been evidence of the demand for unity and strict decisions on how different groups should be represented, have worked against the ability of the higher education institutions to adjust to their own special preconditions. ... My principal view of the universities and colleges stems from the traditional meaning of the concept of university: an autonomous academy composed of students and teachers who freely choose each other. (Gov. Prop. 1992/93:169, p.93)

In line with such a view on the autonomous academy, the Minister's ideas for the tasks of the management of the higher education institutions included:

> The most important task for the board and the rector is long-term strategic planning. This planning must be based on the freedom of the students to choose their education, and the scientific freedom of the teachers. (Gov. Prop. 1992/93:169, p.94)

Recognizing the difficulty, as well as the importance, of these newly assigned management tasks for the board and rector, the Minister continued, mentioning that:

> An optimal decision must be made in regard to the relation between how available resources are distributed, how quality should be insured, which organizational entities should exist, and in what way the economy of the institution will be handled. (Gov. Prop. 1992/93:169, p.94)

Thus by incorporating into winning legislative proposals some of the classic arguments of how institutional autonomy can support academic excellence, the Minister of Higher Education transformed Sweden rather quickly from a strongly centralized, unified system to one where the individual higher education institutions, and especially their leadership, would be playing an increasingly important role.

A more autonomous system requires accountability: A new bureaucracy with a new role

Since the H-77 reform, the higher education bureaucracy in Sweden had been quite stable, with change being a rather slow, drawn-out process. Ten years after the passage in Parliament of the H-77 reform, the Minister declared that 'the main tasks of the National Board for Universities and Colleges should be to initiate and administer different types of follow-up reports on the activities of the higher education institutions' (Gov. Prop. 1986/87:100, Appendix 10, p.220). However, these reports were to concentrate largely on economic issues and how best to allocate resources within the framework which was established by the government and Parliament. An evaluation of an institution's overall quality was not conducted, instead the National Board carried out national evaluations of the individual study lines/programs. But one year later, the Minister of Education at this time stressed a new role for the National Board declaring that:

> The National Board should, according to its instructions, be responsible for the following up and evaluating of the activities of the higher education institutions. ... A part of the National Board's tasks, since the first of July 1988, is to conduct oversight of the activities in the higher education institutions. That the National Board takes seriously its new role as oversight authority (*tillsynsmyndighet*) is a condition for the decentralized higher education institution to function according to the guidelines established by higher education policies. (Gov. Prop. 1988/89:65, p.19)

However, not much time was given for the bureaucracy to adapt to the new tasks. One of the largest changes for the National Board occurred later in the spring of 1991 when the government and Parliament decided that the higher education institutions would directly report their requests for financing to the government, thus eliminating the task of financial allocations, which had been one of the constant and dominant tasks for the National Board (Gov. Prop. 1990/91:150, p.6). But it is impossible to know exactly what these changes would mean for the National Board, as approximately four months later the new Conservative Coalition government took power and dismantled the National Board entirely.

A new national bureaucratic structure was created (see Chapter 3, p.61), reflecting the increased responsibilities on the higher education institutions themselves to be accountable under a more autonomous system. No longer would an extensive, large National Board of Universities and Colleges collect data on, report about and plan for the future of the higher education institutions. The Minister, in closing down the National Board, declared, 'The changes now confronting higher education and research also motivate changes in the organization of the central authorities. The need for central authorities steered from the government and the Parliament has decreased' (Gov. Prop. 1991/92:76, p.4). The new Minister's view on quality also influenced the way in which the new bureaucracy was structured, with the establishment of a Secretariat of Assessment and Evaluation which would work to initiate, coordinate and publish evaluation results. However, the actual evaluations would be closely connected to the academic world and the Minister explained:

> The main responsibility for conducting the evaluations of the higher education institutions' activities will be connected to various bodies, which are independent in their relation to the government and to the higher education institution – mostly the scientific and scholarly academies, and also international expertise, which will have a large role. (Gov. Prop. 1991/92:76, p.3)

Soon after this bureaucratic reorganization, it was clear that the higher education institutions were also to develop systems for quality control on their own. This change was reflected in the government letter to the higher education institutions when the Minister of Education had 'a dialogue with all the higher education institutions and mentioned the measures they [would] need to take to insure quality. If this was not to be done, sanctions would be possible' (Parliament Education Committee UbU92/93:14, p.32). This was seen more as an interim step during the preparation of quality criteria which a State appointed commission, known as 'Resursberedningen' was in the process of formulating. These criteria were to be used by the Chancellor's Office (previously known as the Secretariat of Assessment and Evaluation) in their evaluation and judgments prepared for the government. The Chancellor's Office was also to prepare judgments which would be used in the government approval process regarding the right of higher education institutions to award 'degrees' under the new degree system which had replaced the study lines (Gov. Prop. 1992/93:169, p.77).

However, as mentioned in previously, the attempt to establish specific criteria – or performance indicators – failed to gain support by the public investigative commission, which instead suggested that evaluations be conducted on the higher education institutions' quality assurance programs (SOU 1993:102). The results of the quality assurance evaluation were to be connected to a 5 percent 'quality premium'. As explained by the Parliament's Higher Education Committee, 'All of the institutions' programs for quality development, as well as the carrying out of these, will be reviewed by the Chancellor's Office, which will judge if the institutions are to collect the complete, half or no 'quality premium' (Parliament Education Committee UbU93/94:12, p.56). The Minister declared that this would provide the institutions with a 'direct stimulus to systematically develop quality in their activities' (Gov. Prop. 1993/94:177, p.39). Under this new system, the Chancellor was to report yearly to the government with a complete description of the Chancellor's Office's conclusions regarding quality in the higher education system. (Higher Education Ordinance 1993:886.)[7] Yet as we will see in the next chapter, the 5 percent quality premium was never implemented, as a change in government in 1994 brought also a change in this quality policy (see Chapter 5, p.139).

Summary of shifts in state governance

In this chapter we have demonstrated how the higher education system in Sweden underwent a change in both the purpose of the system and the distribution of authority in the system between the H-77 reform and the H-93 reform. Changes which primarily characterized the shift in purpose are the emphasis in the 1990s on the needs of a broad 'knowledge society' rather than the needs of a narrowly defined job market, and the relinquishing of using the higher education system to reform society and instead focusing the system towards various market demands and the need for 'academic excellence'. The shift in authority was primarily characterized by the move away from centrally regulated and steered institutions to more autonomous institutions, led by more powerful institutional leaders who were now to compete in an education marketplace. Such a shift in the distribution of authority between the state and the institutions naturally brought about a change in the authority of the central bureaucracy, with a new emphasis on accountability rather than on planning and managing the system.

---

7   For a more complete description of the state's strategies and intentions with
    evaluation of Swedish higher education, see also Askling and Bauer 1997 and
    Kim 1997.

Now that we have described the changes along our two dimensions, we are also able to see that the H-93 reform contained changes in both types of autonomy which Berdahl (1990) discussed, substantive and procedural autonomy. By analyzing both these types of autonomy, it becomes evident that the Swedish higher education system has shifted from a 'social goals' governance type to an 'invisible hand' governance type. The meaning of such a shift for institutional autonomy is not, however, as dramatic as some of the politicians' claims may have been. In our model (Figure 4.2), such a change in type of state governance implies a movement from a 'most restrictive' institutional autonomy category to that of 'substantially restrictive'. In our next chapter, we will describe the various actors in the higher education policy network in Sweden and explain how this change to an 'invisible hand' state governance type came about in the 1990s.

Chapter 5

The Policy Network Changes
Elites, Interest Groups
and Political Interaction

Introduction

The higher education system can be regarded as a policy arena
wherein the core activities – knowledge transmission, knowledge
production and administration – are subject to attempts by different
categories of actors to affect and control the relevant processes and
events in a policy network. These actors may include academic
institutions, interest groups, academic and business elites, bureaucrats and politicians. State domination, autonomous institutions,
elitism and interest group representation (including corporatism)
represent different ways of conceptualizing the structuring of this
policy arena. How an actual policy arena is structured can not be
theoretically predetermined, and the relationship between this
structuring and the policy-making will be the focus of our analysis.[1]
The issue of policy change in higher education has recently been an
attractive topic for scholarly works. Much research attempts to
describe and explain the efforts at the national level to enact higher
education reforms. For example, in *The State and Higher Education*,
Salter and Tapper (1994) focused on the exercise of ideological power
by the state. In *Power and Politics: Federal Higher Education
Policymaking in the 1990s*, Parsons (1997) uses a theoretical approach
grounded in the sociology of translation (Callon and Latour 1981) to
analyze the social relations that form the higher education policy
arenas, and from this an explanation of policy change is presented.
Our own approach to understanding policy formation and policy
change is somewhat broader than Salter and Tapper's focus on

---

1   These ideas were originally presented in Bleiklie, Marton and Hanney (1995)
     and are informed by such contributions as Clark's 'triangle of coordination'
     (1983) and Becher and Kogan's 'synoptic model' (1992).

ideology since we view the role of ideology, epitomized by the political parties, as but one force in the policy formation process. Parsons' emphasis on social relations in explaining power is somewhat closer to our research design, yet we differ in the extent to which we have adapted the policy network concept in our Swedish study. The policy networks approach has recently been applied in studies of higher education policy change in Spain (Sánchez-Ferrer 1997) and in Australia (Marshall 1995), studies which are quite similar in approach to ours. We will discuss the policy network concept in more detail in the next section.

First, we would like to return to the discussion in Chapter 1 which emphasized that our object of study is both change and continuity in two major poles (the values and prerequisites for academic tasks and the policy formulation processes). In Chapter 1, we also justified our reasons for not conducting an implementation or evaluation study. At the macro level, we further suggest that the actual complexity of public policy formulation requires a broader framework than the rationalistic presumptions on the implementation of policy (Brobrow and Dryzek 1987). In our efforts to understand and explain policy change over a twenty-year period in Sweden, we believe that a combination of theoretical tools is most rewarding.[2] Following March and Olsen (1989, 1994), we distinguish between two main classes of ideas that can be applied to the study of policy change. The first class of ideas is based on theories of exchange and rational choice, where one can assume that policies are the aggregate outcome of interest maximizing behavior and exchange relationships. This class of ideas presupposes purposive action and conscious design on behalf of the actors in the policy formulation process. Policy is made to reach certain 'ends' given certain 'means', in a strategic, goal-oriented process. Thus, political reform and processes of policy change are explained by changing relations of power and influence between the actors, in our case, the state authorities, the academic institutions, the elites (both bureaucratic and academic) and the interest groups – who all may have different preferences.

The second class of ideas is based on institutional theories, where it is assumed that behavior is rule driven rather than preference driven

---

2   For a more elaborate discussion of theories of policy change and policy design, see Bleiklie and Marton 1998.

(March and Olsen 1989, 1994). Therefore, political action is understood in terms of a logic of appropriateness, a logic which is reflected in the structure of rules and conceptions of identities. Policy may instead be an outcome of changing beliefs about the nature of a given policy field and the way in which it relates to the rest of society. Outcomes depend on what values and norms the actors feel obliged by, and how the actors in a mutual process of adaptation, shape reform measures to conform with current norms and values in society.

In our analysis of policy change in this chapter, we recognize that there is a coexistence as well as a potential tension between these two logics of action. This tension can best be handled by allowing for the possibility that both logics may be operating, and that it is the interaction between the two that is particularly interesting. In order to empirically identify and analyze the existence of these two logics, we suggest a 'dynamic network approach' which should help us explain differences in the policy formulation processes, and thereby help us to better understand policy change.

A 'dynamic network' approach

Our approach is grounded in the literature on policy networks, a concept which emerged in order to accommodate the increasing variation in the degree and forms of interest representation due to the weakening of the traditional corporatist arrangements which started primarily in the 1980s (a common example is England during the Thatcher years). However illuminating at the time, the term 'policy network' has not to this day resulted in any new theoretical approaches and has instead remained a term which described static, structural arrangements (Atkinson and Coleman 1992; Raab 1994; John and Cole 1997; Richardson 1997). Policy networks have been viewed more as a metaphor, a generic label so to speak, for the different types of state/interest group relationships which exist in the policy process (Jordan and Schubert 1992; Rhodes and Marsh 1992; Raab 1994; Dowding 1995). As a result, the range of network members conducting these policy 'relationships' is broad and much of the literature attempts to classify different types of policy networks (Rhodes and Marsh 1992; van Waarden 1992). The main assumption of most policy network approaches is that networks are based on shared interests of the various actors – rather than values or institutional conditions.

Our position is somewhat different, based on the view that assumptions about the political behavior of and within policy networks should consider both the interaction of norms/values (an institutional perspective) and interests (rational actor perspective) within a specific social and historical context. Thus, we will use the concept of policy networks as an analytical tool to shed light on both types of political behavior.[3] In order to accomplish this task, we will focus on two dimensions of policy networks, the first being the distribution of *influence* over policy-making between the actors in the network, and the second being the level of *cohesion* between the actors in the network, i.e., how tightly or loosely the actors are related to one another. By doing this, we hope to answer questions regarding both the actors' preferences and interests, as well as the values/norms upon which higher education policy is shaped over time.

For the dimension of influence, we focus on four possible ways in which the actors can be structured in order to impact policy formulation. First, under *state domination*, policies are formulated at the central state level and are later to be implemented by the individual subordinate agencies. Comparative higher education research over time and across countries has found that variations in state domination may be due to traditions of political steering, the relationship between the civil service and the higher education institutions, and the role of education and research in achieving national political goals (Clark 1983; Becher and Kogan 1992; Salter and Tapper 1994). The reverse of state domination we call *autonomous institutions*,[4] where influence is exercised by individual government institutions managing their own affairs to such an extent that central government policies amount to little more than the sum of the institutions' actions. Such autonomy in the public sector has often been justified on the idea that authority should be based on

---

3   Initial efforts to apply this approach to comparative empirical data on higher
     education policies were presented in Bleiklie, Marton and Hanney 1997.
4   Note that the term 'autonomous institutions' is being used in a broader sense
     than the term 'institutional autonomy' which is used primarily in the context of
     higher education. Here we refer to the possibility of 'autonomous' relationships
     between the state and a variety of societal institutions (for example the military,
     the national health system, the judicial system, and the higher education
     system).

specialized knowledge, for example in administering areas such as the judiciary, the health care services and the military. In addition, there is the idea that authority should be placed in close proximity to those who are affected by the decisions, such as the principle of subsidiarity promoted by the EU or the ideas of decentralization which are a central element of the new public management ideology.

It is also possible that policy formulation is subject to mediation, and for this we have identified two forms of mediation, via *elites* or via *interest representation*. In the classic version of elite mediation, elites gain power by exploiting their positions in society. Applied to the policy sector of higher education, it is likely that academics can also be 'co-opted' into the policy formulation process, which has been described as 'the process of absorbing new elements into the leadership of policy-determining structures of an organization, as a means of averting threats to its stability or existence' (Kogan 1984, p.69, citing Selznick 1966). There are three ways in which co-opted academic elites may operate:

- through their membership in government appointed bodies
- by internalizing, interpreting and helping to implement government policies
- by creating hierarchies of resource and esteem. (Marton, Hanney and Kogan 1995, referring to Becher and Kogan 1992 and Kogan 1992).

Thus, forms of elite influence can be patterned differently depending on the policy sector.[5] Interest representation is a form of influence where the interest organizations, such as employers' associations and trade unions, act as the main mediator. At a national level, their interest lies in matters of overall policy for a particular sector. At the

---

5   The concept of elites may be rather difficult to discern in the Swedish style of policy-making, primarily for two reasons: 1) the Swedish university system has been based on the presumption of equivalence of institutions across the country, thus a *clear recognition* of an institution as 'elite', or the members of that institution as 'elite' individuals, is not very common; and 2) there is a long tradition of interest group and special representative involvement in the policy process through the use of public investigative commissions. However, we note the 'elite' nature of the 'Professor' title in Sweden, and do pay attention to some interest groups which exist as academic honor societies and/or academic professional associations (but in our usage of the term elite, we do not include the academic trade unions – instead they are seen as a part of interest representation).

same time, they are interested in more local issues such as wages, working conditions, personnel management and workplace democracy. Under the theory of corporatism, political exchange would be limited to a few participants, usually business associations and trade unions, who would receive a representational monopoly from the government. With the rise of liberalism and managerialism during and after the 1980s, there have been indications that corporatist arrangements are weakening – an assumption which will receive further study in our empirical analysis.

In addition to the distribution of influence over policy-making, our dynamic network approach also aims to identify the level of *cohesion* between the actors in the network. Rhodes and Marsh's (1992) idea of the policy network as a continuum, with 'policy community' and 'issue network' at the two opposing ends is helpful in this regard. A 'policy community' would thus be characterized by: its limited membership; frequent interaction with shared basic values; all participants having a resource base and the ability to deliver their members' support; and the power among the community's members relatively equal in distribution. On the opposite end of the continuum is the 'issue network', characterized by: a large and/or wide range of affected interests; fluctuations in contacts, access, and level of agreement; unequal resource distribution combined with varying abilities to deliver members' support; and unequal powers among the groups. Thus, corporatist arrangements of policy-making can be seen as a type of policy network, most often leaning towards the 'policy community' side of the Rhodes and Marsh continuum. Loosely coupled networks of elite decision makers or autonomous institutions, on the other hand, may operate like issue networks.

As stated, in order to explain the policy shifts in Sweden, our study uses the policy network concept as a tool to analyze the dimensions of both cohesion and influence in the policy formulation process. Our empirical sources in this analysis are primarily membership of the SOUs (public investigative commissions), interview data and documents from the 'remiss' process. One should not underestimate the importance of the remiss process in Sweden. It is a legitimate institution for Swedish policy-making and takes place after the public investigative commissions have completed their reports (see Introduction to Part II, footnote 1, p.71). The final report of the SOU is sent to all interested organizations and bureaucracies, who then, in writing, send their comments to the Government. In this chapter, these written comments are a crucial part of our empire since they explain each organizations' official standpoint on policy issues. It is only after this remiss circulation that the government's propositions should be presented in Parliament. Furthermore, it is important to note that a largely negative remiss could lead to the appointment of a new commission or a modified government proposal (see Sannerstedt 1989).

Interest mediation and the strong state: a 'policy community' in the late 1960s and 1970s

Politicians, bureaucrats and interest groups

Swedish policy-making since the 1940s has been characterized as social corporatism (see Introduction to Part II, pp.69). Structured consultation and corporate representation (Heclo and Madsen 1987) were an established part of this policy-making style. During the late 1960s and 1970s, this corporatist style mainly dominated higher education policy-making as well (Ruin 1982; Bleiklie 1994b) and helped to ensure that the function of the system would be the satisfaction of politically defined welfare goals (Nybom 1985).

As mentioned in Chapter 3, the reform ideas from U68 finally passed Parliament in 1975, with a 'principle' proposition launched by the Social Democrats (*Socialdemokratiska Arbetarepartiet*). Shortly thereafter, the Social Democrats lost power to a coalition government (led by Prime Minister Fälldin of the Center Party, *Centerpartiet*). Yet this coalition was too fragile to make any major changes in the field of higher education, and the H-77 reform passed with some small modifications. Many aspects of the H-77 reform were grounded in traditional Social Democratic ideology which focused on the need for a steady expansion of the welfare state (public services in addition to social insurance benefits; an active labor-market policy emphasizing training and job programs; a solidaristic wage policy; and a supplementary pension reform (ATP) which created significant pension funds under public management). However, as Sainsbury (1993) stated, the 1970s represented a more radical Social Democracy[6] with 'a stronger advocacy of state intervention in the

6   Based on the following Social Democratic party documents: Program for an Active Industrial Policy 1968, Towards Equality 1971, and Industrial Democracy 1971.

economy, the reassertion of equality as a major party goal, and the call for greater employee influence' (p.44), all elements which are evident in the H-77 reform. It was also during this time period that the wage earner's funds policy was implemented and the new democracy in the work place laws were initiated.

The 1975 Social Democratic party program outlined the major goals for the party as: solidarity, equality, economic liberation, democracy, the right to work, a planned economy, and regional development. The party's focus on economic liberation at this time in history also influenced the view on democracy with statements such as, 'For Social Democracy, the need for economic democracy is just as obvious as the need for political democracy. Social Democracy is opposed to a system which gives owners the right to exercise power over people' (p.5). This was extended into the belief that 'Every person has a right to work which they see as meaningful' and '[t]herefore, the right to decide over the means of production must rest with all the people' (Social Democratic Party 1975, p.6). It was the purpose of Social Democracy at this time to 'realize a system of production which is not steered by a one-sided and limited profit-interest' (p.16). Rather, '[t]he whole entire economic sphere must be organized by a planned economy under the control of the citizens' (p.16). This contributed to the party's belief in democratic control of technology and research advances evidenced in the party statement that, 'A goal of the planned economy is to steer technological development. Scientific and technological advances are the basis for thorough changes in the structure of business and in working conditions' (p.17). Lastly, equality was to pertain to the various geographic regions as well, with the goal being that 'all the country's regions are equivalent in regards to access to work as well as social, commercial and cultural services' (p.19).

As for specifics on higher education and research policy, the 1975 party program lists that:

- a no-cost higher education should be provided
- students should have influence on all levels
- the most important task of research policy is to widen the possibilities for a democratic order to influence the future
- society should be responsible for the planning of investments in research and development so that technological developments can be prioritized according to the citizens' interests.

In order to accomplish these goals regarding research, the party program states that:

- research is to shed light on the need for reform
- a free research environment for basic research should be encouraged
- the role of researchers to critically comment on society should be guaranteed as well as the right to publish and to think freely
- the researchers' and the scientific communities' contact with society in general should be developed and deepened. (pp.47–48)

During the 1970s, the Social Democrats were very successful in turning their 'higher education ideology', represented in the party program, into higher education policies. At the start of this policy formation process (which led to the H-77 reform), we see a very tight-knit group of politicians and bureaucrats comprising the U68 Commission. Heading the Commission as Chairman was Lennart Sandgren, the Deputy Secretary from the Department of Education, with other key members being Bertil Olsson, the Head of the Swedish National Labor Market Board (known as AMS); Jonas Orring, the Head of the National Board of Education (known as SÖ), and the University Chancellor Hans Löwbeer and the former University Chancellor Gustaf Rosén.[7] In addition, reference groups representing the political parties, the trade unions and the educational interests were formed, however they had no formal decision or voting right over the Commission's work. Such a composition was very unusual and raised much contention among the opposition political parties (who felt the bureaucrats should be regulated to the position of reference group, with the politician's having the voting rights) and among some of the trade unions (TCO and SACO) who felt that their role was not to act as a reference group for the bureaucracy.[8] However,

7   It is important to remember the restructuring in 1964 whereby the University Chancellor's Office was created and the Chancellor was appointed by the Government. Thus, the primary role of the University Chancellor was to head this newly created intermediary body, a role which we characterize as 'bureaucratic' and not as 'academic elite'. See Chapter 3, p.50.

8   TCO, *Tjänstemännens Centralorganisation*, is the Confederation of Salaried (White-Collar) Employees which had 1.167 million members in 1993 (981,000 members in 1978). SACO, *Sveriges Akademikers Centralorganisation* is the Swedish University Graduates' Central Organization and had 271,000 members in 1993 (168,000 in 1978). See Statistiska Centralbyrån 1982, 1996a.

the complaints from these trade unions were mitigated by the genuine satisfaction that a Commission had been appointed to look into the issues of higher education in Sweden (Lindensjö 1981).The National Swedish Labor Market Board (AMS) had a special role in the formation of higher education policy at this time, given the goal of the welfare state to connect higher education to job purpose and job creation (see Chapter 4). In addition, the blue-collar trade union LO[9] was very much involved through its connections with the Social Democratic Party, with both groups viewing the reform of higher education as an instrument in providing economic and social equality. The connection to the labor market was very much supported by LO, which in its U68 remiss response stated, 'education should be mostly dominated by preparation for work. ...the higher education institutions [should] develop to a greater extent than before contacts with *arbetslivet*,[10] in the planning and prioritization of research as well as in the form and content for teaching' (Remiss: LO, 4 February 1974, p.3). The overall goal was to reform society, where 'The higher education institutions must, like the other parts of the educational system in general, be an instrument which supports a more equal distribution of economic, social, and cultural values and a wider development of democracy' (p.1). It was important to LO that the higher education institutions have a governing system which 'would give society outside the institution – not the least being the large workers' groups – a dramatically increased influence than that of today' (p.3).

Other major trade unions to be reconciled within the policy formation process were SACO and TCO. TCO was overwhelmingly favorable in its remiss response and agreed that:

> a complete reform of the entire higher education system was absolutely necessary.' ... The traditional isolation of higher education must be broken and replaced with a cooperation and relationship with society in general. Higher education must be integrated in societal planning in a totally different way than currently. Higher education's role in society and therewith its responsibility for ful-

---

9   *Landsorganisationen* is the Swedish Trade Union Confederation for primarily industrial (blue-collar) workers. In 1993, LO had 1.664 million members, 1978, 1.679 million. See Statistiska Centralbyrån 1982, 1996a.

10 For an explanation of the word *arbetsliv* see footnote 6 in Chapter 4, p.82.

filling societal goals must be strongly emphasized. (Remiss: TCO, 5 February 1974, p.2)

Premfors (1980, p.169) also mentions how TCO was an influential player at the very early stages of the policy process with its 1966 report entitled *Post High School (Secondary) Education.*

The union which represented university educated, white-collar workers (SACO), was somewhat more critical of the reforms during this time than TCO. SACO did feel, however, that their long time argument for the need to discuss solutions to limit student admissions was finally being addressed in the U68 Commission.[11] With concerns for an overproduction of humanities students, SACO was very supportive of the connection to the job market, evident in statements such as:

> If an important starting point for planning is society's need for an educated work force, than it is natural to also take into consideration the job market's demands for workers with higher education as a starting point for the formation of different types of education. This must inevitably lead to that many types of education – and predominantly at the Faculties of Humanities, Social Science and Natural Science which have to this point had a high frequency without a corresponding need from the job market – must decrease in volume or be totally replaced by other types of education. (Remiss: SACO, 23 November 1973, p.4)

Thus, SACO was in agreement with the intentions of the U68 Commission to have total limits on the size of the higher education system. But in contrast to the U68 proposals, SACO did not see any role for individual educational demands to be calculated into the national planning for system size. Instead, SACO declared,

> The primary factor with the size of the HE system is ... the demand of the job market for educated workers. Individuals' demands for education are to a large extent only a function of the job market prognosis at the time of student registration. SACO is of the opinion that the prognosis of the job market's demand for workers with higher education should determine the size of the higher education system totally as well as in regards to the division

---

11   In particular, SACO mentions their previous remiss answer to the U55 Commission and a letter to the Minister in May of 1962 (Remiss: SACO, 23 November 1973, p.3).

between different types of education. (Remiss: SACO, 23 November 1973, p.83)

Yet SACO did warn that the emphasis on the connection to the job market should not mean that the education would be focused towards narrowly defined work categories. In SACO's opinion, it was still important that the demand placed on higher education – to give insight into scientific methods, support critical thinking and give possibilities for the students to solve larger, independent tasks – should be maintained (Remiss: SACO, 23 November 1973, p.83).

SACO was also critical of the U68 proposals on the organizational structure of the higher education institutions. This was SACO's strongest point of contention, evidenced by their request for a new proposal and a new remiss process on this topic. SACO was negative to the idea that the departments would have different boards for research and for teaching, which would mean a 'definite break with the characteristic of higher education and its necessary research connection' (p.88). In addition, SACO argued against the use of educational boards (under the 5 main vocational areas we mentioned in Chapter 3) in the faculties of humanities, social sciences and natural sciences). Regarding the controversial topic of representatives of the general interest forming the majority on each university's and college's board, SACO was also critical and stated that more members should be gathered from within the higher education institutions (pp.88–89).

In addition to the trade unions, another major actor in the labor market to contend with during the policy formation process was SAF, (*Svenska arbetsgivareföreningen*, The Swedish Employers' Federation) which combined its remiss answer with IF (*Industri Förbundet*, Federation of Swedish Industries). The general summary statement at the beginning of their remiss was very critical, mentioning that U68 devoted too much attention to organizational issues instead of issues of pedagogy and method, and that U68 tried to find one-sided organizational solutions to higher education, which SAF/IF found 'unacceptable' (Remiss: SAF/IF, 28 January 1974, pp.1 and 4).

SAF/IF however did primarily agree with U68's plans for the size of the higher education system in terms of judging the development of various sectors of the labor market in relation to one another, and also supported the idea to have a large amount of individual courses available to the students. However, SAF/IF expressed concerns regarding the difficulty in using a prognosis based on job market needs as a basis for establishing admissions levels, stating:

> to steer the size directly from a needs prognosis is hardly advisable on the grounds of the difficulties in making sound judgments of a satisfactorily long term nature and because there are so many different types of demands even for the same type of education. ... The determining factor for the size of higher education should, according to our understanding, be the availability of resources. (Remiss: SAF/IF, 28 January 1974, p.5)

In terms of organization, SAF/IF suggested a more flexible organization for the higher education institutions and thus it was proposed that an oversight authority for all education (including education at the university level) be created. Such an organization would be divided into sectors, and the sectors would handle education as well as research issues (Remiss: SAF/IF, 28 January 1974, p.7).

Academic institutions, elites and students

But what of the academics themselves? How did they respond to a reform which had such significant meaning for their working conditions? Premfors (1980) has written that the proposals were met with strong hostile reactions among parts of academia.[12] We have reviewed the remiss responses from some of the universities as well as some of the major research councils. Our review supports Premfors' findings, with the universities extremely dissatisfied with the lack of attention paid to the 'content, quality and renewal of education' (Remiss: Uppsala University, 27 November 1974, p.1). Of particular concern was the application of the work-related study line system to the faculties of humanities, social sciences and natural sciences, with the universities supporting a subject-based division instead. In discussing the study line committees, Stockholm University wrote that it was, 'an example of such a forced intervention in an established, functioning organization, which has shown its innovative abilities' (Remiss: Stockholm University (Utbildningsledare), 28 November 1974, p.4). This same remiss states that the U68 proposals were 'built on an incomplete understanding about the conditions for

---

12 Premfors' review was based on a summary of the higher education institutions'
    remiss answers which was attached to UKÄ's remiss answer to the Govern-
    ment. Our study has instead reviewed each individual remiss answer.

university education and therefore did not take into consideration that a reformed university system must begin with the stimulation – not the restraining – of the productive units' ability to develop and to take initiatives' (p.1).

In regards to the U68 ideas that society must have stronger oversight of the higher education institutions in order to put an end to the university's 'isolation', Uppsala University's remiss includes many pages of argument highlighting how U68 is wrong in its interpretation of the conditions at the universities and colleges. Uppsala states that the assumption from U68 is that the university lives completely separated from representatives of society's interests, and that these representatives have no possibility to observe the activities taking place within the universities. Of these conclusions, Uppsala University declares:

> This is however not the case at all. One can first constitute that the Government and the Parliament not only decide the framework and the guidelines for the universities activities, but through their regulation letter, they also decide over the university's activities. There are probably few countries which have such a detailed formulation for central steering as that of Sweden. (Remiss: Uppsala University, 27 November 1974, p.8)

Some of the institutions mentioned the tension between the traditional autonomy of the universities in Sweden and Europe in order to secure freedom of research versus the view of the university as an instrument to reach political goals. Umeå University's response mentions this unhealthy tension between the state and the higher education institutions and sees this as detrimental:

> Simply put one can say that the education system's very important social and cultural role requires that a high level of responsibility must be placed on the reform activities within the education system; eventual mistakes can result in serious negative effects for many people and for a long part of their lives. (Remiss: Umeå University, 25 November 1974, p.1)

The major research councils also sent in remiss answers, with nearly full unanimity of criticism. The Medical Research Council (*Statens Medicinska Forskningsråd*, MFR) pointed out that the U68 document was incomplete in three important areas: a) the need for changes in the organizational structure, b) calculations of the costs to carry out the organizational transformation, and c) an analysis of the advantages such an organizational change would bring (Remiss:

MFR, 6 December 1973, p.1). MFR concluded that 'these proposals, which in many cases mean an over-organization with the establishment of further decision-making levels, will ... lead to a worsening of the work done in the departments and faculties, and will thus decrease efficiency (pp.1–2). The Humanities Research Council (*Statens Humanistiska Forskningsråd*, HFR) was very positive to the cultural and social goals of the reform and mentioned that it was 'urgent that the educational walls be open for new groups in society' (Remiss: HFR, 24 January 1974, p.1). However, that was nearly their only positive comment. The council was very much against the division of teaching from research, and the 'inadequate clarity and the lack of emphasis on the importance of scientific research to society and to teaching' (p.2). In regards to the proposals for a new governing board at the higher education institutions, the council interpreted this as a 'clear risk for political steering. From an international standpoint, such a development stands out as remarkable. Research freedom must be reflected in the construction of the university' (p.5). The Social Science Research Council (*Statens Råd för Samhällsforskning*, SFR) was concerned about the negative effects on quality in the U68 proposal to spread educational programs (study lines) to new locations around the country:

> Even if these new higher education institutions, at least at the start, are intended to conduct shorter educational lines which are to a limited degree dependent on research, it is predictable that within a rather short time frame significant quality differences will arise between study lines at such new locations and the corresponding education which takes place in contact with a research environment and where teacher recruitment, library resources etc. provide conditions for higher quality. (Remiss: SFR, 30 January 1974, p.2)

Another representative of the academic interests responding to the U68 proposals was IVA (*Ingenjörsvetenskapsakademien*, Royal Swedish Academy of Engineering Sciences). IVA, like the research councils, was very concerned over the lack of attention paid to research, and the way in which U68 only dealt with undergraduate education, 'while [undergraduate education's] content and relationship to research and research education were not covered' (Remiss: IVA, 30 January 1974, p.2). Another important area of comment for IVA was the size of the higher education system and how to determine future student numbers. IVA found that even though it was possible to try to improve the methods for prognosis making, it was necessary to recognize that a degree of uncertainty would also exist. This uncertainty must have consequences for the formation of education. IVA explained, 'Uncertainty makes it necessary to direct education towards rather broad sectors with an emphasis on basic knowledge, which can provide the foundation for continuous education' (p.9).

An additional large player in the policy process was SFS (*Sveriges Förenade Studentkårer*, Swedish National Union of Students). SFS was extremely critical in its remiss answer (Remiss: SFS, 4 March 1974), going so far as to call for a new Parliamentary Commission and stating that the entirely bureaucratic composition of U68 was wrong from the start. A Parliamentary Commission with all political parties represented as well as representatives from the higher education institutions was needed. SFS thought it particularly troublesome that undergraduate education and research were separated and, because of this, U68 could not comment on the consequences which would arise in relation to the connection with graduate education and research. Further critique was leveled at the lack of attention to the content of the different types of education and also to the fact that a proposal which appeared to be so focused on decreasing social class differences at the higher education institutions did not consider the relation to financial aid packages for the students.

The differences in opinions as to the U68 reform were also reflected in the public debate. Ulf af Trolle's review (1990) shows that many well-respected academics spoke out vehemently about the effects of the U68 reform. In particular, Stig Strömholm, at the time Professor of Law at Uppsala University, initiated the debate with his 1972 book *Försök till en lidelsefri betraktelse* (Attempt at a Dispassionate Reflection), followed by the Rector of Uppsala University, Torgny Segerstedt's *Hotet mot den högre utbildningen* (Threat to Higher Education) in 1974 and Torsten Husén, Professor in Pedagogy at Stockholm University with his book *Universiteten och Forskningen* (The University and Research), 1975.

Policy formulation for the H-77 reform: a summary

After reviewing the empirical data above, we can characterize the membership and actions of the policy network during 1960s and 1970s as a policy community of the corporatist kind, with the state primarily dominating. The membership was small and controlled, with the Government exercising its strong influence by appointing only politicians and bureaucrats to the U68 Commission. Cohesion between the actors in the network was rather high, with shared common values, similar resource bases and somewhat equal powers. Trade unions that had favorable relations with the Social Democratic Party, such as LO and TCO, also exhibited a shared value base, for example, a similar understanding on the role of higher education in reforming society. Thus, we know that there was much cohesion between these actors, with the trade unions agreeable to the U68 proposals and the H-77 reform. However, in discussing TCO during the 1970s, Nybom has written:

> If one were, in a very much simplified way, to characterize the politics of Swedish research and higher education in the 1970s in terms of principle responsibility, one should, instead of considering the State – consider TCO as the 'prime mover' with its outspoken ambitions to change the university to a socially useful and labor market adjusted cadet school. (Nybom 1997, p.145)

We would instead argue that the corporatist nature of the policy community during the 1970s favored input from trade unions such as LO and TCO, but that policy outcome was still very much connected to the Social Democratic Party. Those who were critical – primarily the academics and the students – were not allowed an opportunity to really shape the policy outcome. Although some academics did participate as reference groups, it seems that no efforts were made to co-opt the academic elite. Certainly, the universities, research councils and student groups participated in the official remiss process by sending in their comments, but the tight-knit policy community had already been established and used its strong influence to dominate the policy formulation process.

Below we can graphically summarize the policy community for the H-77 reform, which demonstrates a high level of congruence with the policy outcome for such actors as the Social Democrats, the bureaucracy, and trade unions such as TCO and LO. Other actors are also strongly cohesive in their policy views, resulting in two major groupings – one being, SACO, SAF/IF and the other being the academic elites, universities and SFS.

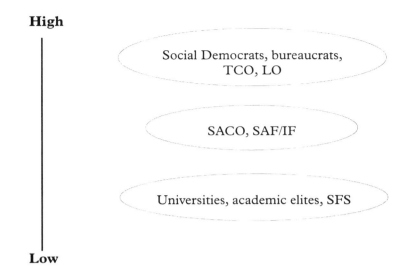

High

Social Democrats, bureaucrats,
TCO, LO

SACO, SAF/IF

Universities, academic elites, SFS

Low

Figure 5.1 Congruence and cohesion for H-77
Note: Level of congruence between actors' policy goals and policy outcome. Ovals
represent cohesion among actors' preferences.

Elite mediation: an emerging 'issue network' in the late 1980s and early 1990s

In our introduction to Part II, we briefly described how corporatism in Sweden has declined in the 1980s and 1990s, replaced by pluralist tendencies. Our research shows that such a decline affected the higher education policy arena as well. No longer was this policy arena primarily reserved for politicians, bureaucrats and trade unions, but rather a dispersion in the policy network membership and influence is evident before and during the formulation of policy resulting in the H-93 reform. In addition, data point to a shift in some of the ideological underpinnings of the Social Democratic Party, a shift which also contributed to policy changes in higher education.

Pressure for change

Some of the early rumblings of dissatisfaction with the state domination of the higher education system were evident as early as the autumn of 1980 in the *Svenska Dagbladet* newspaper series on the 'University in Crisis'. Prominent academics participating in this series included Torgny T. Segerstedt (former Rector of Uppsala University) who declared that the study line system must be abandoned in order to re-create an intellectual university environment. Also participating was Professor Leif Lewin (Uppsala University), who criticized the attempts to create work-related subject areas that did not exist in the international academic community. These debates left a somewhat minor imprint however, until the autumn of 1982 (af Trolle 1990). At that time, Sverker Gustavsson, a political scientist at Uppsala University and later to be the Social Democrat's Deputy Minister of Education, wrote his famous debate article in *Tiden* (1982) commenting harshly on the 'anti-intellectualism' of undergraduate education:

> We who are now adults, have to think of Sweden in the world which awaits us in the 1990s and beyond the year 2,000. Is it not knowledge in the foundations of philosophy, economics, physics, politics, geography, biology, sociology, and psychological theory? How are we who will be living at that time, and our children, to be otherwise able to continue our education and follow what happens? ... Demands must be set higher for every year which goes – not lower such as the case now with all these proposals for misdirected vocational accommodation which flow over our desks. (Gustavsson (1982) cited in af Trolle 1990, p.152)

But change did not come quickly, although it was clear that many were dissatisfied (see af Trolle 1990). Instead, there was an effort to co-opt the elites into the policy network, evidenced by the appointment in 1985 of Sverker Gustavsson as Deputy Minister of Education. Interview data suggests that this appointment reflected a desire to move away from the H-77 reform:

> Lena Hjelm-Wallén [the Education Minister 1982–1985] and Erland Ringborg [the Deputy Education Minister 1982–1985] were very connected with 1977. So, they took Bengt Göransson [as Minister] and Sverker Gustavsson, the academic, instead. This was a very conscious decision on behalf of the Social Democrats, in order to create different relations with the universities and colleges. (former Ministry official)

With Gustavsson as Deputy Minister, dialogue with the academics was strengthened, and was broader than just official remiss answers. Seminars were arranged at the Wenner-Gren Center in Stockholm during 1986 and 1987. Yet it was discussion that was occurring, not proposals for dramatic change. As brought forth in one of our interviews:

> With Sverker Gustavsson a change came, well, a swing actually. He was known as a researcher who also taught. Then his debate article came, and he discussed how the role of the state was to determine basically which [educational] programs we needed, but that the higher education institutions and the students were to determine how these programs would be accomplished. But when he got to office, you didn't hear so much about it anymore. This sort of thing happens… (researcher)

By 1987, the Social Democratic party was also engaged in efforts to rewrite the party program under the leadership of the Prime Minister, Ingvar Carlsson. After work by various commissions and committees, an action program for the 90s (*90-talsprogrammet*), was presented. In comparison to the 1975 party program, some of the significant ideological changes/developments in the 1991 party program included changes in the idea of equality and economic liberation. The document stated that achieving equality was no longer a 'fight' and that it was important to strive after an equal distribution of resources which had meaning for the possibility of people to influence society and their own life (Social Democratic Party Program 1991, p.6). There was some doubt expressed to exactly how economic democracy was to be achieved, evidenced by the statement that it was not self-evident that economic democracy could be achieved by societal organizations having influence over the means and results of production (p.24). The 1975 goal of a planned economy was relinquished, evidenced in the statement:

> The question of a societal planned economy or a market economy is …for Social Democrats a question of which method, in each individual case, is best suited to reach the goal of a just distribution of welfare, an effective usage of the nation's economic resources and planning for environmental and natural resources. (Social Democratic Party Program 1991, p.26)

There was an absence in the party program of the general need to steer technological developments, which was replaced instead by the need for technological developments to be geared towards environmental products and methods (p.28).

Also of importance in the 1991 program was the mention of pluralistic developments in Swedish society:

The knowledge society supports the questioning of authority. People want to themselves, in using the strength of their own knowledge, influence and decide. ... Citizens' involvement in individual political issues is increasing... These factors lead to a more pluralistic society but at the same time, a society that is more divided. ... Urbanization, regionalization, and decentralization lead to different experiences and values, dependent on where one lives. (Social Democratic Party Program 1991, p.18)

As for higher education and research, the 1991 party program also reflects some of these pluralistic and decentralized trends in society. For example, rather than an emphasis on the role of the higher education institutions in reforming society (see Chapter 4) and the need for democratic control at the state level, this party program demonstrates a need for increased interaction with a variety of organizations. The document states that 'Businesses, municipalities and regions must take increased responsibility for [research] development which has direct connection to their own activities' (p.56). There is also mention of the need for diversity in the sources of financing for research activities:

The state-controlled higher education system's most important task in regards to research is its responsibility for doctoral education and the carrying-out of research in line with the best international standards. In addition to the universities and colleges, there shall be, with the intention to support diversity, more varied organizations which decide on the financing of research. (Social Democratic Party Program 1991, p.56)

In addition, the need for a stronger relationship with business was evident:

It is of strategic importance that industry's research and development activities function well, and they should thus be stimulated. It is an important task of business policy to stimulate technical research and development and to encourage the spread of new technology. Research and educational policy should be connected with business and regional development policies. (Social Democratic Party Program 1991, p.56)

There is also an indication that the strong state steering of the study lines is no longer adequate and that 'colleges and universities should give more specialized education in accordance to the students' choice and the needs of the job market' (p.55). The document continues to reflect a utilitarian view on research, however, the role of research in reforming society is downplayed. Rather, this utilitarian view is expressed in statements such as 'It is important that the results of basic research are connected to applied research' (p.56) and 'The percent of employees working with research and development at the colleges should increase in order that competitiveness is strengthened' (p.56). The role of higher education in society is somewhat vaguely presented, but it is declared that 'the entire scientific communities' contact with society should be deepened' (p.56).

With the combination of the Social Democrat's changing views on the role of knowledge in society and the criticisms raised by the academic elites, the time had come to review higher education policy once again.

An invitation to the academics

More than ten years after the H-77 reform, the stage was set for another public investigation into the functioning of higher education in Sweden. As mentioned in Chapter 3, the public investigative commission arranged by the Social Democratic government in 1989 (Högskoleutredningen, SOU 1992:1) was composed entirely of academics (and one student), led by a Chairman who was the Rector of Lund University, Håkan Westling. Interview data reveals that the special composition of 'Högskoleutredningen' was possible because the Social Democratic Deputy Minister of Education at the time, Sverker Gustavsson, was having conversations with Leif Levin (Chairman of SULF, *Sveriges Universitets lärarförbund*[13] and also a political scientist at Uppsala University) about the poor quality in education and the differences in resources allocated for the same education in different parts of the country. They arranged for an all-academic composition for this Commission (former political advisor). Later in 1992 when the new Conservative coalition government (Minister of Education, Per Unckel, from the Moderate party (*Moderata samlingspartiet*) called for a commission to look into a new resource distribution system for higher education (known as 'Resursberedningen'; SOU 1993:3, SOU 1993:102) the idea of having academics in the majority was maintained, with the addition of three other members – the Deputy Secretary of the Ministry of

---

13   Swedish Association of University Lecturers, an organizational member of the SACO trade union.

Education (Bjarne Kirsebom) as Chairman, the Director of the Swedish Association of Universities and Colleges (Lars Ekholm) and a representative from business. The Conservative government also encouraged informal input from a variety of organizations by arranging 'Agenda 2000' – a forum for the exchange of ideas (and publications) dealing with the future of Swedish higher education and research. Organizations contributing reports to this forum included, for example: the Royal Swedish Academy of Sciences (*Vetenskapsakademien*) the Royal Swedish Academy of Engineering Sciences (IVA), and the Research Institute of Industrial Economics (IUI).

When one studies the remiss answers to the major public investigation of higher education (Högskoleutredningen) and to the new coalition government's promemoria (Department Series 1992:1) it is obvious that the reaction is overall very positive. Compared to the intense critique of U68 from the academic community, the Högskoleutredningen Commission was welcomed with open arms. The academics expressed relief that the ideas of strong state steering from the H-77 reform were now fading. Such a comparison was evident in Lund University's remiss statement with:

> Everyone agrees that higher education and research are important for society, but unity has not been as large when it comes to the conditions and rules under which the university and colleges work. Lofty declarations on university freedom have not prevented the lengthy ambitions to regulate the [institutions'] content and forms of work. The 1977 Reform was an expression of a strong belief in the state's ability to plan and steer the complicated and multi-faceted world to which today's university and colleges belong. In retrospect, it has been all the more evident that this ambition to a large extent failed its purpose and led to increased bureaucracy and lower initiative taking, thereby harming the inner life of the universities and colleges. (Remiss: Lund University, 13 April 1992, p.2)

It was obvious that the new freedoms (See Chapter 4) were warmly welcomed. Chalmers University of Technology declared that it:

> agrees completely with the basic view which is presented...to create possibilities to release important parts of higher education and research from today's direct state influence in order to further raise the quality of research and education. It is stimulating to receive greater freedom to organize, use and distribute resources in order to increase the international competitiveness within re-

search and education while continuing to maintain strong academic freedom. (Remiss: Chalmers University of Technology, 15 April 1992, p.1)

However, the overall positive response did not block out all the critical comments. In particular, Umeå University was very critical stating that there was no reason for any drastic changes to the institutional arrangements and that it was not reasonable to connect the students' exam results with the resource allocation system. Due to many concerns, Umeå demanded a new proposal and a new remiss process.

Other respondents were more mixed in their analysis. For example, Göteborg University wrote:

> Freedom is not an unambiguous concept which in every usage has a given, positive meaning and a given intrinsic value. But the increased local freedom means not only increased competition between higher education institutions, but also increased local responsibility to maintain the freedom of research and a long-term and forward looking development of knowledge. (Remiss: Göteborg University, 16 April 1992, p.2)

Many concerns were raised over the use of a quantitative method for resource distribution in the time period before the 5 percent quality money program was finally passed as legislation. In the period prior to this legislation (Gov. Prop. 1993/94:177), the academic debate was not dominated by whether there should be some type of quality connection to resource distribution, but more so by what kind of quality measures would work. The Royal Swedish Academy of Sciences commented that:

> It is thereby important to find reliable measures of quality, rather than just of quantity, for teaching and research. It would be a problem if university departments adjusted to mechanical demands of increasing student graduation rates, and lowered their examination requirements accordingly. (Remiss: KVA, 22 April 1992, p.2)

IVA was also highly supportive of the idea of quality competition amongst the higher education institutions in the new decentralized system, and declared that: 'This entails a systematic evaluation of teaching and research activities, which will affect universities. IVA is in agreement with, and strongly supports, all the thoughts and principles about university freedom, decentralization, and competition, that the Minister of Education advanced in his promemoria' (Remiss: IVA, 22 April 1992, p.1).

Although there was much discussion in the early days of performance indicators, these became very difficult to define and establish for undergraduate education. Support for a strong quality component was expressed by the Rector of the Royal Institute of Technology, who stated, 'It gives the wrong signals ...that one invests only a few percent on quality. [O]ne should have a more obvious quality component, in order to give out signals of quality in the colleges and universities (Janne Carlsson, Royal Institute of Technology in Department Series 1993:9, p.16). Yet finding agreement on the 'obvious quality component' was not so easy, and the final settlement was a 5 percent quality premium.

Another area for concern and comment was the proposed changes to institutional leadership. KVA (*Kungliga Vetenskapsakademien*, the Royal Swedish Academy of Science) wrote:

> In order to enhance the general legitimacy of the universities it may be important that the majority of university board members are non-university staff. Prior experience from both Swedish and foreign universities strongly suggest the value of having access to viewpoints from non-university activities. However, such board members must be selected based on their true interest in the activities of the university. The board as a representative of various interest groups (political parties and action groups, trade unions) should, according to the academy, belong to history. (Remiss: KVA, 22 April 1992, p.3)

Many of the research councils also felt this was an important change, with both HSFR and FRN suggesting that an academic senate be created to work with the new, more powerful institutional leadership (Remiss: HSFR, 18 February 1992 and FRN, 31 March 1992).

Party ideology as a guideline

We have seen previously that the Social Democratic party shifted its ideological base somewhat in the late 1980s and was preparing to review its policy position on higher education with the help of an all-academic public investigative commission (named 'Högskoleutredningen'). We have also discussed (See Chapter 3, p.58) the final report of this commission, which was delivered to the Moderate Minister of Education (Per Unckel) in January of 1992, shortly after the coalition of non-socialist parties (here called the Conservative Coalition) won the election. The Moderates had long been suggesting major changes to Swedish higher education policy, reflecting their opposition to parts of the H-77 reform. And contrary to the Social Democrats, the Moderate party's ideological beliefs were more stable between the late 1960s and the 1990s.

The party's ideology is grounded in the conservative tradition, a tradition based on the individual's own wishes and needs. Freedom and societal responsibility are key values, supported by the rights to private property ownership and a free business environment. The distribution of ownership is seen as the best precondition for increased material welfare (Moderate Party Program 1979).

The party's standpoint on higher education has developed and expanded over the years. The party program from the late 1960s reflects the view that higher education is to generally serve the purposes of the Swedish labor market and the demands from Swedish business for technology. This is evident in concerns about job market prognosis, the need for increases in financing for basic research, and for more freedom in the relationships between higher education institutions and business (Moderate Party Program 1969). In 1984, a new aspect to the role of higher education is presented (that of personal development). The belief in the importance of personal development connects with the Moderate idea to not totally close off all areas of the universities and colleges to students, but to have some faculties continue 'free admissions' for all qualified students. This however is qualified with the statement that economic reasons or strong labor market reasons could make free admissions impossible (Moderate Party Program 1984).

Many parts of the 1984 document directly related to the 1977 Reform and advocated that the policy be changed. For example, on higher education admission requirements, the Moderates believed that the system should encourage goal-oriented studies at the high-school level. There were two acceptable ways to admit students – based either on their high school grades or their results of the national college and university entrance exam. Furthermore, there should not be trade union representatives on the leadership boards of the institutions. The study lines in the faculties of humanities, social sciences, and natural sciences should be abolished so that the students can concentrate on larger subject areas. Finally, the Moderate party commented on the need for a closer relationship between teaching and research, and that the strict division between the two should be abolished.

By 1993, global competition had certainly influenced the party's view on the role of higher education and research. Academic education should increase, and at least match the percentage of those working in the labor market as in other nations. The need to connect the state's economic support of higher education with evaluation of courses, quality, and productivity was clearly presented: 'That the state is positive to a more independent role for the universities and colleges does not however at the same time mean that the state promises to pay whatever it is that the institutions choose to take up' (Moderate Party Program 1993, p.63). Support from the state was to be judged in relation to the availability of economic resources and to student choice. The party program emphasized 'that academic freedom requires that the universities and colleges develop a freer position in relation to the state' (Moderate Party Program 1993, p.62). Given this, the state should not be the only financial source for the higher education institutions. There should be greater freedom to establish connections with other funding sources – such as research institutes, foundations, and international business. In addition, state-owned universities and colleges should be allowed to privatize if they so desired, and new private institutions could be formed.

Thus, it is evident that the Moderates were ideologically prepared to carry through a major reform of Swedish higher education. In the next section, we will review the responses of interest groups to the Moderate inspired policy changes in higher education.

Interest group dispersion

In studying the responses from the various interest groups to the policy proposals, much variance is detected in the level of congruence between the actors' policy goals and the policy outcomes. There were some strong criticisms – on the one hand complaints that too much of H-77 was being dismantled, and on the other hand, that not enough was being done to move Sweden towards an internationally competitive higher education system.

TCO was one of the strongest critics. It appears that some of the elements which TCO found to be positive in the U68 report were not to be relinquished in the 1990s – but rather were to be preserved. TCO continued to advocate an effective government control of higher education, and therefore concluded:

> The proposal entails fundamental changes in the Swedish higher education system. Government control, through democratic insti-

tutions, will decrease in several important areas. TCO is negative to this development. (Remiss: TCO, 21 April 1992, p.1)

The importance of the role of higher education in solving societal problems also continued to be emphasized and was reflected in comments such as:

> The proposals...will lead to a larger distance between higher education and the surrounding society and *arbertslivet* ... The economic crisis, unemployment, regional imbalances, and the increasing international competition are examples of societal changes leading to higher expectations on the teaching and research of universities. (p.2)

TCO maintained its position on the need to connect education to the job market and to *arbetslivet*. The remiss document states that 'TCO is of the opinion that cooperation between *arbetslivet* and higher education institutions should increase rather than decrease. ... TCO wants to keep the wording in the law about higher education being a preparation for *arbetslivet* (Remiss: TCO, 21 April 1992, pp.6–7). Furthermore, TCO was very concerned about the abolition of the study line committees, and suggested that 'unless specific organizations are created to replace the study line committees..., TCO wants *arbetslivet* to have seats on departmental boards for issues regarding the content and organization of the programs' (p.11). As for the proposal on freedom over admissions, TCO did not agree and advocated that admission should be centrally organized and coordinated 'in order to guarantee students maximum choice' (p.11).

LO was also sceptical of many aspects of the proposals, and continued to emphasize the themes of equality and the connection to society (major reforming themes of U68). LO wrote: 'Higher education should be of equal and equivalent quality in the whole country. Several of the proposals ... work against this goal, such as the proposal for a new degree system. As a consequence, the country will have A and B universities, which is unacceptable to LO' (Remiss: LO, 3 April 1992, p.2). There was a fear that higher education would return to the sphere of the elite, closing out other members of society. LO believed that the proposal's goal to strengthen academic values would mean that 'Decisions will be made by an elite within a closed university system. Contacts with the surrounding society, *arbetsliv*, and businesses, is not considered necessary, (p.2). Consistent with such concerns, LO suggested that 'the collegial structure be replaced by a societal leadership' (p.3).

The connection between 'freedom' and 'quality' which the government suggested, did not seem to be self-evident for LO. LO was not supportive of the suggestion for increased decentralization:

> In order to conduct a high-quality university education, and to reach the desired goals, a good local organization is needed, with knowledgeable administrators and heads of education, good planning of research and education, and an efficient use of resources. LO does not see any reason why this is facilitated through decentralization. (Remiss: LO, 3 April 1992, p.6)

In addition, the new resource distribution system did not receive support from LO, who saw a risk with the allocation of resources based on the number of degrees awarded by the higher education institutions. LO explained:

> According to the proposal, universities will set their own requirements for admission, which may entice them to have high requirements in order to become more cost efficient. This involves the creation of a strong financial incentive for each university to try to attract only those students that can 'most easily be taught'. LO's basic view that higher education should be of equal and equivalent quality nationwide makes us skeptical towards simple, quantitative measures. (Remiss: LO, 3 April 1992, p.3)

Unlike LO and TCO, SACO was generally more favorable. Citing the past difficulties with the uniqueness of the Swedish higher education system, SACO stated:

> From a Continental perspective, Swedish higher education policy has appeared unusual and obsolete. ... The proposals for deregulation and more power to the higher education institutions is a very important policy shift. Swedish higher education policy will now agree with important aspects of European and North American university traditions. (Remiss: SACO, 21 April 1992, p.1)

SACO was, however, hesitant about some aspects of the abolition of the study lines and of the new degree system which was to come as a replacement. SACO's first concern was how the connection to vocations would be maintained, evident by:

> SACO wants to point to the need for continued cooperation between the vocations and education, even after the abolition of the study line system and the study line committees. It will be the responsibility of each individual university to create the framework for such continued cooperation. (Remiss: SACO, 12 April 1992, p.2)

Other problems with this degree system were also raised, with SACO pointing out 'the negative aspects of allowing each university to develop study programs. There is a clear risk, as some of the unions have pointed out, that this will result in too many different types of degrees' (p.4).

The business establishment appears to have been united in their favorable reception of the proposals. Their concerns for international competitiveness of Swedish business are evident in their remiss comments. SAF stated that 'Combining the liberation of universities and competition through quality is a key aspect of strengthening Sweden as a knowledge-based economy and thereby increasing our competitiveness (Remiss: SAF, 24 April 1992, p.1). Both SAF and Industriförbundet did not see the proposals to deregulate higher education as the key factor however. For example, Industriförbundet mentioned the lack of a functioning market for higher education: 'Even though unnecessarily detailed regulation is removed, it will take a long time before any Swedish universities become so financially strong that they become independent from government regulation, and are free to react to signals from a market for education' (Remiss: Industriförbundet, 22 April 1992, p.1). SAF emphasized that global competition put pressure on Swedish universities and colleges, stating that, 'It should also be pointed out that the gradual inter-nationalization leads to Swedish universities having to compete more with foreign universities, regardless of whether Swedish universities are deregulated or not' and that 'the market reaction is often the best criterium for evaluations' (Remiss: SAF, 24 April 1992, p.2). In this regard, the role of the students as a market player is mentioned, 'A functioning system for the evaluation of teaching quality is a necessary form of customer information for students, who are about to make one of their biggest investment choices when they select a university or college' (Remiss: Industriförbundet, 22 April 1992, p.4).

The response from the student union was mixed, with concerns primarily related to the new forms of institutional leadership. The students were worried about preserving their right to representation, and in their remiss declared:

> SFS would strongly like to point out that we want a democratic governance of universities, and therefore we say no to both the hi-erarchical and the collegial models for governance. Student representatives should be on all decision-making levels, including

the boards responsible for recruiting faculty. No group should be in the majority in any board. (Remiss: SFS, April 23 1992, p.6)

In regards to other policy areas, SFS was in favor of open admissions to all qualified students and favored the proposal for local admissions, but proposed that the selection criteria remain nationally determined.

Policy formulation for the H-93 reform: a summary

During the 1990s, higher education policy formulation has moved along both the dimension of influence and cohesion. On the influence dimension, a movement from the state mediating with interest groups towards mediation of a more elite nature has taken place. As for cohesion, the 'corporatist' policy community (with the key members being the bureaucrats, politicians and interest groups) seemed to fade, replaced by a looser group of academic elites and business groups who were able to find new possibilities to express their policy goals. A wide variety of participants from outside the previous 'corporatist' arrangement were active in this new 'issue network', including not only the individual academic elites, but also scholarly organizations, institutional leaders and business leaders who were invited to participate in different types of forums (Agenda 2000 is an example). Industry and business, affected by the weak Swedish economy in the early 1990s and the need to compete in the global markets, were very satisfied to be able to have some influence in higher education policy again. As explained in an interview:

> In the 1960s, industry had many contacts with the universities. ... But after U-68, with the increased influence of other types of rep-resentatives on the Boards, the voice of industry was drowned out. Nothing really changed until around the 1990s, when the higher education institutions were than encouraged to get financing from the outside. (interest group representative)

Also, Minister Unckel could more easily heed to the demands of business than could the Social Democratic party with their roots in the workers'/trade union movements.

As mentioned, efforts were made to include the academics, and the all-academic composition of the public investigatory commission called 'Högskoleutredningen' (Higher Education Commission) marked a dramatic change from the 1970s. Their supportive position can be attributed to the fact that:

The academics were unhappy with the steering system. People wanted a genuine change – undergraduate education was not working like it should. Academics were unhappy with the study line system, with the total planning. The Högskoleutredningen Commission was an example that such was the case. And this unhappiness had been there since the 1960s. (former political advisor)

The level of cohesion between these policy actors also varied, given, for example, their unequal powers and unequal financial resources (for example, compare industrial/business groups such as SAF and IF with the academic honor societies such as KVA). Thus the policy network in the 1990s can be characterized as leaning towards an issue network on our dimension of cohesion. This type of issue network exhibited fluctuations in the level of policy agreement, with the academic voice not always unified (a case in point being the inconsistent support for performance indicators; see Chapter 4, p.100) and with the business community advocating that the reform should go even further to meet the demands of the market for internationally competitive education and research.

In Figure 5.2 we can graphically summarize this type of issue network for the H-93 reform, which shows a high level of congruence with the policy outcome for such actors as the Moderate party, SAF and IF. In comparison to Figure 5.1 for the H-77 reform, much more dispersion in the network is evident as the actors are less cohesive in their policy views.

Policy formulation explained: comparing the H-77 reform to the H-93 reform

In the Introduction to this chapter, we discussed two main classes of ideas that are useful in studying policy change: the first being an actor-preference logic and the second being a logic of appropriateness – based on current norms and values in society. We also recognized that there is the possibility that these two logics can coexist, albeit with a potential for tension between them. If we now return to our empirical case of explaining policy change in Swedish higher education during a time span of approximately twenty years, our evidence demonstrates that these two logics did coexist at various times and under strained circumstances.

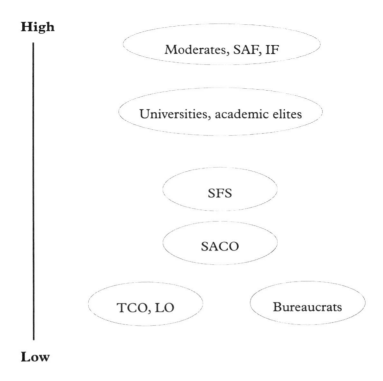

High

Moderates, SAF, IF

Universities, academic elites

SFS

SACO

TCO, LO   Bureaucrats

Low

Figure 5.2 Congruence and cohesion for H-93
Note: Level of congruence between actors' policy goals and policy outcome. Ovals represent cohesion among actors' preferences.

First, we can explain part of the Social Democratic policy formulation in the 1980s from the logic of appropriateness – seen in a new understanding and belief that societies were developing in a more pluralistic manner, a change in 'world-view' that was common to many Social Democratic governments in Europe at that time. This was also reflected in the spread of the 'new public management' philosophy as the basis for bureaucratic reform in many countries. As mentioned in the Introduction to Part II, the Swedish public sector underwent major reforms in the late 1980s characterized by decentralization and deregulation. This was possible in part due to the Social Democrat's renewal of the public sector in face of budget constraints and increasing public demands for quality improvements and flexibility. With the movement toward decentralization and deregulation, it was natural that a reallocation of public administration responsibilities from the central and regional levels down to the municipalities was also advocated. Thus, in higher education, it was recognized that the individual universities and colleges should not be as strongly steered by the central government as was the case in the 1970s and new forms of institutional governance with less regulation were being discussed by the Social Democrats in the 1980s. We also find that the Social Democrats shifted somewhat their view on the role of higher education in society during the 1980s – recognizing the connection between pluralist tendencies and the need to adopt new ideas like that of the new 'knowledge society'. It is possible to trace this shift in values/norms to the party's change in accepting more market initiatives and less steering of research and technology.

Yet, we can also explain the slow pace of reform during the late 1980s from the actor-preference logic. The network analysis shows that organizations such as LO and TCO were not keeping pace with the change in the 'world-view' which was becoming evident in the Social Democratic party. Much of LO's and TCO's critique of the H-93 reform can be associated with the stability of their ideological views from the 1970s – for example, their views on the role of higher education in reforming society, and the need for a strong centralized system to improve and insure social equality. Our analysis shows that the ideas of TCO (and LO) were very much in line with the dominant views of the Social Democratic party during the 1970s. It is difficult, however, to know how TCO and LO would have reacted in the 1990s had the reform of higher education been carried out by the Social Democrats. It seems that a tense situation would have developed as the Social Democrats transformed their views based on what was seen as appropriate policy in the field of higher education in the 1990s, but LO and TCO were still operating with ideas from the 1970s. Thus, the fact that the Conservative Coalition won the election in 1991 certainly added to the ease of putting through the policy change, with increased speed and intensity in the H-93 reform.

The changes which occurred with the H-93 reform do, to a large extent, seem to be actor-preference driven, with the Moderate party leading the way. For many years the party had been advocating a freer position for higher education in relation to the state, and that privatizations should thus be possible. In addition, the party has long favored increased autonomy for the universities and colleges, with more freedom over admission rules, and the formation of curriculum for example. And in the debates on the distribution of resources, the party has long maintained the need to connect this to the results of quality evaluations. Thus, the majority of the policies which were finally enacted were very much in line with the Moderate's long-term preferences on the goals for higher education and the means to achieve them. They were thus implemented as soon as the party had the political power to do so.

The longstanding differences between the two largest political parties encouraged the Moderates to act quickly while they were in office (1991–1994). The prevalent attitude among these new policy makers was that the Social Democratic policy legacy demonstrated 'too little, too late'. Interview data from a former high ranking politician at the Ministry suggest that the Conservatives

> did not think the Social Democrats were going far enough. In the 1989/90 Proposition, their ideas for change are very cryptic – and even at that time they were still keeping the study line system. All talk of change was as if it was just an administrative change. There was no discussion of the totality of the system – of research, of the role of the faculty, the total structure – no changes were thought of in these things.

It is certainly possible to detect a sense of urgency on behalf of the Conservative Coalition politicians in quickly formulating and legislating new policies before the end of their three-year term. As one interviewee put it: 'Unckel did not follow the 'remiss' procedures, the most important thing was to have a quick pace. For example, in October 1991, he held his first Rector's Conference, then one week later, the Ministry released proposals' (former Ministry official). This was confirmed by a political advisor working for Unckel at the time:

> We did a lot of changes in a very quick time frame to get the changes in process. The old system of long remiss processes with all the special interest groups involved actually could create its own opposition process – and this needed to be prevented. We didn't have any time to waste and we felt the changes were very important to the functioning of Swedish education. We sometimes went directly to the researchers. Sometimes we by-passed totally the bureaucrats, the rectors, the trade unions and this led to many good ideas. Per Unckel had an idea about what direction he wanted to go in, but the reform grew in dialog with the universities and the researchers.

Many of the university and college leaders also referred to this quick pace of the reforms, but there was also a 'resigned' acceptance to the way things were because they were in favor of the new policies. As an institutional leader stated at the time:

> A point that I am critical of concerns the remiss process. I presume that the background is that the mandate period in this country is short. Every government wants to get out so much as possible during their mandate period. But this causes a problem for the universities and colleges, which are open systems. ... I would like it to be known that we at Karolinska Institute do not appreciate that we do not get an opportunity to express ourselves in a normal remiss process. This is almost the only point we are critical of. ... I think that the proposal contains so many positive components that we should bet on it. (Lars Ekholm, Karolinska Institute in Department Series 1993:9, pp.26–27.)

Our evidence shows that the Moderates also selected a well-known and respected politician to lead the way on higher education policy. Interview data confirms the favorable standing of Per Unckel as a politician and that this played an important role in his ability to quickly get policy proposals through the system. As a former Ministry official stated:

> Per Unckel was a very heavy Minister. He was close to Carl Bildt, just like when Palme was Minister of Education – a central political position in the government. No one wanted to have a conflict with Unckel because they knew he had the support of Bildt. And he [Unckel] was even able to make increases in the budget against Anne Wibble's [the Finance Minister] wishes.

In conclusion, evidence from the comparison of the policy formulation arena over twenty years demonstrates that two types of logic of political behavior were in action. The period after the H-77 reform and up to 1991, mostly reflects a logic of appropriateness – where some policy change can be explained by the changing beliefs in the Social Democratic party on the nature of higher education in a modern knowledge society. Yet we see that it was also difficult for the Social Democrats to put through any major reforms during the 1980s. This may be explained by the strong preferences of groups such as LO and TCO and the power relationships between them and the Social Democrats. The period during which the H-93 reform was formulated seems to be best explained by preference driven behavior of powerful actors, actors who were very aware that their access to power could soon be limited in a new election.

Confusion in the recent time frame 1994–1997

In the autumn of 1994, the Conservative Coalition lost power to the Social Democrats. This change of power in the higher education policy network has had an impact on policy outcomes, reversing some of the policies implemented by the Conservative Coalition. It is impossible for us to review this recent power shift in its entirety (as we have tried to do for the change from H-77 to the H-93 reform), yet some of the recent changes by the Social Democrats illustrate well the dominance of political 'actor-preference' based, purposive action in changing Swedish higher education policy.

Many of the recent policy developments under the Social Democratic government can be perceived as using the higher education system to respond to general societal problems. One of the new government's first steps was to increase student admissions in the natural and technical sciences – using special financing from the Labour Market Department (Gov. Prop. 1994/95:100, 1994/95:139). To further expand the number of student places, the government has embarked on a controversial expansion of the colleges by allocating to these smaller colleges, for the first time, financing for research and doctoral student training. This has caused quite a heated debate among academics at the larger universities and those at the smaller colleges (see Demker and Bjereld 1996). Supporting this development, recent legislation was quite favorable to the colleges in the allocation of student places as well as the allocation of research funds (Gov. Prop. 1994/95:100, App.9, 1995/96:150).

The extent to which quality judgments are incorporated into the new government's distribution of financial resources to the institutions is unknown. The Social Democrats canceled the 5 per cent quality money soon after arriving in office, stating that:

> According to the Government's understanding, internal quality work is supported best if it is done without connection to resource distribution. Such a connection is based on evaluations which necessarily contain subjective judgments. The system would give room for a level of discretion and lead to centralism and politicization (Gov. Prop. 1994/95:100; Section 4.6.2).

Yet the Government did not abandon the idea that such evaluations could be tied to resource distribution. Rather, it emphasized that these evaluations would be a component of the Government's material upon which decisions are made for each institutions' educational 'task'. This was rather ambiguous compared to the previous Government's ambitions however.

Another controversial area has been that of the 'affirmative action' plans for the universities and colleges (see Pandolfi 1996). Decreed by the central government (Gov. Prop. 1994/95:164), this plan entails the establishment of research assistantships and 30 professorships, where the 'under-represented gender', i.e., women, can be favorably treated in the hiring process. The government proposition is based on the public investigative commission completed by Ebba Witt-Brattström and colleagues entitled 'Desire to Know and Desire to Understand' (SOU 1995:110).

A partial return to some of the ideas of centralization and a corresponding strengthening of the state bureaucracy appeared in the recent policies. In particular, the bureaucracy was reorganized once again, creating a 'new' National Agency for Higher Education (HSV, *Högskoleverket*) by combining the smaller units of the 'old' National Agency for Higher Education (*Verket för högskoleservice*, VHS), the University Chancellor's Office, the Appeals Board and the Council for Undergraduate Education (Gov. Prop. 1994/95:165). Justification for this recent bureaucratic reorganization (effective 1 July 1995) was primarily that the previous structure was confusing and too divided. The previous program of evaluating quality development, which was to have been carried out by the University Chancellor's Office, is now to be under the control of the new National Agency. The University Chancellor, Stig Hagström, is now the Chairman of the Board of Directors of the new National Agency.

In contrast to the previous government's efforts to increase university autonomy, the new government has reclaimed part of its previous powers from the 'social goals' era of the 1970s. For example, it had reinstated its power to establish professorships at all state controlled institutions of higher education, but only to be exercised when necessary to prioritize research areas that are of particular concern to the nation (Gov. Prop. 1994/95:100, App. 9). This was changed again approximately two years later (with a new policy on academic titles in higher education) where the Government gave up its right to establish professorships (Gov. Prop. 1996/97:141).

Regarding admission requirements, the institutions are no longer able to determine these solely themselves, and new nationwide rules and procedures have been announced by the central government (Gov. Prop. 1995/96:184).

The structure and autonomy of Swedish research have also been under study by the new government (SOU 1996:29). The government attempted to reverse the 'private foundation' status of the research foundations created by the previous government with the wage-earners' funds. This attempt was hindered by the Swedish Legal Council (*lagrådet*). Instead, the government has rewritten the foundations' charters so that it can appoint and dismiss the board of directors. Additional attempts to influence the direction of research appear to be underway after the passage of legislation in the winter of 1997 which increases the Ministry's influence over the structure and admissions procedures for doctoral programs (Department Series 1996:35, Gov. Prop. 1997/98:1).

It is of course, impossible to predict the future. However, what we do know is that quite a few policy changes continued after the H-93 reform. Thus, a large part of the content of higher education policy seems to be preference driven, connected to the actors' strategies and political powers at a given time. According to this, one would expect that as the relations of power and influence change between the actors, so too will the policies concerning issues such as quality and resource distribution, efficiency of education (especially on the doctoral level), structure of the national bureaucracy, admission rules and size of the system, and the extent and type of utilitarian purposes for the higher education system. Yet a logic of appropriateness is also evident, meaning that some major policy changes are most likely here to stay. Changes relating to new public management ideas – such as deregulation and decentralization, evidenced in the new resource distribution system and new freedoms for the institutional leaders – have not yet been reversed by strategically-driven actors, and therefore, may remain intact.

Conclusions: part II

In Chapter 4, a two-dimensional diagram was presented to model four types of state governance ('security guard', 'honor society', 'social goals' and 'invisible hand'). This was followed by an analysis of the policy developments between the H-77 reform and the H-93 reform in terms of the two dimensions. We can conclude that on the vertical axis representing 'authority', a substantial downward shift took place as strong state steering was relinquished and new freedoms concerning, for example, institutional organization, curriculum and distribution of funds, were granted. On the horizontal axis representing 'purpose', it does not seem evident that a dramatic shift from utilitarian to cultural purpose has taken place. Rather the situation is more complex, allowing for a mixture of both cultural and utilitarian purposes, but with a stronger emphasis on utilitarian. The question in the 1990s is also one of 'what type' of utilitarian purpose is being pursued. In the 'social goals' type, the purpose is state-determined, incorporating goals such as social class equality, regional development and needs of the job market. This type dominated in the 1970s and 1980s. During the early 1990s, the Government's legislation provided a shift towards the 'invisible hand' type, with the movement toward decentralization also changing the nature of the 'utilitarian' purpose – with a variety of different needs raised by various 'market' actors. After the election in 1994 and the policies that followed, it is somewhat questionable how much support remains for the 'invisible hand' type. If we now return to our model of four types of state governance of higher education (Figure 4.1),we

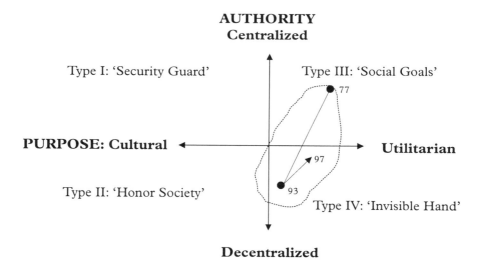

Figure 5.3 Summary of shifts in state governance of higher education in Sweden 1977–1997

can trace these changes over the years (Figure 5.3), allowing for some space in which these changes can vary due to their complexity.

In our study of the policy formulation arena (Chapter 5), we have used a dynamic network approach to study both the influence of actors on policy outcome and the extent to which the various actors are cohesive in their policy demands. By using this approach, we characterized the 1970s as a period of state mediation with interest groups, where policy formulation was conducted in a tight-knit 'policy community'. The state (both the government and the bureaucracy) certainly played a strong role in this community, but one which allowed for mediation by the large trade unions. A significant change was evident in the 1990s as the type of groups involved in mediation differed, with the government side-stepping the bureaucracy and entering direct discussions with various elite groups in a new 'issue network'.

All actors under study at the macro level were confronted with various conditions outside of higher education to consider as they shaped and influenced higher education policy. Certainly some of the most important conditions for the macro level were high unemployment levels and the large budget deficit. As mentioned earlier, the H-93 reform seems to be a result of political action based on a logic of appropriateness combined with a logic of preference-driven behavior by various actors. Discussions involving the needs of the new 'knowledge society' seem to reflect this logic of appropriateness which also contributed to the adoption of new public management techniques by both Social Democratic and Moderate politicians. Yet we have also noticed how the limit of a three-year election mandate affected the Conservative coalition, encouraging them to quickly put in place policies before their political power could be lost in the next mandate period. Thus, a preference-driven logic was also at play in the formulation of higher education policies in the 1990s.

The issue of quality, and how to develop and assess it, was also largely dependent on which actors were formulating the policy. Throughout the 1970s and 1980s, the Social Democrats viewed the issue of quality in undergraduate education as an issue of maintaining quality for the entire higher education system, which was thought to be accomplished at that time by having equivalent standards in the study line system (see p.88). Not until as late as May of 1991 did discussions in the Parliament deal with the need to evaluate quality based on international comparisons, possibly at the sacrifice of detailed steering. Yet with the change in government in the autumn of 1991, much emphasis was placed on quality indicators and performance related distribution of funds. Although the original idea of performance indicators was abandoned in the face of pressure from leading academics, the University Chancellor, and some institutional leaders, the idea to connect resources to evaluation remained as a way to provide incentives to improve undergraduate education. Thus, the program to evaluate each institution's quality development work was developed (see Chapter 4). Here we see that the process of mediation with the academic elite resulted in a change of policy before legislation was passed. However, with the return of the Social Democrats to power in the autumn of 1994, the connection to the distribution of resources was removed (further evidence of the preference-driven nature of the quality issue.)

The continued change in policies which occurred during the most recent time period (1994–1997, see above), seems to also render support to the preference-driven nature of the actors shaping Swedish higher education policy. However, even after these recent changes, the H-93 reform can still be regarded as significantly widening the space of action for the universities and colleges. Of substantial importance was the cancellation of the study line system, with its central controls on curriculum and course development. In addition, the end of detailed, central regulation of the institutions' internal leadership has provided a new freedom to the universities and colleges to organize themselves in ways which they deem necessary to meet their own goals. Finally, the new resource distribution system allows the institutions to focus and plan their educational programs in new ways and to take responsibility themselves for the management of their budget. Much of this newly granted space of action, dramatically increased compared to that allowed under the H-77 reform, appears to be favored by both Social Democrats and Moderates. Thus a return to the days of intense state steering seems unlikely, as does also the possibility of Sweden having totally autonomous institutions. Rather, based on what we have observed of preference-driven political behavior, policy changes in the near future will most likely be the outcome of mediation between the politicians and the various interest groups and academic elites whom these politicians support, depending of course on the political power which the politicians muster.

Part III

Institutional Governance and Management in a Context of Policy and System Changes

Introduction

The purpose of this meso-level study is to examine how the expectations of changes in structure and governance were met by the institutions during the years immediately before and after the new ordinance was put into effect and how they and their leaders used (and intended to use) the widened space of action which, in turn, determines the space of action of the academics on the basic level.

Key elements of the 1993 reform were the increase of the autonomy of the institutions and the expectations of a self-regulative model of institutional governance. More specifically, many of the tasks of the former intermediary bodies have been delegated to the institutions. As a result, the institutional leaders, in cooperation with the university boards, have to shape a new kind of 'intermediary body' between the government and the academics for defining and fulfilling tasks which are quite new in the institutional contexts in Swedish higher education. Fixation of student number and allocation of study places was formerly one of the major planning tasks of the National Board of Universities and Colleges (UHÄ). After 1993, the institutions themselves took a more active part in this planning procedure.

The H-93 reform was implemented in a period of rapid changes. In Chapter 6 we give a brief description of how the institutions met the expectations on expansion and renewal of missions and tasks and what kind of effect these quantitative and qualitative changes might have on the structure of the higher education system. We also examine, in Chapter 7, how the leaders define their roles as academic leaders and how they meet the demands for strong leadership. In Chapter 8 we focus on the autonomy of the institution and how the devolved authority has been regulated in internal orders of delegation and in models of institutional governance. The overall theme for these three chapters is to study how the institutions responded to the government's deliberate move away from a state-regulated model of governance towards what could be characterized as a model of self-regulation.

Chapter 6

A Period of Rapid
Expansion and Renewal

Expectations on expansion and renewal

Not until the end of the 1980s did Sweden begin to follow the track of most other European countries and increase the number of study places for higher education. This was the start of an almost linear expansion of student numbers.

Expectations of internal renewal provided a strong argument for decentralization already in the 1970s, although the meaning of decentralization has changed since then (Askling and Almén 1997). At that time, cooperation and democratization were considered important mechanisms for releasing the innovative capacity for continuous internal renewal of curriculum and teaching, within, however, the overall framework of a fairly uniform structure. In the 1990s, the academics were challenged to contribute to the renewal of the higher education system in a climate of competition and sensitivity to markets. This time, the expectations on renewal were not just restricted to issues concerning curriculum and teaching within the established programs (the so-called study lines), but also on creating variation and profiles of whole programs.

In 1994, The Ministry of Education formulated the challenge which lay ahead as follows: 'The old centralisation has been replaced by autonomy, pluralism, institutional competence and individual choice. That is in my opinion, the only possible way, for any country, to create a structure for schools and universities which can deal with the demands for flexibility and quality in an uncertain tomorrow' (Unckel 1994, p.12). Thus, the institutions and their academics were faced with expectations on extensive but non-prescribed qualitative changes, in addition to fairly explicit expectations on increase in student intake. This combination of quantitative and qualitative change was supported by the government, but its administration lay in the hands of the institutions themselves and depended on their innovative capacity.

Institutional responses to expectations on expansion

By the end of the 1980s, the government allocated more resources to the higher education sector and the institutions received more 'freedom' from state regulations for, among other things, expanding their student body. Since then, the increase in undergraduate student numbers is almost 50 percent at the large universities. At one of the medium-sized universities and at all of the colleges the numbers of undergraduate students have almost doubled. When all figures were brought together and examined in retrospect, this extensive expansion of undergraduate places was a surprise for the institutions themselves. No one had expected that such a rapid expansion was possible and that there was so much 'space' in the system. See Table 6.1 below. (Current figures for the Swedish higher education institutions of all categories are presented in Appendix 7. Appendix 8 gives the changes in student and staff numbers from the academic year 1985/86 to 1995/96.)

As was the case in the 1960s, the main expansion has taken place within the faculties of humanities and social sciences, although there has also been a substantial increase of student number in the faculties of natural science and technology. It may be noted that the latter increase was mainly in order to meet the demands for qualified personnel in this sector of the labor market, which is crucial for the Swedish economy that is a part of a more competitive international market.

From Table 6.1 we can clearly see that the universities are responsible for about one third of the expansion, while the relative increase is largest at the colleges, some of them having almost doubled their bulk of undergraduate students. The expansion is surprising since some institutions deliberately decided *not* to expand at the end of the 1980s. Evidently, since then, these institutions have followed suit and taken measures which sometimes are contrary to their own spontaneously declared intentions.

**Table 6.1 Increase in total number of undergraduate students
between 1990/91 and 1994/95**

Institution	1990/91	1994/95	Increase in number	Increase in percent
Universities	77.155	10.1154	23.999	44.1
Specialized institutions	11.942	17.246	5.304	44.4
Private sector		11.173		
Colleges	29.764	54.056	24.292	81.6
Colleges of Art	1.662	1.722	60	3.6
Colleges of Health Ed.	15.655	17.561	1.996	12.7
Others		606		
Total	142.953	215.666	72.713	50.8

Source: Högskoleverket (1996d)

As an example, in 1989, when the rector at one of the universities was re-elected, he prepared a letter of intent for his new six-year period. The starting point for the plan was the belief that the period of expansion was over and what followed ought to be time for consolidation and internal improvements. Several measures for improvements in particular areas were presented, such as programs for staff development and for academic competence development in terms of a doctoral education for junior lecturers. This was done in order to overcome the earlier mentioned longstanding separation of teaching from research in the lecturer position. Measures aimed at improving the research connection of undergraduate teaching were also presented. The influence from the contemporary Higher Education Commission, which published its final report at that time, was evident. This extensive strategic plan formed the basis for the quality development program a few years later. This also indicated that there was a readiness both to interpret quality issues in terms of development activities for academic staff and to improve undergraduate teaching. At about the same time, similar decisions were made at other universities.

The new resource allocation system resulted in a very powerful combination of governing and framing factors for imposing changes. Through this new model of funding, the government also introduced quite new issues for internal decision-making. In the earlier system, the institutions got a predictable and pre-allocated income. The fixed price tags gave no incentives for internal considerations to be taken and did not imply any risk-taking. Now, after negotiations with the government, each institution is individually obligated for a period of three years to produce a certain number of degrees in undergraduate education for a fixed lump sum. Each institution agrees to commission a certain number of students in each one of these price (and study) fields in a triennial appropriation proposal.

There are a number of different 'price-tags' for different areas of study, for example, medicine, humanities, and natural sciences. Before they sign a three-year contract, in order to secure adequate funds, the institutions have to calculate how many students they might examine for a certain total amount of funding and how many extra students over the so-called 'ceiling' they ought to admit in order to compensate for drop-outs. In our interviews with rectors and deans and other persons belonging to the institutional leadership, the impact of this new system is an often mentioned issue:

> The change towards the new three-year planning system has had an impact. We have had such a tremendous change during this time. (leadership, university)

The model requires internal collaboration between the faculties and departments before deciding on the number of students to admit and the amount of costs to claim. This requires a very careful weighing of the risks and benefits for the faculties, the departments, and the entire institution before the contract is signed in the name of the institution. As the manager of the institution, the rector and his/her staff are responsible for all the figures and calculations presented in the 'offers' made to the government. This new model of negotiations and its consequences for the system were not fully realized by the organization when the first series of contracts were to be signed. As one rector said:

> The distance between the university rector and the departments is great. Those at the grassroots level do not know what is going on. (leadership, university)

When the outcome of the first three-year period was summarized (Högskoleverket 1997c), it was evident that the institutions had expanded their undergraduate activities by about 50 percent since the beginning of the 1990s (see Table 6.1). However, they have not dared to take the risk of a corresponding expansion in staff numbers. Figure

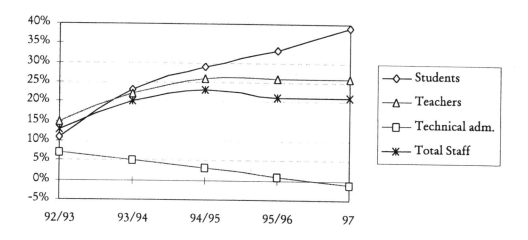

***Figure 6.1 Number of students, academic staff and technical
administrative staff between 1992/93 and 1997***

6.1 gives data from one university and demonstrates clearly that while
the number of students has increased by about 50 percent, the
academic staff has increased by about 25 percent and the administrative staff has decreased by a few percent.

Consequently, the expansion in student numbers has been cheap
for the state. Almost all institutions allowed for a certain number of
drop-outs among the students and, therefore, they admitted more
students than the corresponding funding allowed for. This was done
to avoid not reaching the predetermined number of exams contracted
by the funding estimate. Over the three-year period, every institution,
with just a few exceptions, made a small 'over production'. When the
figures were finally available and the total 'over production' was
summed, it became evident that the institutions had offered study
places to about 40,000 students without claiming corresponding
resources. This is the same as saying that they have offered teaching
which, if regularly financed, corresponds to 537 million Swedish
Kronor. Thus, with regard to the three-year contracts, one could say
that the higher education system at large provided, without any extra

funding, education equivalent to that of one university for one year (Dahl 1997; Högskoleverket 1997c; Utbildningsutskottet 1997).

Renewal of programs and courses

Another prominent impact of the H-93 reform, in addition to the above-mentioned further expansion, was the appeal to the institutions to examine their potentials for creating new programs and courses, as well as for creating new combinations of already existing ones. For example, within a few years, Uppsala University created new programs and courses for about 4000 – 5000 students. Expressed another way, it is as if the university had established a whole new college within its regular framework:

> The reform released a lot of energy and developmental capacity. (leadership, college)

> We can prepare new programs without having to get approval from the Ministry of Education before we start. (leadership, university)

The institutions were eager to attract students by being noticed as innovative and creative. Some universities and colleges even engaged advertising agencies to prepare attractive information materials and course catalogues.

This renewal also reflects a substantial shift from a disciplinary to a more interdisciplinary-structured education. Within a few years, a substantial number of interfaculty and interdisciplinary activities were introduced. A variety of new courses and programs were added to the line structure of the H-77 reform, but many of the 'old' study lines were simply renamed after the H-93 reform as so-called professional study programmes.

> We now create programs and courses which in many respects are quite new: they are interdisciplinary and offer students quite new combinations of fields of knowledge. Before the reform in 1993, this was almost impossible. One consequence is of course, that teachers have got a heavy workload. We have put these demands on them and not just asked them to do more regular teaching. (leadership, university)

In general, such efforts have been rewarding, since these programs get far more applicants than there are study places and contribute to the image of the institutions as innovative and flexible.

A similar trend is evident in graduate education, and new kinds of graduate and post-graduate programs have been prepared. The establishment of various 'Graduate School of...', mainly with interdisciplinary programs, is something quite new in the Swedish context of discipline-bound graduate education.

In the H-93 reform, the universities with their permanent research resources were granted the right to establish new professorates and also to give professorates new directions when the chair holder retired. Formerly, the institutions were obliged to apply to the Ministry before a professor position could be replaced, and this was one important tool the government used to steer research in one or another direction. This opportunity can now be used by a university board as a deliberate measure to shape, or rather reshape, the research profiles of the institution. For example, Uppsala University, within a period of a few years, changed the direction and content of 30 professorates when the chairholders retired, taking an active role in redefining disciplines and in establishing new areas of knowledge.

Thus, the changes which started in the late 1980s were not just impressive quantitative changes. The changes also involved an extensive renewal of the curriculum of undergraduate and graduate education. Compared to the thorough changes of structure and curriculum in the 1970s, which were imposed on the academics by the government, the initiatives to renew during the 1990s originated in the institutions and from the academics themselves.

> The resource allocation system allows us to try out new ideas our-selves, and if we recognize that it does not work, we can cut off the funding and switch to something else. That is better than the days when the government or the National Board made all the deci-sions. (leadership, university)

The new funding system, with its sensitivity to student progress, makes the institutions eager to recruit motivated students with solid backgrounds. Evidently, a new way of looking upon the students as 'customers' is emerging – despite the fact that the students have not become powerful customers as they were expected to evolve into. As long as there are far more applicants than study places, the admission system and thus the higher education system has more power than those students admitted into the system. In addition, the close links between individual point-production and access to study loans also give the students a dependent position *vis-à-vis* the departments.

The dependency on external 'income'

There is a substantial variation among institutions regarding the relative proportions of direct governmental funding and external funding for research commissioned from national councils, private companies, or contract teaching. The state is still the major financier of research, through direct funding for research and graduate education to the faculties, and, increasingly, through research councils and strategical research foundations. The number of faculties and departments, the particular specialization into research fields, the existence of prominent and successful researchers, and the skillfulness in preparing research proposals are all important factors for receiving more or less additional income. Of course, this external income is welcomed, but it is also looked upon as a threat.

> There is a risk that the internal research criteria will be second to
> the external, market-oriented ones. (leadership, university)

Within each institution the faculties vary with regard to total income, as well as to the proportion of funding for undergraduate education, graduate education and research, and the proportion that comes from external funding (see Figure 6.2).

This diversity implies a variation in authority and autonomy among the faculties and also among the departments within one particular institution, and is an important source of the internal so-called centrifugal forces (which are discussed in chapters 7 and 8). Different parts of the institutions interact with different markets and also with different kinds of actors (public and private). Some departments, mainly in the faculties of technology, medicine or natural sciences, may obtain as much as 80 percent of their income from external financial sources, mainly representing the private business sector and international and national research foundations. Some of the departments belonging to the faculty of Humanities or Teacher Education, on the other hand, obtain only a small percentage of the total income from external sources, mainly in terms of contract teaching and in-service training of comprehensive school teachers, which are less generously financed by public funding. Thus, behind the facade of the institution as an entity, there is an uneven distribution of economic power. This is to some extent controlled by the legal decision-making bodies and by the formal leaders, while to some extent controlled almost solely by the departments and the individual academics.

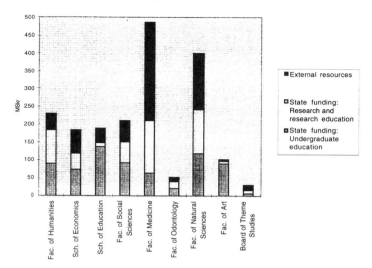

Figure 6.2 The income of one institution, separated on faculties, and on undergraduate education, research and graduate education and from external sources (in millions of Swedish Kronor)

There is also variation within one particular department between individual researchers or research groups. At one of the large universities in our sample, we made a small study of the external income at two departments, belonging to one and the same faculty, the faculty of social sciences. The departments differ with regard to the size of the external funding and, thus, also with regard to how relatively independent they are of the state funding, or expressed in other words, how dependent they are on the continued success of the researchers receiving research grants. Although the total sums are fairly stable year after year (see Table 6.2), a closer scrutiny indicates that there is a substantial annual variation in funding from each source, which means that from one year to another the projects replace each other and new constellations of researchers contribute to the total sums.

Although the departments benefit from the external incomes as they take a considerable percentage for overhead costs, the external funding is less predictable than the government funding. With such a reliance on external funding, in combination with unpredictable fluctuations in the actual level of funding, staff management has turned out to be an almost impossible task for the heads of the departments.

The departments (and the university) are dependent on external resources. These are brought to the university by individual researchers. Therefore, it is much more difficult now than in earlier days to draw a strategic plan for the management of the future development of the faculty. (leadership, university)

In earlier periods, differences in resources, competence, and profile within and between the institutions were not paid any attention to (see Chapter 3). Now, these differences are intended not just to increase but to be used as promising forces for promoting creativity and flexibility in the system. The system is now challenged to become even more diversified.

This diversification also has implications for the inner life of the institutions and calls for a more flexible use of internal incentives, such as recruitment and promotion. Within the national framework of state regulations concerning the collective of academics, individual agreements on such issues as the level of salary is now a rule and not an exception (Askling 1998b). In this respect, Swedish higher education is on the same track towards the 'flexi-university' as many other Western systems are (Farnham 1998).

The quality issue in a period of expansion

At the end of the 1980s, the word 'quality' was introduced more systematically in the higher education context with direct implications for the institutions. Since then, the word quality has been rather frequently used. However, there are many points of reference in the usage of the word, and also in the creation of various measures launched for enhancing and controlling quality.

The Higher Education Commission was set up by the government at the end of the 1980s as a response to student criticism on poor teaching quality. In its references to quality, the Commission followed in the footsteps of the UPU Commission from the early 1970s, and focused mainly on teaching tasks and teacher–student relations. The Commission also made references to the perennial problem of competence development for teachers without doctoral degrees. In addition, but to a lesser extent, the Commission made references to quality in academic standard and to the evaluative and accountability-oriented aspects of quality.

Sociology and Economics

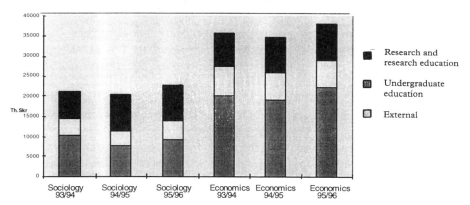

Figure 6.3 Sources of income (divided in undergraduate education, permanent research resources and graduate education) at two university departments, Sociology and Economics, belonging to the same faculty (in thousands of Swedish Kronor)

Table 6.2 Sources of income at two university departments, Sociology and Economics, belonging to the same faculty in thousands of Swedish crowns

	Sociology			Economics		
Income	*93/94*	*94/95*	*95/96*	*93/94*	*94/95*	*95/96*
State funding: Undergraduate education	4,268	3,896	4,737	7,465	9,778	6,916
State funding: Research and research education	6,944	8,822	8,767	8,265	8,822	8,767
State authorities, etc.	3,034	1,971	943	12,802	10,682	11,012
Commissioned teaching and research	74	320	254	999	2,050	2,118
Senior research council	3,141	2,463	3,007	3,539	4,048	3,320
National research council	2,799	1,762	3,935	1,768	1,735	5,119
Others: Organizations, associations etc	963	1,074	968	840	504	557
Total	21,222	20,310	22,612	35,678	34,620	37,809

In 1993, the government allocated earmarked resources to the institutions to be used for quality work. Each institution was requested to present a quality assurance program. Influenced by the debate of that time, the government replaced the word 'assurance' with the concept 'quality development programs'. The government also gave examples of activities to be included in these programs, such as pedagogical courses for university teachers.

Thus, when launched in the H-93 reform, the issue of quality was not a new one. However, while the earlier approach to quality had focused on teaching, the perspective taken now was more system-oriented. In the reform documents, focus was on performance indicators (called quality indicators) which were to be linked to resource allocation and on evaluation of the standard of the academic 'production'.

After an intense debate, the government's proposal for quality indicators was withdrawn, and a new proposal calling for audits of the institutions' quality development programs was prepared and accepted. The Chancellor's Office (the former Secretariat of Assessment and Evaluation incorporated into the National Agency in 1995) was responsible for instructions and manuals for these audits.

During this period of turmoil, the advisor of the Chancellor, Martin Trow, took an active part in clarifying the different functions of internal and external, supportive and controlling approaches to the assessment of quality (Trow 1994; 1995). From the standpoint that quality is a dynamic concept and through the device 'scrutiny for improvement', the Agency underlined its supportive role and its strong commitment to a 'soft' approach to its evaluative task. This standpoint has, however, been questioned by Bohlin and Elzinga, who claim that the Agency still tries to integrate an absolute definition of quality with a relativistic one as the point of reference for its evaluative activities (Bohlin 1998; Bohlin and Elzinga 1998).

Thus, within a few years, the quality issue was approached in quite different ways and four distinct sets of quality criteria were presented, concerning:

1. teaching and preconditions for good teaching practice (the teaching process)

2. the standard of academic outcome (the product of teaching and learning)

3. performance indicators (mainly in terms of preconditions for quality in teaching)

4. the institution's management of its quality work (an aspect of institutional governance and management).

In the instruction to the new National Agency ('Högskoleverket'), the government defined the role of the Agency, concerning quality judgment and evaluation, in the following way:

The Högskoleverket shall

- monitor and evaluate higher education, research and development-work of the arts within higher education institutions, and thereby consider their role and way of functioning in relation to society and to the development and demands of competence in the labor market

- summarize and publish the results of its monitoring and evaluation

- support and promote the activities in the institutions to raise the quality of education, research, and development work

- lay down the rights for public universities and colleges to issue degrees and diplomas

- decide whether institutions without faculty organization shall obtain the right to establish professorial chairs. (SFS 1995:945, §3, our translation)

The Agency was allocated an important, but double, role as the executor of evaluations, with a focus on quality, and as the missionary of a supportive evaluation culture. Both aspects of the role were presented as responses to the new ideas of the higher education institutions as 'self-regulating and learning organizations' (Bauer 1994; Askling and Bauer 1997; Kim 1997; Massaro 1997).

The various types of evaluation undertaken by the National Agency of Higher Education were organized into four programs:

1. Assessments for the right of institutions without permanent research funding to award degrees.

2. Assessments of the right to establish professorial chairs at institutions without permanent research funding.

3. Quality assurance audits of the higher education institutions.

4. National evaluations.

The first two programs are directed towards those colleges which take the initiative to apply for the right to award degrees and/or the right to establish professorial chairs. The criteria set up by the Agency are very explicit and have had a strong impact on the institutions. The theoretical foundation for defining criteria is provided by basic educational theory (goals–preconditions–process–results) and practical experiences from accomplishing graduate education and research.

In the National Agency's program for national evaluations, only a few programs have so far been evaluated. The low number indicates the Agency's fear of executing its control function in a too centralist manner and in a way which opens to interinstitutional comparisons. For this program, educational theory provides the foundation for defining criteria, in combination with criteria set up by important stake-holders.

Regarding the audits, the Chancellor took an important step when he decided that the frame of reference of the audits should be the 'learning institution' and that the focus should be on the governance and management of the institutions and, in particular, of their quality work. The theoretical foundation for defining criteria for these audits is derived from organizational theory and, in particular, from the conceptualizations of the self-regulative model of institutional governance. The instruction prepared by the Agency, however, allows for alternative interpretations of 'quality work'. This might have obscured the controlling and management-demanding dimensions of self-regulation and the 'learning institution' model of governance.

Taking into account all proposals and measures taken by the two successive governments (the Conservative and the Social Democrat) and the intermediary bodies (the Secretariat, the Chancellor's Office and the National Agency) since 'quality' was brought to the fore by the Higher Education Commission, one notes that the whole process of national evaluations indicates an uncertainty among the many actors on the national level regarding their own role in a decentralized system in the public sector (Askling and Bauer 1997).

Although the Agency and its forerunners have been criticized for their ambivalence with regard to the evaluative approach, they have received much credit for introducing quality assurance and evaluation as regular features in the governance of higher education. Comparing Sweden with 20 other OECD countries, Massaro maintains that

Sweden has developed an enlightened and thorough approach, and I should imagine that it will have little difficulty in getting academics to accept the process. (Massaro 1997, p.22)

Further, according to Massaro, the National Agency of Higher Education has

a dynamic concept of quality assessment and enhancement as having the best chance of achieving improvements, with an emphasis on supporting the institutions in their task of developing a culture of continuous improvement. (Massaro 1997, p.22)

Referring to Clark's power triangle, one could claim that the Agency has chosen a position in the triangle which is closer to the academics than to the state authorities or the market.

Led by the Chancellor, the National Agency has now nearly completed the first round of quality audits and has published the audit reports. The impressions from the first half round are summarized by the Agency in the following words:

The overall impression is that the culture of Swedish universities and university colleges is developing in a positive direction, but that the goals of systematic, communicable and comprehensive quality program still lie in the future. (Högskoleverket 1997d, p.7)

However, the relationship between enhancement processes and improvement of actual operations remains unclear, even if there are a number of indications that improvements have taken place. Such indications include the introduction of new study programs in response to new needs of local industry, improved student services, and improved working environment and curriculum changes, all measures taken as a result of different kinds of evaluations. (Högskoleverket 1997d, p.8)

It has been questioned by some of the audit teams themselves, however, whether the audits really have any impact on levels below the faculties, especially at the large universities, and how deeply into the organization the quality assurance and enhancement work has reached. Any causal effects of the institutional quality work on the quality of teaching or on the quality of student outcomes have not been identified and documented, which is not the same as saying that such effects do not exist (Högskoleverket 1996b; 1997b).

Towards increase in diversity and in homogeneity

In summary, two distinct patterns emerge out of the development trends during the years around the H-93 reform. The first pattern indicates a rapid quantitative development that has affected the structure of the system at large in a fairly uniform manner and also caused a heavy overload on teaching. The other pattern presents us with a picture of many simultaneous but miscellaneous processes of change that have brought about more diversified and, at the same time, less stable and predictable working conditions for the institutional leaders and the academics. The interaction with external interests is also causing an increase in diversification within each institution (see further chapters 7 and 8). Boundaries between faculties and departments have become more distinct, and at the same time, in other respects, more fluid.

The system is apparently moving towards increased variation in what concerns students, programs, teaching tasks, research activities and additional assignments. There is both expansion in student numbers and in knowledge at the same time. In addition, the institutions are also encouraged to distinguish themselves. However, supported by local funders and interests, each institution is also eager to contribute to the renewal of its own region by offering almost the same kind of undergraduate programs and courses as are offered by other institutions. This trend is most evident among the colleges and contributes, in this respect, to a national homogenization. Thus, the institutions have become more alike in some respects, as well as more distinct. The same tendency has been noted by Scott as an international trend: 'With the massification of higher education differences between institutions, universities and the rest, are eroded and may finally be abandoned. But, within mass systems with multiple missions, new types of institutional differentiation emerge' (Scott 1995, p.169). Universities were often blamed for being old, stiff, and without the capacity for change, compared to the colleges which impressively met the need to support the development in their regions. Evidently, however, not only these creative colleges, but also the universities, have undertaken radical quantitative and qualitative changes. The universities are apparently trying to become more international, and at the same time more regional without losing their traditional national importance.

At the same time, Swedish colleges are almost invited to 'compete' for university status by presenting development plans. Some of the colleges are preparing plans for establishing graduate education and professorships and are being financially supported to do this by the government. Thus, with regard to access to research resources, the system might also move towards homogenization. Thirty years after the split was introduced by the government in order to solve the problems of expansion at that time, the institutions themselves are using their widened space of action, supported by the government, to overcome the shortcomings of those measures. The criteria used by the National Agency in assessing institutions which apply for the right to establish professor chairs might also, in the long run, contribute to the homogenization of the higher education system (Andrén 1996).

Since the late 1980s, Swedish higher education has made remarkable development from a static, firmly structured and state funded system to a flexible, dynamic and expansive system based on diversified funding. The 1993 reform has brought about a combination of state steering and institutional autonomy which apparently has supported not just a quantitative expansion but also a substantial qualitative development. The entire higher education system is moving towards both diversity and homogeneity. Formerly the institutions were kept together by strong state governance. The state was the main consumer on their market. Now, with much more reliance on other consumers in the market, the issue of institutional leadership and governance is quite different.

The institutions responded positively to the expansion requests in the late 1980s. The successive deregulation at that time had an encouraging effect on the institutions' willingness to take the extra burden of expanding their activities when additional funding was available. When, in 1993, further economic incentives were at hand the institutions used their widened scope of action and innovative capacity to take further measures. As many of the institutional leaders have emphasized in the interviews, the reform codified what was already going on and facilitated for further steps to be taken. Through this expansion and renewal the higher education system was saved from drastic budget cuts that affected other parts of the public sector. All institutions increased their total assets during the first three-year contract period, and in doing so they also avoided the need to dismiss staff. They have received more funding in total, but in reality they have ended up with more work for less pay.

This increase in variation, diversity and differentiation on the national system level must be considered against the backdrop of a significant characteristic of the Swedish context. First of all, almost all students in undergraduate education are examined by their own teachers and second, degrees from different universities and colleges should in principle be equivalent.

Chapter 7

Academic Leadership in Transition

Demands on strong leadership

Since 1964, a series of intermediary bodies for higher education have replaced each other (see Chapter 3). Despite differences in instructions, they have all released the university boards and leaders from having to deal with authoritative and delicate decisions concerning allocation of resources, priority of activities and appointment of professors. Also, since 1964, the universities have been requested to have their own apparatus for internal administration and annual follow-up reports to the National Board. Therefore, the registrar position was introduced. The rector acted mainly in the honorable role of *'primus inter pares'*, which was not too demanding with regard to executive decision-making duties. The rector was appointed by the government but elected by the academic staff, that furthermore was employed by the state, a fact which also contributed to a restricted and ceremonial role. Together, the rector and the registrar formed the Rector's Office.

In 1993, when the independence of the institutions was strengthened, a strong academic leadership was emphasized by the government and the divided university leadership was abandoned. The rector was designated as the ultimate leader of the institution and the universities were no longer formally requested to hold a registrar position. They were free to make their own composition of the Rector's Office. However, most registrars continued as heads of the central university administration.

Nowadays, the rector is not only an academic leader but also the head of a large organization. One crucial issue for the university board, to which we will return in Chapter 8, is to decide on the order of delegation, i.e., to which organizational level(s) the decision-making power is to be delegated. In the Higher Education Ordinance, the strong leadership was emphasized on all levels in the institutional organization. 'The new situation gives the leaders on various levels a changed role, which is difficult to integrate with the other pronounced principle of leadership at universities and colleges, namely the traditional collegial model of decision-making' (Gov. Prop. 1993/94:177, p.38). The expectations of the H-93 reform – expansion, renewal, efficiency, quality and sensitivity to external interests – also form demands on the institutions and their leaders. They are now less protected by state regulations. The rectors at the universities, more than the rectors at the colleges, are faced with double loyalties – both to the government which appointed them and to the academics of their own institutions who nominated them or, as is sometimes the situation, to the fraction of the academics who preferred them rather than other potential candidates.

External representatives are now the majority in the university boards. From 1 January, 1998, the institutional board is chaired by an external representative, appointed by the Government. Many of the new board members have long experience as senior managers and leaders in the public or private sector. In their duties as board members, they have to examine the internal affairs of the institution, and in doing so they introduce a new and strange kind of external monitoring of the institution's internal affairs (Askling 1997b). This circumstance also contributes to the new role of the rector and the Rector's Office in 'serving' the board with propositions and basic data.

The many references in the reform documents to 'strong academic leadership' provide the university rector with a potential space of action for transforming governmental policy into internal regulations. These regulations, in turn, set the conditions for the basic units and the individual academics. Each university leader has to shape his or her own new style of academic leadership and to establish a new kind of relationship to the university board and the academics, in order to realize the expectations of an expanding, innovative and quality-minded self-regulative institution. For the colleges, where the dual leadership was never introduced, the reform did not mean the same substantial shift in conditions and expectations on the rectors.

This chapter addresses how the leaders met the reform, how they perceived the new demands on themselves, and what kind of experiences they had.

Leadership in self-regulative academic institutions

The current concern for the execution of institutional leadership is neither new nor unique in Sweden. The importance of leadership in Swedish higher education was identified already at the end of the 1970s by Berg and Östergren (1977) in their study on innovation and change in higher education. They argued that the leadership at all levels in the organization must be stressed and that leading positions must become attractive. They also claimed that training was an important issue for leaders.

In the path towards decentralization of the public sector, which started in the 1980s (see introduction to part II), the consequences in terms of new demands on leadership were also identified. Many parallels were drawn between management in private and public sectors. However, incompatibilities between the two sectors and their leadership were also emphasized.

At the end of the 1980s, academic leadership was also raised as an issue by the Higher Education Commission. The Commission undertook a few studies (SOU 1992:15) where the point of departure was that the leadership role was changing, and that there were no simple models to copy from the business sector, not even from the knowledge production companies. The new leadership was to be formed, the Commission argued, with respect paid to the distinctive character of higher education institutions as multiprofessional organizations.

Examining a corresponding trend in Norway, Bleiklie claims that this new kind of leadership calls for a balance between a democratic and an authoritarian leadership. The role of an institutional leader, thus, is a combination of a civil servant operating in a hierarchical organization, a senior academic as the disciplinary coordinator, and an executive leader in an organization devoted to knowledge production (Bleiklie 1993).

According to Middlehurst, leadership is an elusive concept which has encouraged researchers to view the subject from different perspectives, drawing insight from a range of disciplines and utilizing a variety of investigative techniques. While in earlier periods the theoretical framework for analyzing leadership was dominated by personal trait theories the tendency nowadays is to consider the entire organization and not just the individual leader in its particular framework of continuously changing external conditions. Today, the practice of leadership is related to different images of academic organizations, such as 'the entrepreneurial and adaptive university' and 'the university as a cybernetic system', and to what kind of constraints the academic organization provides (Middlehurst 1993).

Evidently, as was also pointed out by Dill and Sporn, it is not enough to focus on individual personal traits: 'University leadership will become more critical. Not necessarily leadership by individual personalities, but rather leadership vested in collegial groups and collective processes for planning, resource allocation, and quality assurance' (Dill and Sporn 1995b, p.138). Kerr, in his broad international overview of ongoing trends in higher education systems, comments on the new kind of leadership in the following way:

> leadership will be both more necessary and more difficult. It must, under current circumstances, be based less on power and more on persuasion. Even more than in the past, the leaders of the future will need to be like the legendary Proteus, who both knows all things, and has the power of assuming different shapes in order to escape being questioned'. (Kerr 1994b, p.33)

A more entrepreneurial model of leadership is often suggested as a solution. But such entrepreneurial leadership places the academic leader in a sandwich-position: 'Operating between the superstructure of controls above the institution, and the understructure of departmental faculty control, how does entrepreneurial leadership for the university as a whole emerge?' (Clark 1995b, p.8). In his reflections on the reform of Swedish higher education, Trow points to the key element of leadership and the new pattern of authority. In the Swedish reform,

> there is a clear and substantial increase in the responsibilities carried by the universities, and in the first instance by their rectors. But here we see the danger of assigning greater responsibility without greater authority. In universities as in other organizations, the power to innovate, to be entrepreneurial, to promote change lies in the strength of the chief executive. Academic communities are on the whole culturally and organizationally conservative, even when they are scientifically innovative or politically radical. (Trow 1993b, p.26)

Attitudes towards the reform

Almost all leaders in our sample had their first academic experiences in the 1960s. Since then, for shorter or longer periods, most of them have held one or another leading post within the university system.

They have personal experiences from the 1977 reform, although from various perspectives, roles and functions. They have met a series of demands on structural, organizational, and curricular adjustments and changes in earlier periods of their professional academic life.

Together, the leaders in our sample represent a body of substantial knowledge about the Swedish higher education system. Following the Swedish pattern of low geographical mobility, most university leaders have spent the major part of their professional life at one and the same university. Most of them have their current position at the same university that they entered as young undergraduate students and where they passed their first exams. Most of them have remained at their universities for the sake of research:

> I would never have been a university teacher, were it not for the op-
> portunities to do research work. (leadership, university)

Although many of them have long and usually successful experiences as study directors, heads, deans and pro-rectors (often following what in retrospect seems to be an informal career ladder for academic leaders), most of them emphasize their basic identity as researchers. Some of them will never return to a life as an academic researcher:

> Some of the deans don't return to their departments. They turn
> themselves into some kind of professional administrators. (leader-
> ship, university)

Most of the registrars and head administrators in our sample also identify themselves as academics with deep respect for the values of research, although they themselves, for various reasons, entered into an administrative career within the university.

All leaders declare that the new model of governance has brought about a heavy administrative workload at all levels within the institutions. There has been a substantial increase in, and also diversification of, duties for all those who are directly engaged in decision-making and administration. The responsibilities have expanded, the administrative tasks have become more varied, and the management of the institution has become a much more complex and challenging task.

The number of organizational levels differ between institutions. At the fully-equipped institutions (the universities), institutional boards, faculty boards and department boards form a three-level hierarchy of decision-making bodies. At the colleges, on the other hand, the lack of permanent research resources also implies a lack of faculty boards. Thus, there is just a two-level decision-making apparatus, more focused on undergraduate issues. Besides, at the universities, the academic perspective is more formally represented and protected by the presence of deans and faculty boards.

Despite a generally positive acceptance of the reform, the leaders express their attitudes towards the reform differently:

> This is a major reform. Ideologically, it makes a great difference. This reform has changed everything for us. (leadership, university)

> This is really not a reform, not in the way the 1977 reform was. This is just a predictable continuation of something that started in the 1960s, and we were well-prepared. (leadership, university)

> This is not to be called a reform. It is rather a summing up in a hurry of ongoing changes and an adjustment to changed international and national conditions for higher education. (leadership, university)

One may ask why this reform is not perceived as a true reform. Perhaps 'reform' in the Swedish context is so loaded with memories of extensive structural changes, derived from radical ideological policy statements and imposed through a top-down implementation strategy; while this reform, with its references to the autonomy of the institutions and the authority of the institutional leaders, lacks prescriptions and regulations and so is not interpreted as a reform.

Some comments are fairly cynical, saying that one must not pay too much attention to what the government says, since everyone knows that changes come and go:

> If you really want to do what you find important (your own research), you cannot take all these reforms seriously. Solutions change, ideas change. (leadership, university)

> Policies change and reforms change and you must not bother too much. There will soon be changes again. (leadership, university)

However, despite this variation, there is an overall acceptance of the new division of labor which is being established between the government and the institutions. Most of the institutional leaders are stimulated by the new freedom and the new responsibilities, and are also very determined to use them. It is now up to the institutions to use their widened space of action, and of course the institutions have to show that they have the creativity, flexibility and energy to do so. The positive acceptance of the reform is also reported from the government's own follow-up study, RUT-93 (Utbildnings-departementet 1995).

From a research methodological point of view, you could say that it must be almost impossible for an institutional leader in an interview to confess any objection to their new responsibilities as institutional leaders. However, an indication of the validity of the positive responses is that although workload and responsibilities have increased, no one wants the former system back.

Why, then, is the reform so accepted by the leaders? A basic reason for the wide acceptance of the H-93 reform among the university leaders is, with a reference to Lane (1989), that the reform did not hurt the core of the institution. On the contrary, the use of words such as 'knowledge', 'academy', and 'academic freedom' in the reform, has contributed to its acceptance.

There is also complete agreement that the former system with its fixed student tags (a resource allocation system that was not sensitive to whether the students were successful or not), did not support productivity and efficiency, and did not invite the institutions to improve their offer of undergraduate programs. The institutions were not encouraged to care about their own 'image' and their own students. There were few incentives, economic or otherwise, for improvements.

Evidently the leaders were, perhaps with some exceptions, well-prepared for the reform. The reform had a rationale, which was logical also from their point of view. At least some of the institutional leaders, in the late 1980s, had already foreseen the consequences for higher education when steps were being taken at that time towards the model of public sector goal-outcome steering. They started their internal preparation several years before the new model of higher education governance was set into motion (see Andersson 1997). For them, the H-93 reform meant just a confirmation of ongoing changes in other parts of the public sector, which sooner or later were to also affect the higher education system.

However, when the Minister of Education, Per Unckel, prepared the reform, he was criticized for hurrying. Proposals were not properly prepared. They were sent by fax to the institutions, and the institutions were expected to react almost immediately. The entire official remiss process was abandoned, there was no time for such procedures. In this respect, the 1993 reform was as much dictated by politicians as was the 1977 reform. However, from time to time, Per Unckel invited the rectors to meetings in order to inform them, but also to listen to their opinions. In that respect, Unckel introduced what may be called a new 'instant' model of the remiss process. He was also sensitive to the rectors' responses, consequently, many of them felt that they had taken an active part in the preparation of the reform. In retrospect, this is a good example of a network strategy, in which actors on the arenas of policy formation and policy realization are brought together (see Chapters 4 and 5).

Leadership as a new academic profession

Initially, at some institutions, decentralization was mainly interpreted positively as a smooth continuation of the decentralization wave of the 1970s. However, this time it addressed the academics without the elements of corporatism which was much criticized earlier (Askling and Almén 1997). From such interpretations, the faculty boards and their deans, the departments and their heads, and of course all academics, as they were directly referred to in the reform proposals, expected increases in authority and autonomy for just themselves.

However, it was made explicit in the Higher Education Ordinance that the institutional leader was responsible for the entire institution in a more executive and demanding way than ever before. The authority of the rector as an academic and an executive leader was enhanced by the elimination of the registrar function. The reason for this arrangement was, from the point of view of the government, to establish the leadership and responsibility of the institution in one single identified person once the state regulations were reduced and the local variations increased.

In addition, the more outspoken dependency on external funding and external commissions have to be met by a more publicly active rector, who must operate in markets in which the academia is not considered the self-evident and best provider. In many cases, international funding bodies also request that the rector of the university, not just the research group and the engaged department, personally take an active part in negotiations and writing contract. Although the executive role of the rector is emphasized, no rector can 'survive' as a leader by just being an executive. The rector is dependent on the capacity, competence and willingness of the academics to take an active part in the renewal of programs and courses, in the preparation of research proposals, in the creation of new centers and in the management of extensive research projects. The rector is, thus, dependent on the loyalty of the deans, the heads of departments and the academics. The rector is also, as a manager, dependent on a qualified staff of administrators in order to undertake investigations, and prepare background materials.

These expectations are similar to the ones that Kerr describes as the 'presidents make a difference model' (Kerr 1994b): 'Here the president has more responsibility than any other single person for holding the organization together internally, for defending and advancing it externally, and for selecting or assisting movement in new directions' (Kerr 1994b, p.39). In the interviews, the new aspects of rectorship are described by the rectors as stimulating and rewarding but also demanding and time-consuming. Although an initial key word in the reform was 'freedom', several times during the interviews the institutional leaders refer to the word 'responsibility' as the main key word for illustrating the major change brought about by the reform. This responsibility pushes the institutions and their leaders to create new ways of acting as managerial leaders:

> The decentralization has transmitted downwards a tremendous amount of work. (leadership, university)

Experiences as a university leader provide new perspectives and have an impact on the leaders' professional identity as an academic:

> When you are a university leader, you get a more Humboldtian view. You also realize that there are other ways of looking at things, other ways of searching for knowledge, and that there are other cultures, other values and other norms at the university. (leadership, university)

So far, we have discussed the rector's role at the universities. The colleges, on the other hand, had from their very start as higher education institutions in 1977 a more managerial leadership. Without deans and without the former registrar position, the rector's role was to be shaped within a power structure different from that at the universities. The existence of two, instead of three, levels of decision-making bodies gives a simpler pattern of decision-making:

> The rector at a college has a much more operative role than has the rector at a university. (leadership, college)

Some of the colleges have been successful in defining common goals for their strategic plans, such as, to become universities and to get the right to establish professorships. As a result, they have also defined a more explicit role for their leader.

Another difference between the universities and the colleges is income from external research funding. At the colleges this income is more modest and provides a better balance between the rector and the departments. That is, it makes it easier for the rector to be the ultimate leader of the institution. On the other hand, the colleges have to meet demands on 'usefulness' from their nearby environment of small-scale companies. This might make the distinction between corporate business-oriented functions and public agency functions blurred in the new rector's role.

The leaders' views on missions and functions

In their responses to our question about missions and functions of higher education (important as a background for understanding how they define their role as leaders), leaders in many ways expressed similar opinions, although their answers naturally reflect the substantial variation between the universities on the one hand and the colleges on the other hand. Some key words in the responses from all leaders are 'independence', 'autonomy', and 'creativity'. Another key word in the responses is 'knowledge', although the points of reference for knowledge differ.

For the university leaders, the unique role of higher education is to create knowledge, and to arrange programs and courses in such a way that the students will be encouraged by the creativity of the university.

> Our mission is to produce knowledge and to transmit knowledge. The university is the only authority which has that as its sole task. This also means that we have to produce such knowledge which we today might not understand that we need. (leadership, university)

Many leaders define the ultimate mission of the university as producing unique knowledge, giving room for teaching as well as research and promoting the students' critical thinking and deep understanding:

> The university must create independent individuals, critical thinkers. (leadership, university)

The independence of the universities and their responsibility to have a service function to society are also emphasized. The relationship between university and society is, however, a delicate one:

> The function of the university is to produce knowledge and play a role in society and also in the region, but not to such an extent that

we become consulting institutes commissioning investigations and teaching. (leadership, university)

The university need not solve the problems of society, but, on the other hand, the university must help students to get a training that is important for society. (leadership, university)

The uniqueness of the universities, according to the university leaders, is of course the rich opportunities to establish links between teaching and research, and also the opportunities for preparing interdisciplinary courses and programs. The very idea of the university is to allow various fields of knowledge to interact and to shape new fields of knowledge. In this respect, the difference between universities and colleges is significant:

The university must be a multi-disciplinary and multi-faculty and multi-science institution. There must be cross-interaction and cross-fertilization. The university must keep its integrity and its independence. (leadership, university)

The university's main task is knowledge production. The students have to get a deeper understanding of knowledge, and also learn how to search for it. (leadership, university)

The colleges also refer to knowledge, but in a more pragmatic way. The role of the institutions in producing knowledge is more often considered in a regional perspective and related to enterprises and firms, as well as other employers and stakeholders in the neighborhood.

Thus, the leaders of the colleges are more sensitive to external (regional) interests, while the university leaders refer to internal as well as international values and norms of the academia and to the idea of the university as a unique collection of beliefs, norms and assumptions which has survived political attacks and threats. What is striking is that the colleges, which have almost doubled their size in a few years and live with regional demands on 'usefulness', have such strong aspirations with regard to their relations to the students:

We want to create something which is a re-establishment of what we missed in the expansion period: the direct relationship between students and teachers. (leadership, college)

Another difference is evident between the universities and the colleges. The latter group has been more alert in preparing official mission statements of the institution. In many cases, such statements are used very deliberately as manifestations of a more offensive way of managing and marketing the institution. The universities, on the other hand, have moved more slowly, well aware of the fact that mission statements for a university can easily be turned into just a collection of non-demanding rhetorical phrases. As such, mission statements have to reflect the wide variety of functions, missions, as well as traditions and rationales of the university. In this respect, the university leaders express the same kind of skepticism which Rasmussen (1998), among others, has declared.

With regard to Figure 4.2, p.81, which has the two dimensions of Purpose and Authority, the leaders are apparently quite happy with being able to leave the upper right quadrant, the model of 'Social goals', and move somewhere else. However, with reference to what they said about 'knowledge', they hold fairly pluralistic views on missions and functions of their own institutions. They have apparently no clear preference of where to move. Their comments on missions and functions indicate that they are open to being responsive to various academic and social demands of higher education, as long as a substantial amount of their autonomy is not threatened.

With reference to the Authority dimension in the typology, the institutional leaders highly appreciate the devolving of authority from the state level to the institutions. Some of them have, as will be described in Chapter 8, shaped quite new models of institutional leadership and governance.

New relations with the government

The issue of *trust* is brought to the fore by the leaders. In 1977, many of the measures taken by the government were interpreted by the academics as a lack of trust from the government. The measures taken at that time imposed issues that were strange to the academic community.

In this respect, the H-93 reform is interpreted as a complete contrast to the earlier H-77. The governments (the Conservative more than the following Social Democrat) have challenged the capacity of the academia to contribute in the creation of a 'knowledge society'. By the extensive deregulation and devolution of authority, they have also made evident that they trust the institutions and the academics in defining what kind of knowledge to produce and transmit. However, from the point of view of the institutions, the question is: Can the institutions trust the government? Will the current rules be kept or will there be changes again in other directions?

Despite the heavy workload the institutional leaders are satisfied with the new model of governance, with some major exceptions. There must be a mutual respect for the new rules, which implies that the government ought to be careful not to break its own contracts by offering additional assignments and introduce alternative tariffs for these tasks or by changing the accountability procedures:

> We now need a stable development, we cannot have ups and downs. (leadership, college)

The institutional leaders have been faced with situations where they have to balance the risks of refusing proposals of additional assignments from the government, and perhaps being considered uninterested or non-innovative, against the risk of being internally blamed for being unpredictable, dishonest, untrustworthy, and ignorant of how staff members are pressed by new demands and obligations.

The universities must keep, and claim and defend if necessary, a long-term perspective to their main tasks of teaching and research. Further, they must keep (and be respected in keeping) a certain amount of independence relative to the government and the environment. This integrity of the university, according to the leaders, is important to respect, protect and defend.

This unfamiliarity with the system at the Ministry of Education, in combination with a lack of consistency in keeping to its model of governance, initially gave, in 1993, rise to many contradictory signals from the institutional leaders to the faculty boards and the departments: to take in more students, to increase the number of courses, to make cuts in the offering of courses, to accept a lowering of the payment for the courses, to prepare to fire staff members and, in addition, to accept sudden increases in offering and study places and to withdraw the announcements of firing academic staff members:

> We are allowed to be more creative, but, on the other hand, the university is not protected in the same way as before. (leadership, university)

There are several examples of other measures taken by the government in the following years, most of them with economic consequences which might, in fact, undermine the position of the institutional leaders. Shortly after the first triennial contracts were signed, the government presented additional 'offers', 'expectations' or 'demands' (there are alternative interpretations of the very nature of these assignments) which broke up the plans just decided on. Another example of contradictions is that after having introduced the term 'quality assurance', the government changed both vocabulary and arguments and asked for 'quality development programs'.

The quality issue: a tool for institutional management

When approaching the quality issue in our interviews, the leaders are evidently well prepared for discussing this theme. In their responses, they also illustrate the wide range of aspects which have been brought to the fore since the end of the 1980s under the common label of 'quality'.

Many leaders formulated quality in terms of desirable outcomes:

The university must create independent individuals, critical thinkers. (leadership, university)

For other leaders it was equally evident to talk about the need for debate, critical awareness, openness, cooperation and the spirit of the creative seminar. The quality issue has contributed to satisfying such needs:

The most important thing in this quality issue is the internal debate. (leadership, university)

Another group of leaders directly refer to the new demands on accountability and define quality as related to the administrative and controlling obligations of the institution:

We cannot go on year after year. We need to look backwards and assess what we have done. (leadership, university)

Some of the leaders refer to management-oriented criteria and pay attention to how the institution is managed with regard to its attractiveness for prospective students and staff members:

The quality of our institution depends on what kind of staff we get, how we recruit people, how we take care of them and how we pay them. (leadership, university)

One positive effect, according to one leader, is that the students have become more important for the institutions than in the earlier system, both as applicants and as contributors to the examination rate:

The recruitment of students is important. We must get motivated students and one way of getting motivated students is to create new and interesting programs and courses. (leadership, university)

The overall impression from the interviews is that attention to quality has been strongly stimulated by the reform and that the quality issue has provided an analysis of missions and functions and also brought about a concern for institutional management. However, the interview responses also show that a wide range of issues are brought under the common label of quality. This, at least partly, reflects the successive approaches to quality made by the intermediary bodies during the turmoil around the reform.

The different aspects of quality also reflect different views on what to give priority to in institutional management. Thus, reference to quality:

- provides discussions about the ultimate mission of higher education
- pays attention to academic and cultural values within the institution
- reminds staff members of the need for qualified internal administration and control
- calls for sensitivity to customer and external interests
- highlights the importance of staff management and student recruitment.

The concern for quality had to be demonstrated in times of many simultaneous changes, for example, of the funding system, the rate of expansion, the new models of state and institutional governance, and the new kind of institutional boards. Due to a combination of preconditions, the approaches differ – these preconditions include the rector's personal interest in and awareness of the importance of the issue, the special competence at hand, as well as the internal organization and engagement of the university board. The complexity of the quality issue is evident in the responses from the leaders, as is the initial confusion about how it was handled by the government and the National Agency. Regardless, all the responses have in common the belief that the quality issue is considered an important part of the new model of institutional management. In particular, the audits by the National Agency have helped the institutional leaders to make evident the new demands on institutional responsibility and to attain acceptance for a certain amount of managerial centralism within their institutions:

> We must manage the university in a proper way. The university must be broader and it must be deeper. The university must have a critical mass, and that is an important aspect of quality. (leadership, university)

Many rectors established councils, committees or delegations, formally commissioned by the university board, to address the whole issue of quality assessment and quality assurance within the institutions. Such committees were in general chaired by a senior academic, for example a pro-rector, a former dean or a vice-rector, and had representation from the faculty boards and the student unions.

One important task for these quality councils is to explain the ideas behind the quality development program and the new relations with the government in such a way that an institutional quality assessment program will be looked upon as a means of quality improvement and not just for inspection and control, and punishment of bad performance. Another task for the councils is to support 'horizontal learning' in the university organization by coordinating and facilitating exchange of experiences. Many councils are responsible for preparing staff development programs. In addition, some of the councils have proposed the establishment of support centers for teaching and learning, evaluations, and staff management, thus encouraging the development of a kind of infrastructure for development-oriented supportive service activities at the institutions. Such councils can also be looked upon as a way of supporting the development of a collective consciousness and, at the same time, strategic institutional management.

In the institutional quality programs, self-evaluations play a predominant role as tools for internal reflection on strengths and weaknesses in the organization as well as in teaching and research. The preparation of the self-evaluation reports for the audit teams have initiated an interplay between 'internal' and 'external' monitoring between the institutional levels. The external quality monitoring acts as a catalyst (Harvey 1997) and the audit visits contribute to an increased organizational transparency (Askling 1997b, 1998a). They also bring to the fore the vast variation of current definitions of quality as well as the variation in models of institutional governance and management adopted by the institutions (see Chapter 8):

> First we decentralized and then we found that we had to elaborate a quality assurance system in order to have control over the system as well. (leadership, university)

It is worth noting that self-evaluation strategies were launched in the 1970s as an aid to self-help in what was then considered an ongoing decentralization. However, they had little success (Bauer 1994). Now, self-evaluations are at work at many institutions, and one can ask why they were not used more regularly when they were first launched. One answer might be that it is not until now, when the institutions have received more evidently demanding managing functions, that the relevance of undertaking self-evaluations has become more obvious.

One tendency is clear: the quality councils did not assume the role of an executive assessor of the quality, as such, of the institution, the students outcomes or the institutional management. They have tried to distinguish themselves mainly as supportive bodies and to respect the responsibility of the faculties and departments for the more explicit defining and assessing of quality. At one of our universities, the first quality council was expected by the university board to undertake evaluative tasks, but refused to execute them and, consequently, asked to be dismissed.

A common trend at the colleges is that the quality matters have been put, more directly, on the rector's own agenda as a crucial strategic issue. One reason might be that the lack of faculty boards also means a lack of boards with the ultimate responsibility for defining quality in academic terms (according to the Higher Education Ordinance). Another reason might be the eagerness of the colleges to define their concern for quality in terms of strategic measures in order to apply for permanent research resources. When compared to this urgent and long-standing issue of research connection, almost all other aspects of quality were considered as being of less importance. This particular issue has a dignity that must be treated at the very top level of the institution. Therefore, the quality work has taken a slightly different direction at the colleges, more directly reflecting the strategic development plan of the institution.

Taking the standpoint of Brennan (1995) that at the macro level, quality is about power and control, we can say that, so far, neither the power aspects nor the control aspects have been predominant in the management of the quality issue. This is true for both the national level and the institutional level. However, at the institutional level, the quality issue has, at least at some institutions, given the rectors incentives to establish interfaculty bodies and, in doing so, strengthen the institutional leadership.

Leadership in transition

For those who hold overall responsibility for an entire institution, the shift in tasks, duties, responsibilities and workload has been dramatic. A great number of issues taken together form a quite new context for the institutions and a great challenge for the institutional leaders:

- delegation of procedural autonomy to the institutions, the increase in financial risk-taking by the individual institution
- increasing number of students
- decline in funding per student
- expectations on efficiency and quality, and verifications of that
- intensifying complexity of activities
- increased dependency on international and national additional financial resources and the increased competition for this funding
- competition for the very best students
- development of cooperative research activities and commissioned teaching and research and development activities with industries and other external interests and 'customers'
- proposals from the government for additional assignments, quality audits and accountability reports
- in some respects, also an intrusion in the individual autonomy of the academics.

The many reconstructions of the intermediary body, described by Askling and Bauer (1997), also contributed to a confusion as to what the rules of the game were and undermined the work of those who tried to set one particular model of governance to work.

Chapter 8

Institutional Autonomy in Practice
New Models of Institutional Governance

A new framework for institutional autonomy

The proposition of the H-93 reform can be read as 'a textbook case of change from a "State Control" to a "State Supervision" model' (Bauer 1996). The state intended to steer from a distance and, accordingly, an increased autonomy was awarded to the institutions. Regulations were to be replaced by evaluations, and an *ex ante* steering by an *ex post* steering.

However, it was easier to define what was to be replaced than to outline what it should be replaced by. The proposal for indicators, linked to funding, was heavily criticized and finally withdrawn (see Chapter 5). After confusion and ambiguity, a model for the national audits of the institutions' quality development programs was set into action, focusing on governance of the institutions in general (leadership and organization) and on the quality work in particular.

The National Agency formulates the aim of the audits in the following way:

> Our aim is to strengthen the individual institution's own ability to i) formulate goals and choose strategies for its operations, and ii) make these goals and strategies manifest, evident and openly communicable within the institution itself, as well as in its relations to the government and other interested authorities, organizations and bodies. (Högskoleverket 1996c, p.13)

It is in the instructions for these audits that the self-regulative model of institutional governance was explicitly introduced for the first time. The instruction reflects the influence from the work of Kells and van Vught on self-regulation as a model of institutional governance, as the state steps back from its former regulative and prescriptive role (Kells and van Vught 1988; van Vught 1989):

In several countries, a governmental steering-concept is being developed in which the government tries 'to step back'. By strengthening the autonomy of the higher education institutions, government hopes to create fruitful conditions for quality and the enlargement of creativity and excellence in higher education. Instead of more planning and control, in this strategy a choice is made in favor of more institutional autonomy and self-responsibility. Government, however, does not disappear from the scene. It tries to influence the institutions by means of rewards and sanctions.

This strategy may be called the *strategy of self-regulation*. In this strategy emphasis is put on the self-regulatory capacities of higher education institutions within a regulatory framework provided by government. The strategy of self-regulation is a combination of (less) governmental control and (more) institutional autonomy. (Kells and van Vught 1988, p.17)

As described on page 25, the strategy of self-regulation is based on the logic of the cybernetic perspective on decision-making, and the principle of feedback is emphasized (van Vught 1989). The consequences of this strategy on their internal management for the institutions are obvious:

When the institutions want to answer this challenge, they will have to develop a type of institutional management in which the traditional guildlike arrangements are respected, but in which also the institutional decision-making capabilities are strengthened. (Kells and van Vught 1988, p.21)

The idea of self-regulation is one of the predominant issues of the reform (see Chapter 1). The operational target, according to Kells is twofold: to provide better assurance over time to the public regarding quality, costs and general benefits of the system in a way that is more effective than governmental monitoring and inspection alone, and to provide a better effectiveness over time through continuous regulation and feedback. In both cases, the main idea is that all levels in the system are to be engaged (Kells 1992).

Kells and van Vught admit themselves that it is an open question whether this strategy can work:

the strategy of self-regulation in higher education has two different faces. It is a combination of two fundamentally different theoretical conceptions. In this strategy aspects of the classical model of central planning and control are combined with aspects of the natural selection model. The result is a strange hybrid which may be interesting to watch in practice, but which is not very clear from a theoretical point of view. (Kells and van Vught 1988, p.28)

In spite of the frequent use of the concept of self-regulation and some development of its implications (for example, Kells 1992; Trow 1993b; Maassen 1996) it is still a rather unspecified concept as concerns what is required from a self-regulative higher education institution in order to be able to develop its own steering and regulation. Neither in the literature of Kells and van Vught nor in official Swedish documents are any recommendations given as to *how* the institutions ought to design their internal organization or how the devolved authority within the institution ought to be dispersed (within an overall framework where strong institutional leadership is also sought for).

The various shapes of and instructions to the intermediary bodies (the National Secretariat and its successors the Chancellor's Office and the National Agency) reflect the search for an adequate balance between governmental control and institutional autonomy or, with reference to Becher (1997), between direct and indirect governance. They also reflect the efforts to integrate supportive and controlling forms of evaluations, as well as functionalistic and relativistic definitions of quality. The focus on quality and the institutions' quality programs, in combination with the generally supportive and moderately controlling approach, which was eventually adopted as the Agency's main strategy, might have concealed the fact that the audits examine the institutions' responses to the expectations on self-regulative governance and not just their quality work in a narrow sense. An informal scrutiny of the reports from the audit teams confirms such an interpretation.

Shifts in institutional governance are currently taking place in many higher education systems in Europe and many examples of institutional models of governance set into practice are reported (Maassen and van Vught 1994). There is also a growing literature in which new models of institutional governance and leadership are examined (Höllta and Pulliainen 1993; Middlehurst 1993, 1997; Trow 1994; Dill and Sporn 1995b; Clark 1995a, 1995b, 1997, 1998b; Bargh, Scott and Smith 1996; Höllta and Karjalainen 1997; Ramsden 1998). Within the framework of system changes, the institutions may react and respond in various ways. The internal academic growth can move the institutions in one direction or another, as can the history and structure of the institution. The sharp division between academic tasks and administrative ones will be blurred by an emphasis on the academic engagement in the leadership (Kogan 1996a; 1996b). The traditional organizational separation of responsibilities and tasks between academic layers and units will be affected:

> The organizational map of a modern responsive university can no longer be seen as comprised of boxes and arrows of direction showing the hierarchical relationships between organizational layers and units. Instead, it could be visualized as transparent layers of structures with blurred boundaries between entities, each having different functions, and each connected with others not so much by the lines of administrative authority, but by the coupling mechanisms of values, goals, information, leadership, tradition and practice of academic work. (Hölttä 1995, p.143)

The normative message from higher education researchers such as Clark (1998b) and Dill and Sporn (1995a) is that the solution to the increase in demands on the universities lies in a more entrepreneurial approach to the institutional management. In this approach, respect has to be paid not just to the institutional leadership but also to the collective sharing of responsibilities and obligations: 'Self-defining, self-regulating universities have much to offer. Not least is their capacity in difficult circumstances to recreate an academic community. Towards such universities, the entrepreneurial response leads the way' (Clark 1998b, p.148). Scott has identified the intention behind the shift from state control to state supervision of higher education to be an increase of 'institutional adaptivity, flexibility and propensity to innovate – in other words, to be more reflexive' (Scott 1996, p.122). Dill underlines the implications of self-regulation for the institution as an organization, when he says that in 'this new context it is reasonable to expect that many academic institutions may need to re-consider the basic organization and governance of their system for teaching and learning' (Dill 1998, p.6).

However, there are few reports concerning positive or negative relationships between models of governance on the one hand and outcomes in terms of the capacity to innovate on the other hand. Clark, in his explorative study of innovative universities, has identified some common features which might 'be conceptualized as essential elements in the formation of the entrepreneurial/innovative university' (Clark 1996b, p.427). These elements were, for example, an innovative institutional idea, an integrated administrative core and an innovative developmental periphery.

Institutional management and administration

The H-93 reform was introduced as a reform of 'freedom'. However, it soon became evident that the new system called for more local planning and accountability, more local control, and more responsibility for those who were in leading positions and thus also for a stronger and more pronounced institutional management. As such, it became a good example of the so-called decentralization paradox (Askling 1994).

The concept 'decentralization' implies that there is a transmission of power or influence away from the center of the system. The concept does not say, however, to where in the system and to whom in the organization the authority is to be reallocated. Decentralization can imply a vertical transmission from the top in a hierarchy and downwards. It can also imply a transmission from the center to the periphery, that is from the state to external markets. The same kind of ambiguity is also evident in such concepts as deregulation, democratization and deconcentration. All these concepts are sometimes used as synonyms for decentralization when references are made to changes in the relationship between central authorities, institutions and individual academics (see Askling and Almén 1997 for a further discussion of this theme). Even the concept of self-regulation is a very relative notion (Neave 1997b).

> We reduced the rector's office, but perhaps all too much. The rector needs a staff of qualified experts, preparing data for strategic decisions and for keeping the university together. (leadership, university)

> The paradox is that when you devolve more of the responsibilities, you need a stronger central administration. (leadership, university)

The rectors found themselves squeezed between two contradictory intentions, namely to increase the executive capacity of the rectorate for long-term strategic planning while not increasing the costs for the central administration.

In this last respect, the rectors were carefully watched by the academics, who feared a return to the bureaucratization which was so heavily criticized earlier. An additional argument, at this time, was of course the financial situation. With more students and less funding, all kinds of internal 'taxes' for consolidating a 'top level management' were met with suspicion. As a matter of fact, as was shown in Chapter

6, there was a slight decrease in the proportion of administrative staff to student number.

In order to strengthen the institutional level and without explicitly increasing the administration, some rectors have appointed vice-rectors and formed advisory groups with the deans and vice-rectors, the registrar and other senior administrators in the Rector's Office. Such additional rector positions have at least one of the following functions:

- to establish and extend the interfaculty communication within the institution
- to keep and enlarge the external network of relations
- to bridge the gap between academics and administrators.

At some institutions, the vice-rectors have an operative leadership function for particular units or departments within the central administration of the institution. The formation of such interfaculty bodies has, in some cases, passed through a two-step development process. In a first step, the rector formed a steering group by inviting the deans to regular meetings. However, the experience from such group meetings was mixed. While the rector was the self-evident spokesman of the institution as an entity, the deans were to the same extent self-evident spokesmen of their own faculties (and at the same time expected to have an overall perspective on the institution). With such a formation of representation, these meetings easily turned into a 'one-against-many' game:

> Somewhere in the institution, there must be something telling you that you have to keep together. The faculties and departments must not turn into divergent directions. (leadership, university)

> The deans have been fighting against each other. We must keep the university together. (leadership, university)

In a second step, the rectors proposed interfaculty committees, delegations or councils to be established and commissioned by the university board to cover particular strategic issues. By this second step, the number of people with an interfaculty responsibility for the institution increased. Clark (1998b) has noticed the same strategy adopted at some innovative universities – among them Chalmers University of Technology, a Swedish specialized higher education institution.

Some of these extraordinary bodies are responsible for policy issues (internationalization and quality), while others are more executive (student affairs and external contracts). Thus, a matrix-like organization was introduced. Many deans objected to this matrix organization, in particular if these interfaculty bodies got a formal decision-making power which could be used for generating costs for the faculties. One lesson learned, so far, is that the relationship between the deans (in the vertical line dimension), and the vice-rectors and council chairs (in the interfaculty dimension), must be clear, and that the decision-making power ought to be restricted to the rector and the deans.

There is another reason for the rector to establish a central group of qualified academic and administrative staff. As expectations placed on the rector to represent the university, internally and externally, have increased dramatically, the time for the rector to take an active part in the management of the institution has been reduced. At the same time, demands for qualified management have increased. These expectations also move the rector further away from the ceremonial *primus inter pares* role, for which some of them were nominated, and which at least some had in mind when they accepted the nomination.

Another way for the rector to manifest the strength of the institutional level is to use traditional ceremonies as a kind of symbolic power. The interviews give many examples of an increased awareness of the potential for using this kind of power in the managing of the institution. The use of a common policy or statement is also an example of how the institutions as entities are profiled. At some universities in our sample, the rectors have taken a personally active role in preparing the institutions' own books of rules and in laying down a common policy for appointments and for recruitment of staff members, and for the setting of salaries:

> An extensive decentralization demands a strong central leadership. This in its turn demands a clear and understood policy. (leadership, university)

> The university has to elaborate common policy documents. Such documents can inspire the faculties and departments to prepare their own policy documents. (leadership, university)

The interviews tell us that this new, more managerial, rector role is much more demanding, time-consuming, and laborious than any one of the academic leaders had expected. The amplitude of the changes away from the former collegial academic leadership was unforeseen, as well as the complexity of the tasks and the intensity of the work. The focus on quality and the new demands for accountability have underlined the administrative and controlling obligations of the institution. When the interviews with the leaders are considered together, it is striking how absent references to the professors are in the responses of the leaders. In the power structure of the institution at large, the corpus of professors apparently has no role.

Internal devolution of authority

Formerly, in the Swedish higher education system, authority was located at the top, on the state level, and at the bottom, among the professors. The authority of the institutional level was weak. Within the institutions, the faculties form the academic belonging, the 'families'.[1] Thus, by tradition, the faculty is a strong element in the university's internal organization. For example: although the dissertation work is undertaken in a department and is usually supervised by a professor holding a chair in a discipline, the doctoral degree is awarded by the faculty. The academic staff members have their academic affiliation to one of the faculties, even though they have their appointments in one of the departments. The departments belong to their faculties, and the rector, following this view, is the spokesman of the collection of such 'families'. The dean of the faculty is the chairman of the faculty board and the spokesman of the academic staff in his or her own faculty, while the professors, as chairholders, are the spokesmen for their own disciplines. This hierarchical model of institutional governance followed the German-influenced faculty structure, in which the autonomy of the professors and disciplines is respected and protected. On all levels, the leadership reflects the *primus inter pares* model.

In the new Higher Education Ordinance, the faculty board is the only mentioned internal decision-making body apart from the institutional board. These boards are the formal receivers of the funding for research and graduate education, while the university board is the formal receiver of the funding for undergraduate education.

At the same time as the Ordinance defines the exclusive obligations for the institutional board and the rector, it also stipulates that the

---

1   The faculties in Swedish universities have almost the same function as the
     'Schools of...' in the U.S. higher education system.

institutions themselves are free to decide on their internal organization, such as the internal order of delegation and the number and size of departments. This puts the deans in a delicate position. While the rector is the head and the coordinator of the entire institution, the deans are pushed towards the role of being the protectors of the academically well-defined preserve of his or her faculty.

The first spontaneous reaction among academics in general to the further decentralization in 1993 was that the devolving of authority from the government to the institutions was to be interpreted as to be followed by local measures for a similar decentralization within the institutions for the faculty boards and then further down in the organization for the departments and the academics. Such a vertical decentralization would allow for an allocation of power concerning academic issues to the academics themselves, this time without the corporatist elements of the decentralization of the 1970s (Askling and Almén 1997).

Some institutional leaders came to the same conclusion, and the responsibility was delegated to the faculty boards, together with a wide range of administrative tasks and, with regard to specified issues, further down, to the department boards. They consolidated what can be called a 'hierarchical model' of institutional governance (see Figure 8.1).

> The university adopted almost the same kind of decentralization as the government did to the university. (leadership, university)

The initial experiences at the universities from this radical devolution of authority were sometimes rather frustrating. Questions and issues tended to be transmitted upwards and downwards between the boards, the result being that nowhere was there a qualified overview and enough authority over the other boards that a final decision could be made without any objections from other boards in the line. The same kind of uncertainty about who was actually responsible for what, and who was deciding on what, is also reported by RUT-93, the follow-up study undertaken by the government just a few years after the reform (Utbildningsdepartementet 1995; SOU 1996:21). This internal strictly vertical decentralization also released strong centrifugal forces and gave the deans a very powerful position, all too powerful as was soon experienced by some rectors:

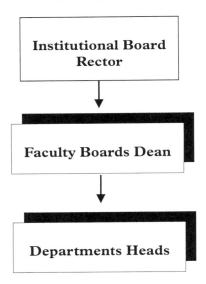

Figure 8.1 The hierarchical model of institutional governance
Source: Askling 1998c

> The deans are powerful, but they think they have to decide on each matter. They don't realize that they now have to make strategic, and not detailed, decisions. (leadership, university)

> The deans have too much power, which leads to conflicts between the faculties. (leadership, university)

> Perhaps we have decentralized too much. At the departments, the competence in economics and business is not there. The same holds for staff management. (leadership, university)

The strongest centrifugal forces came from faculties with the most prestigious professionally oriented programs with the largest proportion of external funding, such as the faculties of medicine, the schools of business and economics and the faculties (or schools) of engineering. These faculties, more than the other university faculties, have to compete with independent institutes, such as the Karolinska Institute of Medicine, the Royal Technical Institute, the private Stockholm School of Economics and the Chalmers University of Technology for qualified student applicants and for external (often international) funding. Through their deans, these faculty boards claim that they must have the same kind of influence on their own affairs, in other words the same kind of autonomy, as the boards of specialized institutes.

At some of the universities, it was considered that the initial devolution to the faculties went too far. At least some of the authority had to be reallocated at the institutional level if an institutional, and not just an individual, self-regulation was to be realized. The institutional leaders admit that they did not fully anticipate the consequences when they initially supported the radical devolving of authority:

> First we decentralized. Then, we found that someone must have control of the system also. We must have someone who is looking at the university as an entity. (leadership, university)

> Now we have tried to break this centrifugal power, and we try to let the deans feel that they have their freedom, but at the same time feel that it is rewarding to belong to the university. (leadership, university)

The centrifugal forces were calmed down by giving each faculty, or groups of faculties, an extensive autonomy of their own. Each faculty established and consolidated its own center of administration and the central administration was reduced. These universities organized themselves almost as a collection of independent faculties or schools

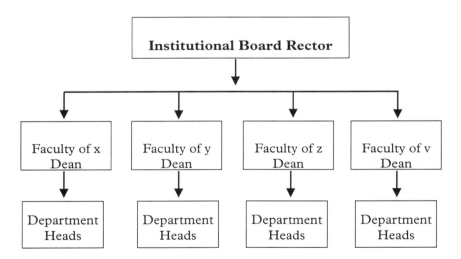

Figure 8.2 The federation model of institutional governance
Source: Askling 1998c

and represent 'a federation model' of institutional governance (see Figure 8.2).

However, not all universities responded to the reform by setting such a radical internal devolution of authority into action. On the contrary, already at the end of the 1980s, when the model of goal-outcome steering in the public administration was presented, the consequences of the application of this model and the shift from *ex ante* regulation to *ex post* control of state steering were thoroughly analyzed at one university (Andersson 1997). A few years later, another university made a similar analysis as a basis for the preparation of its new order of delegation (Askling, Almén, and Karlsson 1995) (see Figure 8.3).

With a strict vertical transmission of decision-making power, the universities anticipated that it would be difficult to make decisions which would imply interfaculty manoeuvres. In particular, it would be difficult to create interdisciplinary or interfaculty oriented programs or courses. Therefore, they explicitly broke up the internal hierarchical structure. The particular types of responsibility and initiative of the university board, faculty boards and department boards were identified and separated, as were the traditional relationships between these boards. Staff are appointed by the university and consequently the university has an employer's responsibility, which ought to be delegated to the departments and the heads. The faculty boards have a particular responsibility for keeping and controlling the academic standard while the departments have an operative responsibility for teaching and research and for staff qualifications and staff development (as necessary preconditions for these activities). From such an analysis, it became evident that if the rector wanted to establish a more executive institutional leadership, the step-wise delegation in accordance with the *primus inter pares* model of governance was not the most effective one. The rector had to establish a closer and direct relationship to the basic units, the departments, and in particular to the heads of the departments.

By conceptualizing the dispersion of responsibilities as a triangle, the unique set of responsibilities of each decision-making body was identified, as was the unique character of the relationships between the corners of the triangle. (For further information about this 'triangular model' of governance, see Andersson (1997) and Askling, Almén, and Karlsson (1995).)

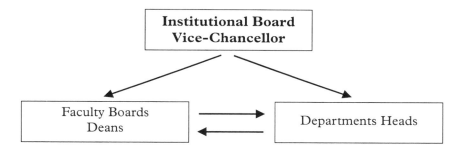

Figure 8.3 The triangular model of institutional governance
Source: Askling, Almén and Karlsson 1995

This model challenged the departments to see themselves as having an active and dynamic role in the university organization, a role that the hierarchical model prevents. The departments can more easily take initiatives of their own, and are not just subordinated to the faculty boards. The rector is also allowed to make direct contact with the departments which the hierarchical model prevented:

> We have regular meetings with the deans and the heads. That the rector meets with the heads of departments is new. That might confuse some of the deans, but it is necessary. (leadership, university)

> The collegial decision-making structure is a good one. It has been in use for centuries. In addition, we are not companies. (leadership, university)

Evidently, this model has implications for the organization of departments. In order to create strong basic units, there is a clear tendency to organize the basic level in large departments. Thus, the implementation of the triangular model has been followed by a deliberate attempt to group disciplines in larger departments (see next section).

The centrifugal forces called for some kind of measure to be taken by the institutional leaders, either towards an increase in institutional management or in its opposite, a division into independent sub-institutions, each one with its own management. The move away from the traditional hierarchical model towards the triangular one can be looked upon as a move towards a more network-like model. This has been argued for by, among others, Dill and Sporn (1995a). With triangularization, the rector can cooperate directly with the heads, thus to some extent reducing the deans' power. However, as was pointed out in the interviews, this model does not implement itself. For the rector this is a more complex, dynamic, and demanding pattern of governance than in the hierarchical model. Following RUT-93, it can also be questioned whether the actual centrifugal forces are reduced in this model or if they are simply just concealed (Utbildningsdepartementet 1995).

The same kind of centrifugal forces are not at all apparent at the colleges, since they have no faculties and no deans. The academic as well as the institutional responsibilities are in the hands of the rector. Since the very start of the colleges in 1977, the rector has been in charge of the entire management of the institution (there has never been a registrar position). The preconditions for devolution of authority to the institutional level, and for turning it into an institutional management, therefore, are better at the colleges than at the universities.

Apparently, with regard to the model of governance, the crucial factor is not what kind of measures were taken *after* the reform was implemented, but rather what measures were taken during the years *prior* to the reform. Expressed in other words, how sensitive were the rectors to the system changes at large and their prospective consequences for the institutions? The importance of such sensitivity towards changes in the environment is a quite new aspect of institutional leadership.

Our empirical data do not allow us to draw any conclusions about the direct relationship between one particular model of institutional governance and the amplitude of the measures taken by the institution with regard to quantitative or qualitative changes in educational and research activities. Nor is there any simple relationship between measures affecting the model of governance and management of the institutions, on the one hand, and such institutional characteristics as age, size, number of faculties, composition of faculties, on the other. There are all too many criteria variables and too many interacting factors, present and historical, to take into account that are not covered in the empirical study. However, with a longer time perspective and with additional data, we might in a few years be able to approach the question about causes and effects with regard to reform intentions and institutional responses and measures.

The merging of departments

Until the 1950s, the universities were small organizations. The individual professor was the main factor for the prestige of the discipline. He (or she) was also the head of the department (the disciplinary-based basic unit). The rector was the *primus inter pares* and a spokesman for the other professors. The H-93 reform gave the rector and the institutional board an extended legal decision-making power. In the Ordinance, the design of the internal organization is left to the institutions themselves. With regard to the division in departments, as well as other working units, the Ordinance gives no stipulations. As a matter of fact, the word 'department' is not even mentioned, even less regulated, in the Ordinance.

Over the years, as the universities expanded and grew into large institutions, more and more of the direct employer responsibilities were devolved to the departments. As a consequence, at the end of the 1980s, the question about optimal department size was brought to the fore. It was argued (among others by the Higher Education Commission and in Gov. Prop. 1990/91:150) that the institutions ought to examine their internal organization and look for opportunities to create larger and more stimulating and creative working units. Too small departments cannot allow for the necessary manpower flexibility and carry the costs for the necessary qualified administration of staff and economy. Since then, the search for an effective model of the internal devolving of authority, mentioned in the previous section, gave additional arguments for a merging of the departments. The increases in research funding and the reliance on additional funding (see Tables 6.3 and 6.4 and Figures 6.2 and 6.3), have also supported this development towards departments as fairly powerful economic units. The same tendency is also identified in Norway (Vabø 1996; Høstaker 1997).

This merging process was first set into action in the late 1980s at the specialized (one faculty) institutions (which are not included in our study). The measures taken there were soon adopted as models for governance at the so-called professional faculties at the universities, and from there spread to the universities at large. At these institutions the disciplinary-bound departments have been merged into large units, to which substantial authority on economy and staff has been delegated. In an in-depth analysis of this process at the Chalmers University of Technology (as one of his innovative universities) Clark (1998b) characterized the measures taken at

Chalmers as a deliberate (and successful) exercise, initiated by the rector, in order to improve the innovation capacity of the entire organization. With reference to Becher's work on academic tribes (1989), another explanation for the readiness among these faculties to merge departments was that because the managerial approach to the organizational issues is more in line with epistemological characteristics in these faculties and their successful models of managing large research projects.

Some universities, and also some colleges, have followed suit and merged related departments into larger new units. However, there is wide variation between the faculties regarding to what extent they have adopted this idea of merging. The process has been carried out in several steps and has resulted in a radical reduction in the number of departments at some of the faculties of medicine and engineering, but has so far only affected such faculties as humanities and law to a much lesser extent. There is still great variation in the number of departments at the institutions. In our sample of institutions, the variation is between 130 and 18 departments. This extensive variation is found between our two medium-sized universities of almost equal size.

This merging might, in the long run, also contribute to a reduction in the strength of the disciplines as academic entities and pave the way for a more interdisciplinary knowledge structure. It has already had an effect on the head position, turning it into an almost full-time administrative job as department manager. As a consequence, it is too complex and diversified to be run by professors acting as a combination of chair-holder and lay-man administrator:

> It is a waste of competence when a professor is a head. From a head you expect the same kind of competence as they have in the administration. (leadership, university)

This statement is another example of how the traditional collegial based *primus inter pares* model of academic leadership is abandoned in favor of a more functionalistic view on qualifications for leading positions.

Institutional autonomy in practice

When the main trends in the responses of the institutions are brought together in a chart, some characteristics of the changes stand out (see Table 8.1). Almost all institutions have responded in a fairly uniform manner with regard to the expectations of expansion and renewal. They have increased their basic activities (teaching and research) and also oriented themselves towards new categories of students, markets and funders.

The devolution of authority, in combination with the changes in structure, has turned the institutions into complex and extremely dynamic organizations. As was noted in Chapter 6, the institutions are changing their structures in many dimensions at the same time. These processes of change, however, do not affect the internal structure of the institutions symmetrically. Some parts are growing more rapidly than others. Their contributions are more requested by the government and by external 'consumers' than the contribution from other parts. Their market value is higher. Thus, as a consequence, there is an increasing internal imbalance between faculties and departments (and probably also between individual academics) in perceptions of goals and values and, also, in their 'political' and economic power.

In order to cope with the contradictory striving towards procedural autonomy, flexibility, adaptivity, strong leadership and, at the same time, internal decentralization and freedom, different solutions have been tried out. Apparently, today, institutional authority calls for another kind of leadership than the one which is legitimated in collegial nominations together with a ceremonial execution. The government's shift towards the state supervision model has aspired to a variety of models of institutional governance. The institutions and their leaders have been struggling with finding new forms of institutional governance which match the new demands on institutional autonomy and, at the same time, each institution's own history, and present structure and actors. The triangular model might be a step on the way towards a network model à la Dill and Sporn (1995a).

Table 8.1 Reform characteristics and institutional responses affecting structure, leadership and governance

The macro level *Chapters 3 and 4*	*Responses affecting structure* *Chapter 5*	*Responses affecting leadership* *Chapter 6*	*Responses affecting governance* *Chapter 7*
The reform * was introduced with a sensitivity to the expertise of the 'field' * coped with some earlier shortcomings * challenged the leaders as professional leaders * allowed for a new kind of 'ownership' * did not prescribe any particular kind of changes – except for general expansion and renewal and quality development and assurance * opened for external economic influence and monitoring * appealed to the academics by using 'freedom' as a catch word * used 'knowledge' in a way that allowed for many interpretations **However, during the implementation phase** increased * financial restrictions * unemployment among young people * unforseen changes by the government of the rules of the game.	**1) Expansion** **2) Improvements in existing programs and courses** **3) New courses and programs** **Thus,** **increase in** – diversity **and** – homogeneity	**1) Individual leadership** (*primus inter pares*) by * reducing the rector's administration and increasing the administration on faculty level **2) Collective leadership** by * appointing senior academics as assistant leaders (vice-rectors) * selecting their own co-workers * bypassing the formal election procedures * establishing steering groups * mixing elected and appointed senior academics in advisory groups * strengthening the institutional administration by appointing academics as vice-rectors etc. * preparing a 'book of rules' and similar documents in order to enhance the institution as an entity.	**1) Hierarchical model for order of delegation:** * the authority is devolved further down in the organization * the existing structure of departments is kept intact **or** **2) Federation model of order of delegation** * the institutions are turned into federations of faculties **or** **3) Triangular model for order of delegation** * a further straight downward devolving of authority is stopped * authority on different tasks is identified * the number of departments is reduced by merging * the tradition of the professor as the chair-holder and the head of department (discipline) is broken.

Source: Askling 1998c

Conclusions: Part III

The H-93 reform implied, as almost all substantial system reforms do, changes of the administrative system in order to achieve desired ends. As was noted by Dahllöf during the implementation of the H-77 reform:

> when many parts of a system are changed at the same time, there is a real difficulty in anticipating the net effect in an economic and social context which is also subject to continuous change. Even if the planners who propose a series of reforms do their best to make their own thinking about the relation between ends and means explicit (which is not always the case), there may be good reasons also for considering alternative solutions. (Dahllöf 1977, p.3)

Dahllöf's reflection at that time, when he tried to foresee the possible impact of the H-77 reform, is relevant for our study. The H-93 reform (as well as the general changes in the 1980s of the governing of the public sector) has had a tremendous impact on the meso level. The H-93 reform meant a redistribution of responsibilities and obligations, not just between the government and the institutions, but also between levels within the institutions. The consequences of this redistribution were more thorough than the actors on the various levels might have predicted or anticipated.

The Swedish higher education system is in the midst of an explosive expansion. It has also moved towards a salient differentiation in structure and function. This differentiation is evident when the institutions are compared to each other and also when the internal structure of the individual institution is considered. At the same time, with regard to distribution of resources for funding and the right to award degrees, the colleges' strive for university status can be looked upon as a deliberate move towards homogenization.

With reference to Figure 4.1 (p.74) and our two-dimensional chart on Purpose and Authority, the higher education system and the individual institutions are getting more pluralistic. On the Purpose dimension, the leaders enhance both intrinsic values and extrinsic goals. They want to defend the academic values of higher education (also evident at the colleges in their striving for university status) and, at the same time, they are fully aware of market demands (and the fact that the State nowadays can be regarded as just one of the commissioners on the market). The responses from the institutional leaders indicate that, in this respect, the institutions have a readiness to transform themselves into what Rothblatt calls a 'multiversity'

(Rothblatt 1995), by using their autonomy for adding new obligations to the current ones and by being sensitive to the demands of new consumers and funders. Evidently, the institutions were in the possession of an impressive innovative capacity, which was released by the devolving of authority from the state to the institutions.

The other dimension of our chart, Authority, has caused the leaders trouble where it concerns internal distribution. The uncertainty in approach and the differences in models are striking. Within the new space of action, granted to the institution, the institutions must develop their internal governance, i.e. organizational and distributive responsibility and authority. The initial internal devolving of authority released strong centrifugal forces which called the leaders to respond in one way or another. Initially, the devolution of authority, in combination with expectations on a more self-regulative institutional governance, was interpreted as a promise of more space for the individual staff member's values, norms and operations to exert influence on strategic decisions and internal conditions. One explanation might be the simultaneous references to decentralization, freedom and academic autonomy which preceded the reform. Decentralization from the state to the institutions was looked upon as a logical continuation of the decentralization movement in the 1970s, but gave no indications on how much authority to locate to the top level of the institution and to the deans and to the academics in general. The miscellaneous models of internal devolution of authority and the various arrangements to strengthen the institutional leadership, indicate that there have been varying degrees of awareness and insight about the very nature of the self-regulative model of governance and its implications on the institutions' internal affairs.

A crucial factor for how the institution's autonomy is actually used is the readiness of the institutional leaders to be sensitive to the expectations of the government, and at the same time, to the particular historical and present preconditions of the institutions as well as to the innovative capacity of the faculty members. A key issue in the transformation towards self-regulative governance is seemingly by whom the 'self' in self-regulation is defined, who this 'self' refers to and who is challenged by this reference. The new demands from the government on institutional management and strong leadership might be interpreted as an argumentation for the 'self' in self-regulation to be located to the top of the institution as a new kind of local centralism. However, there is a rather consistent movement towards a more collective form of leadership, although the movement in that direction has been more reluctant at some institutions than at others. The appointment of additional sub-leaders can be interpreted as a way of replacing the traditional amateuristic, *primus inter pares* leadership by broadening the academics' engagement in the management of the institution rather than by strengthening the individual leadership.

Our findings illustrate the earlier mentioned hybrid character of self-regulation, which was pointed out by Kells and van Vught (1988). The widened space of action calls for a more pronounced institutional leadership. However, a more network-oriented model of institutional governance might encourage the academic staff members to mobilise their own capacity for the benefit of the whole institution.

Our experiences confirm the observations made by Teichler (1988), that deregulation is a powerful means for stimulating initiatives of higher education institutions. To Teichler's conclusion we can add some observations from our own comparisons between the H-77 reform and H-93. The H-77 reform was launched as a decentralization reform where local study line committees were established in order to take the responsibility for innovations and necessary adjustments of content. Why did it not work? Why was the main impression from many such committees that much time was spent on endless meetings which resulted in just small changes? Now, when having an opportunity to compare with another strategy for promoting change, one can say that the decentralization at that time went too far down in the organization and was concentrated on just curricular issues. The prescribed uniformity of the system on the institutional level (see Chapter 3) and the lack of obvious incentives for the study line committees, were not encouraging for the committees. The intended variation, which was one of the purposes of the decentralization, was not identified and rewarded outside the local committees. In the H-77 reform, 'wrong' issues were decentralized to the 'wrong' level.

Within the design and framework of this study, it is not possible for us to draw any conclusions about causal relationships between particular models of institutional management and governance on the one hand and particular outcomes in terms of expansion rate or curriculum changes on the other hand in the way Clark (1996a; 1998b), Hölttä and Pulliainen (1993) and Jenniskens (1997) have tried to do. In order to be able to draw those kind of conclusions, a much more in-depth study has to be undertaken, examining various kinds of innovations and also checking various internal and external factors which, in addition to the model of governance, might influence outcome.

We agree with Kogan (1996c) when he claims that there is a need for more in-depth studies of changes and innovations, before anything can be said about the relationship between innovation and models of governance in a comparative perspective. Kogan argues that the true criteria variables, such as changes in research, scholarship, and teaching, have to be taken into account, before any conclusions can be drawn from the impact of particular models of policy and management: 'Without very fine grained analyses of curriculum change, some of them unique, that kind of generalization will not be true for one country, let alone in comparison across countries' (Kogan 1996c, p.397).

Part IV

Academe in a Context of Policy and System Changes

Introduction

This part of the study focuses on the basic units of higher education institutions and on the professional life that takes place there. Since knowledge and its formation through learning/teaching and researching is the basic substance at this level, any attempt to interpret change occurring in the basic units must start from the values, purposes and operations formed by academic groups in their endeavor of developing knowledge. As stated in Chapter 1, our intention is to investigate change, and variables influencing change in connection with a major shift in government policy, by approaching them from both a bottom-up and a top-down perspective. Consequently, in Chapter 9, our interview material will first be analyzed concerning values and ideas about the university among our sample of present-day academe and how they perceive their own identities, roles and tasks. It is against this value basis that the major issues from the preceding analyses of reform at state, system and institutional levels will be considered. In Chapter 10, the analysis will continue by tracking changes in influence and other conditions at the basic level. Have rules and conditions on the 'arena of policy realization' changed, and with them the space of action and the discretion of the basic units and individual academics? How do changes in organization, management and distribution of authority and resources within the institutions affect responsibility, influence and conditions of faculty within the basic units? How can the reception of the reform and reactions to it by those carrying through the tasks of higher education and research be understood? Are there shifts in professional roles and identities? These are the kind of issues that will be treated in this part of the study.

Background

The academic staff in Swedish higher education can be classified in four major categories: lecturer (*adjunkt*), assistant professor (*forskarassistent*), senior lecturer (*lektor*) and professor. For the latter three categories a doctoral degree is required. For the lecturer (adjunkt) position a doctoral degree is not demanded but is desirable, since this group constitutes nearly one-third of the teachers (lecturers and senior lecturers) at undergraduate level within the faculties of humanities, natural sciences and social sciences in the universities, and as much as 68 percent of the total teacher corps in the colleges. The lecturers, furthermore, usually have more teaching time imposed than the other categories of teachers.

However, the proportions of lecturers with and without a doctoral degree vary considerably between the three faculties within the universities. The faculty of natural sciences has both a lower proportion of lecturers among the teachers (lecturers and senior lecturers) 19 percent (140/140+613) and a higher proportion of those with a doctoral degree 14 percent, as compared to the humanities with 25 percent (196/196+592) and 6.6 percent respectively, and the social science faculty with 42 percent lecturers, 2.1 percent of which with doctoral degree (see Table IV.1). A further step in these proportions is taken by the colleges with 68 percent lecturers (1879/1879+877) and only 1.2 percent with doctoral degree (see Table IV.2).

In Appendix 1, the distributions over gender and age of the academic staff – within these three faculties in the universities and totally within the colleges – are presented.

Table IV.1 Number of Full Time Equivalents (FTE) of academic staff, and number and proportion of those with Ph.D. degree at the faculties of humanities, natural sciences and social sciences 1995/96

	Lecturer	*Assistant professor*	*Senior lecturer*	*Professor*
Humanities				
No. FTE	196	136	592	172
No. with Ph.D.	13	132	527	160
Percentage with Ph.D.	6.6	97	89	93
Natural Sciences				
No. FTE	140	219	613	185
No. with Ph.D.	19	211	585	182
Percentage with Ph.D.	14	96	95	98
Social Sciences				
No. FTE	745	114	1029	254
No. with Ph.D.	16	109	809	241
Percentage with Ph.D.	2.1	96	79	95

Table IV.2 Number of Full Time Equivalents (FTE) of academic staff, and number and proportion of those with Ph.D. degrees at the colleges 1995/96

	Lecturer	*Assistant professor*	*Senior lecturer*	*Professor*
No. FTE	1879	6	877	19
No. with Ph.D.	23	5	614	18
Percentage with Ph.D.	1.2	83	70	95

Chapter 9

Academic Values and Identity

Introduction

Even though academic duties such as administration and communication and cooperation with the surrounding society have increased (Askling, Karlsson and Rydberg 1997, Askling and El-Khawas 1997), there is general agreement about the primacy of the teaching/learning and research activities of the universities. These basic activities are subject to strong pressures for change, both extrinsic and intrinsic. The extrinsic demands and requirements on the higher education system call for raising the quantity, quality and relevance of education and research. At the same time, an irresistible intrinsic source of change comes with the explosive development of knowledge within many disciplines and subdisciplines (see, for example, Clark 1997). This is further fortified by the reactions that extreme specialization and fragmentation lead to, that is, demands for development of multi- and transdisciplinary knowledge and for increased cooperation with other forms of knowledge production (Gibbons *et al.* 1994). The responses and reactions by academe to policy and system changes in our study should be seen in this context and in relation to their basic values.

Academic identities

In the introduction to Part I we have sketched an outline of academic values and some ideas of the mission of the university as they have been developed and reflected in the discourse on higher education and universities during the past century. In our comparative research project concerned with the impacts of reforms on academic values and work, Henkel (1997a) suggests that the issue can be reconceptualized as reform impacts on academic identity, as being a critical concern within academic life and a concept connecting the individual with its context, since 'individual agents and individual actions cannot be identified in isolation from the context and traditions in which they are imbedded and can be comprehended' (MacIntyre 1981, cited in Henkel 1997a, p.1). By analyzing philosophical ideas about personal identity and its formation, Henkel derives some key concepts about 'the distinctive individual' and 'the embedded individual'. Three aspects that Henkel derives on the concept of the distinctive individual are 'as the subject of a unique narrative history', 'as located in a chosen moral and conceptual framework' and 'identified by the good s/he has achieved' (Henkel 1997a, p.2). But the distinctive individual is at the same time an embedded individual. In our present context, we are foremost interested in the personal identity which is being formed by professional roles and practices in institutions with values, structures, languages and myths that differentiate them. In Henkel's words:

> the embedded individual, emergent from, working within and making an individual contribution to communities and/or institutions within their own languages, conceptual structures, histories, traditions, myths, values, practices and achieved goods [and]the embedded individual carrying a range of roles, strongly determined by the communities and institutions of which s/he is a member. (Henkel 1997a, p.2)

The interactive nature of identity formation emphasized in this citation leads to the question: which community or institution that determines the academic professional identity formation is the primary? Henkel asks whether it is at all possible to think in terms of the narrative identity of an individual even within the boundaries of a profession. Given the extent of the competing values and roles in the academic profession, at least over time, the possibility of several professional identities should be considered. On the other hand, taking into account the academic environment as one in which people often shift between roles, it might be more fruitful to consider the construction of identity as a lifelong project and put more emphasis on the continuities and changes over time (Henkel 1998). Clark (1983, p.75) states that academic systems 'provide a plurality of nested groupings that manufacture culture as part of their work and self-interest'. The major sources of culture to be distinguished, according to Clark, are the discipline, the institution (or enterprise), the profession-at-large and the national system. Clark's classic formulation of academic systems as essentially 'matrix structures' of institutions and disciplines exhibits the interaction and the concomitant struggle for authority between them. However, within this major matrix there exist other examples of crosscutting bases. In Sweden, for instance, the whole higher education system has since 1977 been organized in a matrix of the disciplinary departments and general study lines – copied from the model of professional education. Although Clark and others contend that within this structure the disciplines are the dominant force, institutional history and reputation can certainly influence academic self-perceptions – both in venerable universities and in vigorous newly established institutions – and it cannot be assumed that the relationship between them, i.e. discipline and institution, and thereby also their relative influence on academic working conditions and priorities, will remain stable (Bauer and Henkel 1997a; Henkel 1997b). It is an essential issue in our study how the shift of authority and influence within this matrix structure has affected and been perceived by academic staff. That the discipline is a most influential source of academic identity formation, however, has been shown convincingly, for example, by Becher (1989). Enders and Teichler (1994) have reported and compared some results from the Carnegie Study on the Academic Profession, in which more than 20,000 scholars active at institutions of higher education in 15 countries all over the world, including Sweden, responded to a questionnaire. In response to a question regarding their commitments, academics in all countries felt most strongly affiliated to their discipline, second most strongly to their department/faculty and only in the third place to their institution of higher education. Especially illuminating in this respect are studies focusing on the processes of induction into the disciplines through the doctoral studies, which are 'shaped by these conditions, which are designed to optimize the production of new knowledge' (Becher, Henkel and Kogan 1994, p.88). Gerholm and Gerholm (1992) performed an ethnographic study of the induction of doctoral students into different disciplinary cultures within the humanistic and social sciences at six departments in their university. They paid special attention to all the unofficial and unspoken rules of behavior and 'tacit knowledge' (Polanyi 1958) that the novice has to embrace and espouse by being in the world of the discipline (Geertz 1983) in order to become a full member of the disciplinary community. Høstaker (1997) points out that as a disciplinary department may consist of different basic units (sometimes developing into new disciplines), consequently even within the same discipline the academic culture and formation may differ. Another aspect of importance, brought out by Bennich-Björkman (1997a,b), is the way an intellectual leadership is exercised by one or several of the seniors in a research environment.

Analysis of the views of the respondents on academic values, ideals and identities

In the following sections of this chapter, that part of the interviews will be analyzed which concerned the respondents themselves and their values, roles and ideals for the university, within the framework of academic values and identities sketched in the Introduction to Part I above.

Academic values and ideals according to academic staff

The questions concerning the issue of values and ideals for the university led to very few answers in 'philosophical', ethical or epistemic terms, which might be explained by the limitations of the interview situation. Yet, it is striking that a great majority of the respondents, when asked what *ideals* they think should be the guiding principles for the university and the activities carried out there, answered with the primary *tasks*: to do research and teaching, and to do them well.

> The most important is continuously to search for new knowledge and to pass it on and keep up the quality. (professor, modern languages, university)

> Here I have a clear opinion. We have two tasks: Education, under-graduate and graduate, and to search for new knowledge. A university is the only organization that has got the task just to search for new knowledge, the kind of knowledge you don't know what it is good for in the short perspective, i.e. different from for instance a research institute that is limited to a special research area ... Teaching and research go hand in hand and should not be separated. For the university to develop it is dependent on a highly qualified under-graduate education. (professor, biochemistry, university)

Some of these respondents added that an important principle was that the university should be independent and/or that the individual freedom should be as strong as possible. Further, the reasons why freedom and autonomy are essential for the university were for its critical function and for its responsibility for knowledge formation.

> Independence from different groups in society – the business groups, politicians, unions. Critical thinking, respect for ways of looking at things, respect for values, to strive after objectivity. (lecturer, economics, university)

> Freedom is very important, although the term may possibly be used too much. What I mean with freedom is that the university should not be too dependent on the State; you need an opposite to the State's power. The university needs autonomy and integrity ... the university is not a 'market', the students are not 'products'. (senior lecturer, modern languages, university)

> We need to be aware of our relation to knowledge and how we ourselves create knowledge ... If we do this our students will be able to adapt to new types of jobs without needing a lot of further education. (lecturer, sociology, university)

Several respondents emphasized as essential, the issue of teaching and research being interrelated with a continuous exchange of arguments going on:

> It is this about research that it should be free and that the teaching all the time should have channels to research and to the research front. With free research I mean an environment where the arguments and their validity and weight should be decisive and not other things ... and the students already at undergraduate level should meet the argumenting discourse. (researcher, history, university)

This sounds like a conceptualization based on Humboldtian ideals and on a Habermasian communicative process, unaffected by strategic consideration of power and professional interest. There could, of course, be several reasons for the respondents to be unwilling to develop more deeply their 'ideology' about higher education and research in an interview. In the Swedish academic tradition, underpinnings in the form of history, philosophy, ethics or sociology of sciences have not been common, neither in introductory courses nor as essential themes in study programs and seminars, nor probably in coffee-room discussions. Yet Clark Kerr, well-known former chancellor of the University of California, in an essay on 'The Academic Ethic' declares that he has been 'startled at how reluctant academics seem to be to treat ethical issues' (Kerr 1994b, p.137). There might be a hesitance in using solemn words.

> I hesitate to say it ... but the search for truth ... (senior lecturer, biochemistry, university)

> I hardly want to speak about truth and scholarship and all that ... Check if our 'product' is capable of independent thought. (lecturer, national economics, university)

The idea or purpose of the university is more or less taken for granted, and there is not much talk about it, except when considered to be threatened by the state or the market. Responsibilities connected to extrinsic values and demands from society were not often mentioned by faculty as crucial for the university. By some they were seen as necessary obligations due to the major financing by the state. Others saw them as threats to the essential autonomy and therefore to be avoided or counteracted as far as possible.

> That the university is independent, like the idea of the old, traditional university. The development we have in Sweden recently with all these connections to society, they frighten me. (lecturer, physics, university)

> I think that the university should be dedicated to research and teaching in equal amounts, and as far as possible avoid to be steered by politics and business and their wishes and demands. (senior lecturer, modern languages, university)

However, there are also respondents who are very aware of the necessary relationship between society and higher education institutions. It appears from our interviews as if in the universities there are great individual differences in this respect, while in the colleges there is more of a collective insight of the importance of the relationship, particularly to the regional society and the participation in its development.

> My most important task for which I still burn is to see to it that science becomes a resource for society and means something for people in the society ... And that is quite a radical attitude in the university compared with many who think we should close the doors to society and concentrate on becoming best in the world. (senior lecturer, physics, university)

> The most important thing to achieve now is to develop a profile for the department to meet the needs of the region and of the students. We have three primary goals in our institution 1) satisfied students, 2) support regional development, and 3) have competent staff. (head of department, college)

As stated by Clark (1983, p.24), in this century 'the proliferation of materials and groups has stretched beyond credibility the usual global statements of essence'. As a result, when key actors who generally have a well-grounded sense of what they are doing 'are asked to enunciate, in a sentence or two, the meaning and purpose of the entire university, they scratch their heads and revert to trivial statements'. This is evidenced in our interviews in statements like the following:

> This is difficult, the university is so many different things. So many types of people, different types of career tracks and different sciences! The university should be making scholars ... and we, should give something back of the scholarship we received. (lecturer, physics, university)

> Immense question that I can hardly answer. You feel the power of tradition in this big university. It has all to gain from keeping its traditional model. (professor, modern languages, university)

When asked about what constitute their daily activities it becomes clear that ideals and reality do not always concord. The balance and relationship between research and teaching/learning, emphasized by many respondents as an essential characteristic of higher education, is far from being obtained, neither for individuals nor for departments.

> I think the job as a university-lecturer should be such that you could do research regularly. As it is now you can do research during the summer, and research conferences are held during summer-time, but it is very tough to be teaching only through the whole terms. (lecturer, sociology, university)

> I teach 75% now, the rest is supposed to be research, but this is an impossible combination when the teaching demands so much reading and preparation in this expanding discipline. The research has to be abandoned. (senior lecturer, biochemistry, university)

In the colleges where at the time for the interviews (1995) they were still without permanent funding for research, this ideal of combining teaching with research meets with other difficulties. A large proportion of their teachers are lecturers who have not attained a doctoral degree (see Table IV.2).

> Most time goes to teaching, but also to my doctoral training, which is very important, since we do not have so many people here with that competence. But most time is for class planning, preparation work and being the examiner for accounting. (lecturer, economics, college)

It is often claimed that administration takes more time than expected and planned from the primary tasks of teaching and research.

> I am both researcher and teacher and director of studies, which means being responsible for staff, so I am very divided. Both teaching and especially administration take too much time. I wish I had more time for research. I am paid for 50 per cent research, but in reality it is just about 30 per cent. (lecturer, biochemistry, university)

> I spend most of my time teaching, supervising and administrating. For research there is no time. (professor, modern languages, university)

> As a director of studies administration must go before everything. I am supposed to do research on 40 per cent, but feel very divided. The research suffers and subsidizes the administration. It is very embarrassing towards the research financier. (lecturer, sociology, university)

Such statements may be seen as standard responses due to values and interests represented in the academic hierarchies. However, the statistics in Figure 6.1, exemplifying the moderate increase in academic staff and the decreasing technological and administrative staff, while student numbers are rocketing, illustrate that there is a shift in basic operational conditions, that makes such comments more realistic and valid.

Academic identities and professional roles

The first question asked in the interview was: 'How would you characterize yourself with regards to your work and profession?' Of the respondents in the departments about forty percent considered themselves to be primarily teachers, for some of them followed by doing research and also some administration, for others with administration as second task and little chance for research. One-third characterized themselves as primarily researchers within their disciplines, but with some teaching, supervising and/or administrative tasks. A third and smaller group said their principal task was administration with very limited time for teaching or research. This group includes the heads of departments and some directors of studies. Many say their working conditions are very split between these different activities:

> This means that one is divided between four different demanding tasks: research, teaching, management and perhaps also to write

popular science. It is a bit too much to be professional in four occupations. (professor, physics, university)

Yet the primary professional identification is often quite pronounced:

I am a teacher in German. I am also an administrator, director of
studies and doctoral student, but my identity is still primarily
teacher. (lecturer, modern languages, college)

I want to characterize myself primarily as a researcher, but then I
fulfill various obligations to the university. (professor, biochemistry, university)

Whether research or teaching is primary, it means that the discipline
is the basis. Even for those with primarily managerial and
administrative tasks, like heads of departments and directors of
studies, a solid base in the discipline is necessary to be respected by
the academic staff. The overwhelming influence of the discipline on
the professional identity appears clearly in the answers about the
academic careers of the respondents and about which factors have
been of special importance for their professional development. Few
say they were driven by a very early and explicit interest for a special
subject like chemistry or languages. Instead, many talk about an early
history of induction into university studies as a process where chance
played an important role, but once they had detected their area, the
impact of the discipline appears to become dominant. Practically all
respondents mention major influence from various representatives of
their discipline during different periods, from committed teachers
stimulating their interest and curiosity and encouraging them to
continue their studies, strengthening their self-confidence. Many
mention supervisors during their postgraduate studies, and later on
'my professor(s)' and close colleagues, both in their own department
and in foreign university departments. Some of the women mention
the significance for them of having had a woman as a model and as
supervisor or professor, who had convinced them of their ability and
challenged their ambitions to proceed in their academic career. Of
course, important work and authors that have been more or less
decisive for their own academic production and work were
mentioned, but by far not as often as persons in the research
environment and network. A few especially mentioned the positive
atmosphere of their research setting. This kind of testimony of
discipline impact, however, is not discipline-bound to its character.
On the contrary, in this respect it is impossible to perceive any shades
of meaning between representatives of our six disciplines. Con-

sidering the often negative factors of extremely tough competition, uncertainties, the constant struggle for status and positions and the territorial fights for funds and reputation in the academic world, this picture of academic careers may appear idyllic. However, it brings out some important positive factors that encouraged and enabled these people to continue their academic path in spite of all the obstacles that must be faced. Very few of the academic staff explicitly mention their university or college as having had great significance in the formation of their academic identity. Still one can indirectly detect, from their statements about their work and plans, expressions of pride and commitment to their alma mater or to a newer institution, where they have contributed to its establishment or are engaged in its further development. Institutional traditions and rituals have not been so developed in Swedish universities and colleges as compared to England and the U.S., for instance, and associations of alumni are still rare.

> What I miss in this university and what should be more developed are traditions that unite students, faculty and leadership and create a sense of belonging, a special atmosphere ... The university itself is a 'society of knowledge' with specific traditions and ways of being that socialize and relate students, teachers and researchers to each other in a special way. (senior lecturer, sociology, university)

As concerns the relative influence on professional identity from the three principal roles of teacher, researcher and administrator a lot of information can be gathered from the answers to the interview questions: 'What do you most like to do in your work?' and 'What do you most want to accomplish?' Since the largest group (about 40%) identified themselves primarily as teachers, it is not surprising that a large proportion of answers to these questions concern issues of teaching/learning and relations to the students. Although research production is still the dominant criterion for qualification to academic positions, and many respondents consequently regret not having enough (or any) time for research, the most committed comments to these questions are those concerned with the students and the efforts to provide good teaching and learning.

> I really like to teach, but with my present position I cannot do so much teaching, and I do miss it. The most important thing I want to achieve is that the students themselves will like to achieve, that

they be really interested in their studies and develop their analytical ability. (lecturer, economics, university)

Most important is grammar at A level, it is the basis for everything later on. Often our students come directly from high school and their first contact with the university is important. I really think I can do a contribution there. (lecturer, modern languages, university)

The most enjoyable is the contact with the students, but it is also the most demanding. I get totally exhausted. (senior lecturer, biochemistry, university)

For the heads of departments we have not found any significant differences from the ordinary academic staff in their basic values and ideals for the university and its activities. Some department heads regret their failing professionality in management and administrative tasks and some, even in very big departments, mention how when newly-appointed they were entirely inexperienced in these matters and did not receive any professional training or support when they shouldered this role and tasks demanding a combination of leadership and management. All the same, they differ from most of the staff in that, like other university leaders (see Chapter 7), they are more knowledgeable about the university system and how their institution works as well as about the reform. This is an essential difference that equips the heads of departments with a wider outlook and awareness of extrinsic demands. Although this may be advantageous for their departments, it may also cause conflicts and increase their distance to the staff. How far is their professional identity affected by this temporary role? The role as head of department, as stated, implies heavy managerial and administrative tasks, but at the same time usually demands good academic status within the department. Most heads of department hold this office as a part-time task, even in quite big departments, in combination with teaching and/or research. However, they quite often admit that the latter sometimes gets neglected or postponed. Still, all heads without exception said they want and try hard to have some form of direct contact with students or with research. Eriksson (1997), interviewing forty-nine employees at four departments about demands on their heads of departments, summarized as much as twenty-two different roles these were expected to play – an impossible task. Before the present reform, it was quite common that the role of head of department was one that most took on reluctantly in order to fulfill an obligation to the department and to their colleagues. This image, however, does not at all agree with the picture we have obtained in our meetings and conversations with twenty heads of departments. In spite of the often overloaded and fragmented working situations that our interviews reflect (also well documented in Eriksson's study), most of them express an interest in this role and a genuine involvement in the possibilities to act and plan that the position and its authority provide them with.

> It is an important role to be the head of a department. You feel it. There is much one can achieve. A leadership function, a kind of manager. You take initiatives to all sorts of planning. (head of history department, university)

> As head of department I enjoy having influence and being able to see the results. We are going through much development, trying to foster more research in our department. I also like the personal contacts I make in this job. (head of department for modern languages, university)

> I like leading this department. It has a very good environment here, a good atmosphere, and we have a lot of success with our research. I like to make decisions which have an impact on both our educational offerings and our research plans ... I also find it interesting to go out into the international arena. It is good with international competition. (head of physics department, university)

Views on quality and on the 'Freedom for Quality' reform

How do the faculty describe their views on quality in teaching and research, and what do they think could be done to maintain and enhance it? These and other questions concerning quality were asked before questions about the respondents' knowledge about, understanding of and reactions to the higher education reform. A very common feature is that a majority of the respondents showed and expressed great uncertainty, when asked what they 'considered to be quality in teaching and research'. Not only was this something very difficult to formulate, but many also admitted or revealed that this was something they had not thought very deeply about. Quality is often taken for granted in the university.

> That was a difficult question ... I don't know if I have any good answer ... it is difficult ... but we all have a notion of what quality is ... After all we have this peer review system in research, then you try

to base your judgments on quality, but it is difficult to express it in words. (professor, biochemistry, university)

Among those who had a ready answer to the question, the most common was that quality in higher education has to do with the connection between research and teaching.

Connect teaching and research in a good balance! Don't have separate teaching and research staff. (senior lecturer, biochemistry, university)

Others talked about quality in terms of problem-solving, debating and questioning, in terms of the argumenting intellectual discourse, the production of ideas and the critical scrutiny of them.

It is the intellectual discussion that can result in good research. In education too, there is an aspect of intellectual discourse and critical thinking that has to be represented, also in the training for professional jobs like doctors and civil engineers, without being directly connected to research; that would be too limited. (senior lecturer, sociology, university)

Some preferred to describe quality in the results to be obtained or goals to be reached, from coarse formulations like producing well-educated and trained students, to more detailed descriptions of what the students should master when leaving the university. A criterion of quality that was suggested for professional education was whether the basic education given at the university would hold for forty years in the profession, i.e. have the students learned how to update their knowledge. Several added that the reputation of the university among students was an important indication of quality, affecting the recruitment, as well as the attractiveness of the students to the labor market. Less hesitant answers were given when the question was formulated as 'What could be done to maintain or enhance quality?' A common statement was that quality of teaching depends on a well-qualified faculty that could transmit enthusiasm of their subject, and this implied that all university teachers should have a doctorate degree and have the opportunity to do research, or in other ways, the possibility to be in touch with the latest development within their discipline.

Generally you do it by giving the teachers opportunity to do research. It is only when you may do research and deepen your knowledge that you can burn for something … Then you get high quality teaching. Evaluations are just peripheral. (senior lecturer, history, university)

> You need to support a level of professionalism for the teachers ...
> We need a channel for new ideas, and through research you get
> new ideas for teaching. University teachers need to have more re-
> search built into their positions. Teachers get dried up, tired, and
> have nothing more to give if all they do is teach all the time. (lec-
> turer, sociology, university)

A similar ideal was reflected also among teachers in the colleges,
although their present preconditions are very far from being optimal
for the realization of such ambitions (see 'Background' in Introduction to Part IV). In spite of the expressed importance of well-
qualified teachers, very few, on their own accord, mentioned
pedagogy and pedagogical training of the teachers as an important
condition for quality of teaching. When asked about it, some said, yes,
a pedagogical course given at the university can be useful especially
for new teachers; others considered it to be a waste of time and
believed that the only effective way of enhancing quality is to deepen
the disciplinary knowledge.

> There is certainly more attention paid to quality now, which is re-
> ally good. It should have some meaning for the value of teaching ...
> But this course on pedagogy and technology is just a waste of time.
> You need time to train yourself in physics, that is more important
> to your pedagogical talent. (senior lecturer, physics, university)

The few who raised this issue by themselves usually had a positive
experience and were very interested in pedagogical support. Some
mentioned deeper aspects of the development of knowledge and
student learning or epistemic aspects of their disciplines as the core of
quality.

> The most important thing I try to do is to provide a different way
> for teaching physics, a way that provides more opportunities for
> the student to make his own discoveries. I would like to achieve
> that physics could be made simpler. Behind it all are really very ba-
> sic thoughts – this is where we should start teaching, not really on
> the forms, but on these basic thoughts that are more persevering,
> that help you to understand the world around you. (senior lec-
> turer, physics, university)

> Most important is to socialize the students into a discipline that
> demands a certain way to observe the society and a certain way of
> reasoning and develop analytical thinking ... The contact with the
> students is immensely enriching. What I want to achieve with
> them is a radical break with the common-sense mentality, be able

> to argue about social phenomena in a different way, see beyond
> the immediate perceptions … (lecturer, sociology, university)

A few respondents mentioned the need for discussion between
colleagues concerning content, teaching, examination, etc., in order
to maintain and enhance quality.

> Good teachers and good cooperation between them. That the
> teachers talk to each other about pedagogical issues, discuss them.
> It is not enough just to go in and do your duty and then leave, you
> must participate in the pedagogical discourse in the department.
> (senior lecturer, physics, university)

Several departments have regular meetings or seminars for faculty
teaching the same course or program or for the whole department.
Some disciplines also have annual meetings with colleagues from the
other universities to share experiences and ideas. But in others, a
strong individual culture prevails, where each teacher is the specialist
and has his/her own course, and it would be conceived as an offense if
others were to question or even discuss it. Another factor, that was
often mentioned as important for quality in both research and
teaching, is international contacts and exchange of staff and students.

> Various types of international contacts are important for the qual-
> ity. Through exchange programs with outstanding universities for
> both teachers and students you get a yardstick, a criterion for cali-
> bration of your own performance. (senior lecturer, physics,
> university)

Several mentioned the time factor, both for teachers and students,
and many complained about being pressed for time. Good teaching
demands careful preparation and time for renewal of content and
methods. That good research requires concentration during longer
periods is generally presumed. That the same is valid for good
teaching was emphasized in a couple of interviews. On the other hand
there was also the suggestion that 'we could become more effective in
our use of time'. These responses should also be seen in relation to the
reduction of technical and administrative staff.

Evaluation and assessment of courses, programs and research were
mentioned as instruments for quality assurance of some value, but
many expressed some skepticism about their usefulness and thought
that evaluation should be used moderately, since it is time-consuming
and costly.

Concerning research, most respondents felt that it has its quality
assurance system through the international research community with

peer judgments of both *ex ante* and *ex post* forms. A pervading theme was the concern over the strong present trend where research funds, both Swedish and EU funds, shift from basic research to more applied, so-called strategic research. This reaction should be seen in connection with results from the Carnegie Study, according to which, already in 1992, 'the quota of Swedish scholars receiving external grants [i.e. not from their own institution] for research was higher than those of other European countries' (Enders and Teichler 1994, p.20). This fact, however, does not necessarily imply a shift from basic to strategic research.

Towards the end of the interview questions were asked concerning the knowledge about and attitudes to the recent reform. Among regular faculty about a third were rather uncertain about the content of the H-93 reform, a few of them did not know anything and said they were not interested. Among the two-thirds a minority was well acquainted with the reform, and some of them expressed clear appreciation of it. Although the reform has not met with strong criticism and there have been no signs of open resistance to it (as was the case with the H-77 reform), a clear trait in the interviews is that the H-93 reform is often downplayed, i.e. the significance of it is frequently questioned. Many respondents maintained that the various measures taken recently at their institutions were not due to the reform but to 'a new leadership in the university' or because it was 'in the air' or an 'international trend' and would have happened anyway, and very few expected the reform to have any significant long-term impact. This could be interpreted as a strategy used to highlight own initiatives, and perhaps also as a more sophisticated form of resistance to the reform at the dawning insight of the new demands on the universities inherent in the widened autonomy. But it may also be the result of the continuous development during several years which was just codified in the H-93 reform document, and therefore did not raise much attention. Only a few respondents considered the reform to imply a radical change.

Conclusions concerning academic values, ideals and identities

Although most of our respondents were reluctant to enter into a more thorough exposition of their views on values and ideals of higher education and research it seems justified to maintain that within the universities practically all of them, in their ways of describing their professional activities and what they want to achieve, gave cues and indications of basically embracing what could be called academic values within the Humboldtian tradition. That is, the ideal university is an institution financed and protected by the State and guaranteed far-reaching freedom and autonomy, a place where highly qualified people do primarily basic research and teach students, who are learning and training to become independent and critical thinkers and professionals. The rather dismissive attitudes towards the obligations to contribute to the solution of problems in society that were expressed in our sample of academic staff in the universities (but not in the colleges) were somewhat surprising and may not reflect a predominant opinion. However, in the much bigger and more representative sample of respondents in the Carnegie Study, affirmative answers to the statement that 'faculty in my discipline have a professional obligation to apply their knowledge to problems in society' were lowest in Sweden (67%), compared to Germany (93%), the Netherlands (87%) and Britain (79%) (Enders and Teichler 1994, p.24). Perhaps, the various Swedish Government attempts and measures to direct higher education and research more and more towards utility have had an impact of increasing resistance.

Concerning professional identity our sample is biased in the sense that we have selected respondents who have some experience of teaching, and have thus excluded those who are entirely dedicated to research. This can be seen in the answers about activities and primary roles in that the largest group consists of those who identify themselves first of all as teachers. Whether primarily teachers or researchers, a large majority say they prefer a combination of teaching and research in their personal mix of professional activities. For this, different arguments are mentioned: they like both tasks; they consider them to be mutually inspiring and enriching; higher education has to have vital contacts with research and the research front; they appreciate the contact with students and also to be able temporarily to leave one task for the other; etc. Therefore, at least for our sample, it seems motivated to claim that professional identity implies a balanced combination of teaching and research. It is possible that this apprehension of academic identity reflects something of an official opinion, based on the long struggle for the right of university lecturers to use part of their 'teaching time' for research, in which the Swedish Union of University Teachers (SULF) has been deeply involved. On the other hand, results from the Carnegie Study (Enders and Teichler 1994, p.12) show that 'almost three quarters of the European academics report that they are interested in both teaching and research' although they 'frequently express concern that they face problems in keeping a balance between their different tasks and functions'(p.8).

That several professional identities for an individual may develop over time and even be simultaneously upheld seems reasonable and is most clearly exhibited in the interviews with heads of departments (and deans). It is striking how most heads of departments convey an impression of strong commitment and engagement for this task demanding a combination of leadership and management. This may be due to the strengthening of the leadership role of the heads, making it a more challenging task than before the reform. The importance of departmental leadership, not just management, has been investigated by Bennich-Björkman (1997a) in a study of how organization and leadership affect performance. The study covered seven departments, of which four were identified as innovative, while three were considered as stagnant. The significant difference between them was that 'a leadership presence is a crucial characteristic of the innovative departments, while the leadership absence signifies the stagnant ones' (Bennich-Björkman 1997a, p.5). It seems justified to talk about a professional identity as leader and manager of the department, placed on top of the basic academic identity. This can be seen in the similar outlook on values and ideals of the heads as ordinary academic staff, but also in a strong impression from our interviews that, for most of them, this role had implied an enhancement rather than an interruption of their basic academic identity.

Also in this study the impact of the discipline on academic identity is manifest, primarily by the emphasis of our respondents of the importance and impact of some teachers, supervisors, professors and colleagues within the discipline along the academic career paths. We can notice some typical traits within certain disciplines that might affect their views on the reform. Sociologists, for instance are generally more critical to the H-93 reform and also to the organization of their own institution. Some of them mention that this is 'their domain' where they hold expert views. Teachers in biochemistry and physics, on the contrary, often find it difficult to judge and have well-reasoned opinions about the reform or their own organization.

However, any clear differences in responses concerning basic values and identities or views on quality between the disciplines represented in our study cannot be discerned. Although our six disciplines cover the dimensions which Becher (1989) used to identify his 'academic tribes' (hard/soft; pure/applied; urban/rural), in the respects that we asked for, the homogeneity of responses is compact. The unanimity about the affinity between teaching and research may constitute the core of unity between disciplines, and might conceal differences in less crucial quality aspects. However, this basic communality in 'the profession-at-large' seems worth underlining, considering the internal rivalry and dissension undoubtedly thriving in the academic world. Concerning attitudes towards more extrinsic, utilitarian values and tasks there are more perceptible differences between universities and colleges within similar subject areas than between the disciplines generally. The greater dependence of the colleges on the commitment of their surrounding regions make them more apt than the universities to meet and comply with external demands. On the other hand, the ambition of the bigger colleges to obtain university status is reason for their emphasis also on traditional academic values.

Only a few of our respondents gave direct expression to their pride and appreciation of their own university or college. This may appear paradoxical since the mobility of academics between institutions is low in Sweden, and a majority spend their whole academic lives in one and the same institution. On the other hand, not having experienced other institutions might just be the reason for unconsciousness of the significance to you of your own university or college. This does not mean, however, that the institution is an insignificant factor in the academic identity.

With regards to quality issues, most of our respondents, on the one hand, not unexpectedly expressed confidence in the upholding of quality in research and teaching since it was considered to be more or less built into the processes of academic activities. On the other hand, however, many showed great uncertainty when asked to specify what they considered was quality in teaching and research. Again, as with basic academic values, the quality concept was not discussed much among colleagues, rather it was taken for granted. Yet, through their descriptions of what they considered important and what they wanted to achieve, one can see many examples indicating what meaning and action they put into their concept of quality. It was simply uncommon to talk in terms of 'quality', i.e. it is a good example of the tension and disagreement between externally formulated policy and the praxis and understanding among the academic actors.

Some reform impact, however, can be traced in the several assertions (most often by deans, heads of departments and directors of studies) that quality issues had been much more attended to recently at both faculty level and within the departments.

From the fairly comprehensive conversation, following from the many questions in the interview on issues of quality in higher education and research, one can also derive the strong professional influence on their implicit quality concepts. Of the three Models of Quality Control suggested by Rolf *et al.* (1993) (see p.29) the 'administrative', the 'professional' and the 'market' model, our respondents, not unexpectedly, express themselves practically entirely in terms of the professional model. The models do not reciprocally exclude each other and could therefore be seen as complementary. In our interviews, there are, however, few comments that could be interpreted as typical for the administrative or market models. In this respect, as well, any differences between the disciplines are hard to discern. One could expect, for instance, that within the economic subjects there would appear some interest for market models, but that is not the case according to our interview results. The values of the 'academic profession-at-large' seem to prevail.

Chapter 10

Impact of System and Policy Changes on Academic Work, Values and Professional Roles

Introduction

In this chapter we shall describe the changes in responsibilities, conditions and relationships at the basic level following from the H-93 reform and from other structural and policy change during the years immediately before and after the reform. We shall also try to track possible influences on academic roles and values.

The second half of the interview started with questions about perceived changes within the institution and/or departments during the past couple of years. This then led up to a conversation about the H-93 reform and the respondents' conceptions and experience of it as well as their reactions to it. When asked what important changes had occurred during the past 2–3 years the most frequently mentioned items are shown in Table 10.1.

The change expected to take place in the activities at the basic level, due to reform intentions and directives at state level, is not primarily conveyed as a direct message to academic staff to react and act upon. Instead, and in some respects after considerable delay, it is mediated through the policies and operations of the institutional leadership as a consequence of the reform and other simultaneous change in the environment and conditions of the higher education institutions.

We shall consider what space of action for change is offered to staff and leadership in departments and other types of basic units and illuminate factors which exert restrictions on this space and factors which exert a stimulating influence on change in the basic units. How do the new opportunities, obligations and restrictions agree with prevailing academic values? Do they affect professional roles and identities? The analysis is done with respect to the two categories of system change: structure and governance.

Table 10.1 Changes during the past 2–3 years, most frequently mentioned items (approx. 90 respondents)

Items	No. of responses
Impact of the new resource allocation system	31
Development of courses, teaching and examination	20
Change in organization and distribution of authority	19
Increasing competition and market economy	17
Quality awareness and measures	16
Decreasing resources	9
More students	8

Impact of structural change on conditions and reactions in basic units

According to responses to our interview questions about how the H-93 reform message had been perceived by academic staff, the much talk about freedom and the government slogan 'freedom for quality' had had a marked impact on expectations of a widened space of action for the basic units and an increased individual autonomy.

> Freedom! People are tired of homogeneity and that everything should be cast in the same mold. The reform emphasizes individualism, and that is in accordance with my own view. (senior lecturer, modern language, university)

However, several changes in structure at this time, as analyzed and discussed in Chapter 6, had an impact on the freedom and space of action for academic staff and leadership. In what follows we shall focus on how structural factors exerted impact on this new freedom. The examples of the new authority for and expectations on the universities to develop and initiate new courses and programs, on the one hand, and, on the other hand, to set up their own systems of quality assurance, will be analyzed.

Increase in the number of students and staff

As shown in Figure 3.1, the number of first year students increased by nearly fifty percent between 1989 and 1996. The rise in student numbers thus started before the H-93 reform (see Chapters 3 and 6), but as we have seen from Chapter 4 the reform was aiming at further quantitative as well as qualitative growth of higher education, and the number of student places has continuously been extended, also by the subsequent Social Democratic government during years of alarming unemployment figures.

The state funding of undergraduate education, on the other hand, decreased for the first time in the beginning of the 1990s with approximately 10 percent. As can be seen from Appendix 8, during 1985–1995 student numbers grew by 54 percent, while total staff increased with about 20 percent and academic staff primarily for undergraduate teaching with only about 12 percent.

Appendix 7 shows that the distribution of new student places is rather skewed with an increase at the colleges nearly twice as big as at the universities, which reflects government policy. Also striking is the very strong growth in some institutions, like the smaller universities and several colleges with more than 100 percent.

Already this quick growth in sheer student numbers, as well as in student categories, without an equivalent reinforcement of staff has had an impact on planning, administration of courses and students, as well as on the recruitment of new staff, which has often been difficult. All this, in turn, affects the preconditions for maintaining the level of quality.

> It becomes more difficult to keep and enhance quality in teaching with the strong stream of students and different types of courses. These students are more heterogeneous than we are used to, which affects quality, you can't keep the same level as before. It is alarming that student numbers are growing all the time. It becomes a bit factory-like. More and more we have to discuss economy. (senior lecturer, biochemistry, university)

A new resource allocation system for undergraduate education

The reform, as accounted for in Chapters 3 and 4, entailed another major change in structure, which had a thorough impact on the undergraduate education activities: a new resource allocation system, which implied a radical change from input-related to output- and performance-related funding of undergraduate education.

This part of the reform aroused mixed feelings among academic teachers. Sixty percent of the funding was to be dependent on the students' performance, expressed in the production of their credit-points during the academic year. This provoked a rather heated discussion on whether this new, performance-based allocation of resources would force the students through their studies with a lowered quality. Or, on the contrary, as was the policy intention, would it increase the quality of undergraduate education, since it obliged the teachers to give more attention to their students. Some claimed that this new funding system, at last, would lead to due appreciation and reward of excellent teaching.

This debate is reflected in our interviews by the fact that the new resource allocation system is the most frequently mentioned item of change (see Table 10.1), and for some of the respondents it was the only known aspect of the H-93 reform. Some teachers considered this quite revolutionary funding system disastrous:

> My spontaneous reaction when I read this was, that this is so mad that it must be a joke, but it wasn't. It is obvious that it puts quality in danger. Any unfit teacher or weak department, of course, can support itself by letting students pass. (senior lecturer, national economics, college)

More teachers, however, were optimistic about the impact on the quality of teaching and student performance and that this meant that it would stimulate both student care and pedagogical development.

> The new resource-distribution system is the biggest change. You have to develop a strategy, and I see that as positive. We are following up on our students now – not just disregard them as we did some years ago. We must increase our interest in our students, how they learn and develop. We are also discussing the students as individuals more, and we are working more intensively with the courses, evaluating more and making more changes. We do not want the students to choose another university. (senior lecturer, sociology, university)

The drastic reactions by the higher education institutions to this new funding system during the first few years, as reported in Chapter 6, indicate the great uncertainty and worry it brought about at all levels of the institutions, not the least in the basic units, which were exposed to the risk of having to decrease their staff. This overreaction, entailing an even larger intake of students than intended, caused highly overloaded working conditions in many departments, and our respondents often mentioned the increasing work strain and lack of time for the various tasks. This was especially conspicuous within the faculty of natural sciences where the largest increase in student numbers has occurred.

> Yes, it has become tougher, a much tougher climate. You have hardly time to think of anything else than that it must give profit. Especially in the role of director of studies you notice it, but everybody experience it, thoroughly. (senior lecturer, biochemistry, university)

Even if this may have been a temporary situation of extreme strain, and the student intake since then has become more normalized, the demand for greater care for the students and for the progression of their studies also involves a lot of time-consuming efforts. These must be carried through in competition with other rising demands on both research production and participation in various institutional obligations (Askling and El-Khawas 1997).

Explicit responsibility for quality

'At the university we have always cared for quality' is a common reaction by academic staff, when the quality issue is taken up. The new demands on the institutions for explicit quality assurance measures and programs for quality development have met with a fairly weak response from the teachers. These kinds of measures are often considered time-consuming, costly and bureaucratic and are sometimes interpreted as a sign of distrust. In Sweden, judgment of the examination results of undergraduate students is made by individual teachers, something that implies great responsibility and little or no public control, as there is no system of external examiners. This might partly explain the widespread skepticism among academic staff towards the effectiveness of administrative instruments for controlling and enhancing quality. Furthermore, the repeated changes by governments in the content and rules of quality assurance (see Chapter 6) have had a moderating impact on local initiatives.

> We have always worked with quality, and what made me most upset with the reform is that it tumbled down from above that now we shall work with quality. The only thing happening now is that we get delayed and it is much more laborious than before. (senior lecturer, national economics, college)

For research, peer control of both *ex ante* and *ex post* types is generally considered a system necessarily built into the international research community, but few see any need for a similar collective system for assuring the quality of education. There is also among academic staff an aversion to systematic market models, because these tend to neglect existing essential differences between a university and an enterprise.

> Thinking in terms of the market has been discussed a lot … but production of knowledge must not be compared to economic production. Factors influencing knowledge production have other characteristics. You must not let market metaphors steer. The often short-sighted market thinking can carry catastrophic consequences at a university. (senior lecturer, sociology, university)

Among those who consider the quality demands to be among the most important recent changes (Table 10.1) it is usually in the sense of raised awareness and vitalized internal discussions about quality. Only in a few cases are the more strict quality assurance measures referred to as a necessary instrument in a professional organization.

> The reform seems to contain a basic confidence in the professionalism of university teachers and researchers, but conditions must be laid down for it, since professional organizations aren't good enough at self-evaluation. So it must be combined with this type of instruments for quality assurance. I really think it is decisive for the autonomy that you have a real follow-up. (senior lecturer, national economics, college)

At the time of our interviews none of the participating institutions had been subject to the first audit of quality work that the National Agency of Higher Education is to carry out triennially (Askling and Bauer 1997). In recent reports from the agency (for example, Högskoleverket 1997d) in which reactions to and impact from the quality audits carried through are investigated, there are many signs of interest and commitment to quality and quality work by academic staff, but there are also difficulties mentioned. The large expansion of activities and shortage of time were mentioned as major reasons for not having succeeded, for example, in engaging the staff in the self-evaluations that constitute an important part of the audit process. It was also pointed out that the quality work is not well integrated and risks becoming a parallel activity which is looked upon as something that is stealing resources from the primary academic tasks.

> I am afraid that the quality work will become a separate lane beside the ordinary activities. I have reserved one afternoon every month, compulsory for all staff to participate in … It is a bit sad, it ought to have been initiated much more from within, than being pushed from the outside. (head of department, history, college)

This effect could perhaps partly be explained by the soft approach to quality control taken by the Higher Education Agency so far, by not requiring a closer integration of quality aspects into the regular operations of the universities.

Competition between quantity, quality and innovation

The purpose of the H-93 reform was to simultaneously teach more students, enhance the quality of higher education and renew curricula and types of courses and programs. The means provided to obtain these goals were the new freedom to establish courses, a performance-based funding system and institutional systems for quality development.

Freedom to establish courses and programs is a regained aspect of autonomy for Swedish universities after it was strongly restricted during the period of the H-77 reform. It is a change that is in full agreement with academic values and is welcomed at all institutional levels, not least in the basic units where the innovation is to be initiated. The fact that there has been an impressive offer of new courses and renewal of programs in all types of institutions lately (see examples in Chapter 6) can be interpreted as a strong positive reaction after a long time of suppression.

In one way this new opportunity for innovation fits well with the increasing intake of students and the new categories of students. But at the same time, the growing workload that follows from increasing student numbers, and the effects of new resource distribution rules, reduces the time and the commitment for the construction and planning of new courses and curricula. Whatever the attitude is to the new resource allocation system, it cannot be ignored since it has a decisive impact on the economy of the department. The criticism of this system has also been moderate, since most look upon it as both reasonable and fair, with the exception of the claimed misjudgment of the costs for some sectors or disciplines like the languages.

The new outlet for creativity in developing courses and programs and for the academic teachers' commitment to the educative task, in combination with the new resource allocation system, might have also led to an increasing interest in issues concerning teaching, learning and examination. As has been exemplified in Chapter 9, there are several expressions for such a tendency of a change in attitudes among the teachers. At the same time many turned down what they considered to be 'traditional pedagogical courses'.

How can this interpretation of changing attitudes be combined with the rather repudiating outlook on the new responsibilities for quality assurance and enhancement that the reform entails? First of all, these responsibilities are generally not perceived by academic staff as a part of the increasing autonomy, but as central directives to the institutions. Furthermore, they imply the insertion of an administrative model of explicit quality control on top of the existing implicit professional type of quality assurance and enhancement. This does not associate well with the idea of academic values and individual autonomy.

In a situation with increasing demands and a growing workload there is a competition for time and other types of resources between innovation, quantitative and economic growth and new forms of quality control. As a result, the latter is obviously considered the least stimulating and constructive challenge of the reform and apparently the least concordant with prevailing academic values.

Changes in governance, influence and roles

Chapter 7 showed the institutional leadership's reaction to the mixture of empowering and restricting appeals and measures directed to the higher education institutions by the H-93 reform. In Chapter 8 was shown how the new scope for different types of governance models and ways of distributing authority within the institutions were utilized. The mix of freedom and restrictions for the basic units and their staff is dependent on these choices and decisions that concern the entire institution.

On closer inspection, the much highlighted 'Freedom' turned out rather to be a number of new obligations and responsibilities. The radically reduced central regulation and the clearly widened institutional autonomy had to be met with some internal regulation and a strengthened collective responsibility and accountability; and the reform had secured the necessary authority of the rector to facilitate a transition to more self-regulative institutions.

In the following sections we will analyze how the internal distribution of authority and responsibility has affected working conditions and professional roles in the basic units as well as the autonomy and influence of the academic staff.

Changes in distribution of authority and influence

As we have seen, through the reform and other external demands, the role of the higher education institutions has become more important. Their responsibilities have expanded and their managerial tasks have become more complex. Universities are perceived to need both a stronger central leadership *and* devolution of responsibilities to faculties and departments: the paradox of 'centralized decentralization' (Hogget 1991).

> It is called decentralization, but the only thing that has happened is that tasks and responsibilities have been devolved to lower levels, but definitely no control. (lecturer, modern languages, university)

Whichever of the various models for internal distribution of authority that was applied by the institutions (see Chapter 8) it implied that new responsibilities and obligations were devolved to the basic units. It usually meant that these took over from central administration the responsibility for staff and economy. These tasks, however, called for a significantly growing workload, primarily on the heads of departments. Since no additional funding for administration accompanied these tasks, resources had to be transferred to them from academic activities. Not only had the heads of departments less time for their own research or teaching, but also the department secretaries, who used to assist faculty in various ways, were now fully occupied with managing the new systems for economy and staff administration. At some very big and rather wealthy departments, i.e. those with large external funding of research, administrative experts have been employed, while most departments had to manage within their existing staff. Some heads of departments considered this devolution of tasks to non-professional administrators like themselves to be both a waste of academic competence and a very ineffective and costly system, when compared to keeping a few administrative experts at central level for the whole university. Yet, hardly anybody wished to go back to the old system, since the new one, in spite of its deficiencies, meant increased authority over one's own affairs.

The space of action for basic units is dependent on how authority is distributed within the institution. When employing the 'hierarchical model' departments more often grumble about the power of the deans and lack of their own power to make decision. On the other hand in institutions employing the 'triangular model' heads of departments often feel pulled between the rector and their staff, between collegial loyalty and managerial duties.

> As head of department you are chosen by the department but the rector appoints you, and he looks upon you as his representative, so there is a built-in conflict, if the rector and the department would have different opinions on some important issue. But I feel primarily as elected by my staff. I think there is a rift widening between the departments and the central administration. (head of department, physics, university)

In the earlier mentioned interview study by Eriksson (1997) a majority of respondents said that they did not know what decentralization had meant for their department or what the responsibilities of the heads of departments were. Independent of the type of organization model, there appear uncertainties in the distribution of decision authority. This causes some difficult and disputed problems to be shoveled around. As a consequence of all this, in many departments academic staff perceive more of top-down directives than of increased autonomy on the department floor. This also seems to be the case within the colleges, in spite of their tradition of stronger institutional leadership and no intermediary faculty level.

> What we don't like is that our organization has become so centralized and hierarchical. It is so obvious compared with earlier that the goals for our activities down here are formulated up there. They make decisions about money and student performance to be reached and then we are told to do it. That's all. (senior lecturer, sociology, college)

The biggest difference in available space for action, however, is between basic units with a high proportion of external funding and those without (see Figure 6.2) that become totally dependent on the institution.

Another perspective of change in distribution of authority within the institutions is whether there has been any transfer of power and responsibility between academics and administrators. Is there a tendency towards bureaucratization? Kogan (1996b) has pointed out that bureaucratization can mean two quite separate things. The more traditional meaning is the growth of the power of non-academic administrators. Another meaning implies instead the move from individual and academic collegial power to power for the system or institution which results in a new structuring of decision-making.

Are administrators, after the reform, playing a more dominant role in the university or is it rather the academics that are taking more responsibility for administration? Generally, in order to manage the increased institutional autonomy, the institutional leaders need the support of a strengthened staff of experts, and more involvement of academics at all levels in the institution is demanded. An example of this is when academic heads of departments take on a heavy administrative load. At the same time the central administration is said to have increased in some institutions, in others been kept intact while in yet other universities part of it has been transferred to (new) faculty offices. In any case, it seems clear that the new institutional autonomy has brought a total increase in time for and persons involved in management and administrative tasks, and led to a bureaucratization mainly in the latter of the two meanings pointed out by Kogan. Whether the extended academic power over the management of the universities also implies a tendency for these academics to become 'bureaucratized', i.e. to change professional identity, is too early to tell, but there are indications:

> There are quite a few of us who believe that the central leadership and teachers and researchers are not talking about the same thing. I have a feeling that they have entirely different ideas about knowledge and higher education. They have become entrepreneurs and bureaucrats, even persons you could expect to have a more well-reasoned conception of higher education and its role in society. (senior lecturer, sociology, college)

Bureaucratization, as well as representing shifts in power, may also mean a shift in the modes of operation, characterized by, for example, institution-wide rules and the adoption of generic systems. The demand for institutional quality assurance systems, furthermore triennially audited by the Higher Education Agency, is an example both of a shift in modes of operation, that entails more administrative work for teachers, and of a shift from individual or collegial academic to institutional authority.

The conclusion must be that with some variation the relationship between the higher education institutions and the disciplines have changed. Greater responsibility for their activities has been taken within the basic units, but the distribution of authority has moved in the opposite direction and demanded stronger central leadership, while the authority of the spokesmen of the disciplines – the professor corps – has been delimited to their expert areas.

Changes in professional roles and academic identities

Academics have traditionally held a combination of teaching, research and administrative roles, while having a stronger basic identification with their individual specialized form of knowledge and its knowledge community as is confirmed in our interviews. However, this professional role of the disciplinary expert is under increasing challenge from internal and external demands and forces. (Maassen and van Vught 1996)

Askling and El-Khawas (1997) have turned attention to the variation and complexity of the tasks and functions of the academics today. The traditional model including teaching, research and administration is overly simple, they claim, and does not take into account the new aspects of academic work, primarily leadership and management at all levels (treated in the section above) and what the authors name 'special support activities'. These activities include, for instance, committees for student exchange and other forms of internationalization, IT development, gender and ethnic equality as well as special development units such as those for quality enhancement, pedagogical innovation and staff training.

> Decentralization also implies that everybody is expected to participate in new connections and activities. If you compare with a lecturer thirty years ago who did his teaching and then left without asking how his students were doing, the work-load nowadays is much bigger. (professor, statistics, college)

Furthermore, they point to the fact that even the primary functions of teaching and research have been subject to considerable change in conditions and demands. For the researcher role, it is mainly the intensification of demands for productivity and relevance for society and the pressure to meet growing requests for research cooperation with industry. Also, a trend of interuniversity research cooperation in big teams, further reinforced by the demands of EU research programs, entails a considerable increase in planning, writing grant proposals and administrating research work. While, at the same time, the competition for research funding on the whole is sharpening. The role of the teacher, on the other hand, has been put under pressure due to the strong growth of student numbers which brought with it a concern about the quality of the educational mission. The teacher role is being questioned on grounds concerning its professionality (for example, Elton 1992; Rolf 1993). The reform put new emphasis on the quality of undergraduate education and even centered it on student learning and development. This brings forth the dual role of the academic as teacher and researcher and further challenges the adequacy of many academics' strong identification as solely disciplinary experts.

The academics in our study testify to considerable pressure on their traditional roles. In this perspective, our questions concern what impact the increased collective responsibility for the institution, the changes in demands of administrative work and of research productivity and the challenge of teaching professionality have had on the apprehension of the professional role of academics in the department. The strains on the traditional concepts of the academic role seem to demand either further differentiation of staff or some kind of qualitative integration between the roles.

There are indications of a shift towards further differentiation, for example, that the roles as dean and head of department tend to demand more time and commitment as the leadership and management functions have become emphasized. Also there is a need to recruit experts on financial management and other specialties. From our interviews we get a strong impression that the leadership positions have become more stimulating and engaging with the new scope for decision-making and innovation, something which may, on the other hand, obstruct the possibilities of returning to research or teaching.

We have pointed to various forces that fragment the relationship between teaching and research like the growing student population, the pressure for research production and new modes of research cooperation and the proceeding differentiation within the disciplines; all demanding more specialization. These and other forces constitute serious threats to the deeply held belief among academics, also confirmed in our interviews, that the teaching and research roles should be integrated. Compared to the situation in some other countries with a trend towards differentiation of academic roles (El-Khawas 1995; Elton 1996; Fulton 1996; Bauer and Henkel 1997), in Sweden there appears to prevail an even stronger resistance against it than in some other countries and a tendency in the opposite direction, i.e. a striving for a strengthened integration.

In 1996, the government initiated an investigation, where one of its purposes was to upgrade teaching and managing tasks as qualifications for academic appointments (SOU 1996:166). Part of the investigation was an interview study with 25 senior academics. All respondents expressed a holistic view of the academic profession, arguing for one profession including all types of tasks, instead of a split into separate specializations. When the results of the investigation, in accordance with Swedish tradition, was circulated for comments from the higher education institutions and other stakeholders, the proposal that research, teaching and administration would be more equally valued was generally appreciated by the institutions (Askling *et al.* 1997).

The strong negative reactions in Sweden to forces fragmenting the academic profession probably ensue from the experience since the 1960s of separating teaching from research by establishing a university lecturer position that holds a total teaching duty (see Chapter 3). Since then, as the negative consequences have appeared more and more, there has been a struggle to regain the opportunities to combine the two tasks – a struggle in which the Swedish Union of University Teachers (SULF) has been very active. Swedish university teachers, thus, give evidence of still trying to meet the many new claims on their professionality during recent years.

> We must get away from this kind of post for teaching only that I and many others hold. It must become a matter of course that lecturers teach and do research. Perhaps it will take another 10–15 years. You notice the great difference when you talk to colleagues on the continent or in the USA. They can't believe that we are supposed to teach 400 hours. (senior lecturer, sociology, college)

A corresponding struggle for the integration of teaching and research is going on at the institutional level in the colleges that are either aspiring to be turned into universities, or to at least receive permanent funding for some research fields. Both of these aspirations are now being met by the Social Democratic government. It would seem justified therefore, to claim that with regard to this issue, government policy, institutional aspirations and academic values coincide. However, there is also a heated debate concerning the risk of splitting limited research resources to suboptimal research settings.

Changes in quality work and concepts

Raising quality of higher education is pointed out in the H-93 reform as the overarching goal in order to manage the transition to a 'knowledge society'. The reform outlook entails ambitions of reaching academic excellence in international competition as well as meeting market demands, strengthening relationships with the rest of society (see Chapter 4). After protracted negotiations between the government and the chancellor of the Swedish universities, the government's suggestion of a performance-based quality indicator control was abandoned for a process-directed audit of institutional systems for quality assurance and enhancement as recommended by the chancellor. In response to this (as described in Chapter 7), the institutions set up their own quality systems and programs with varying distribution of responsibility over different levels.

The question we are asking here – although as yet difficult to answer – is whether these new demands and responsibilities for quality have had any impact on the academics' work and their views on quality in their activities, as compared with the basic values and thoughts about quality reported in the previous chapter. As pointed out earlier, the many moves and manoeuvres by governments on this issue have had a detrimental effect. The messages have not been taken seriously in the basic units since the rules of the game have changed continuously.

One way of addressing this issue is to ask whether there has been movement from professional, i.e. academic, quality concepts to administrative and/or market quality concepts. It is also interesting whether challenge from or interaction with these two types of concepts has stimulated a development of the ideas about professional quality. An administrative model has stronger requirements for explicit quality criteria than the typically implicit criteria of a professional model (Frackmann 1992). Such demands are also derived from moves towards market models: customers must be better informed about the quality criteria and standards if there is to be effective competition.

The setting up of own institution systems for quality assurance and the demands for accountability, including quality aspects, have certainly emphasized the administrative model of quality compared to earlier voluntary *ad hoc* procedures. This also tends to incorporate within quality criteria more holistic or collective understandings of educational needs and institutional responsibilities. Such criteria are further mediated through the audit process by the Higher Education Agency (Högskoleverket 1996c). Experiences from the audits carried out so far are reported by the Higher Education Agency which has adopted a strategy for stimulating the development to self-regulative institutions (Högskoleverket 1997d). The reports indicate that there is still a long way to go until these new systems and messages will reach ordinary faculty, and even longer before they have been accepted as a constructive instrument for internal self-control of quality, something that is also seen in our interviews:

> The weak link in this, honestly, is that the higher education culture is hard to change, nor is it within the Swedish tradition to take this kind of grip on the whole institution. I must admit it is difficult. We have to embrace, if not all, so many more. It is meaningless if it stays on leadership level. (leadership, college)

Our data tend to support the idea that market models of quality are more alien to academic staff than administrative models. Yet, there are also signs that they constitute a challenge for some. For example, debates about conceiving students as customers raise salient questions about the balance of responsibilities for teaching and learning between students and staff and about what roles, if any, students should have in defining and assessing quality.

> Yes, my view of quality has changed a bit. Earlier I had a more idealistic outlook, being convinced that I knew best what constituted quality. What has definitely changed is my view that we teachers don't have the sole right to interpret quality, but the voices of the students are important and also of others in the environment. (senior lecturer, social sciences, college)

This is one of the rare expressions by our respondents, touching on quality as defined by external stakeholders and extrinsic values. In spite of complaints about the extra documentary and administrative work that the new quality assurance procedures involve, several testify to the positive impact of the internal discussions that have followed from them, and which have stimulated open exchange about the otherwise implicit professional quality concepts. The increasing emphasis on the educational role also challenges professional approaches to quality by shifting attention from criteria connected with disciplinary and research skills to those relating to the teaching and learning process.

Since the whole issue of quality in higher education is generally considered by faculty to be owned by the 'academic society', they believe that they themselves should be trusted to control and enhance it. Interpreted against the particular Swedish tradition of teacher-bound assessment and the non-existence of external examiners and peer reviews of undergraduate education, the new demands for transparency of process and accountability of results arouse strong defense reactions and critique, since they are perceived as encroaching on the individual and the collegial autonomy. As mentioned earlier, these demands can be interpreted as a questioning of the teachers' right and ability to examine students without any public control. But with the many stakeholders in, and definitions of, quality of higher education, it becomes evident that the quality concept is relativistic, something that could easily lead to the reaction that 'anything goes'. However, the point is that the quality concepts must not be arbitrary or gratuitous but should be based on criteria related to the chosen point of departure for the judgment (Bohlin 1998, p.46). The rising consciousness of a relativistic quality concept and the competing definitions from administrative and market perspectives may lead to a vitalizing impact on the development of the academic or professional quality criteria, as well as an openness to the relevance of criteria developed from other points of view. In our material there are several indications of the impact of the new demands for quality on behavior in the basic units and even on changing attitudes among some of the academic staff.

Conclusions: part IV

The analysis of change by means of our two-dimensional chart of purpose and distribution of authority (see Figure 4.1) showed movements in reform policy at macro level of strong decentralization from state to higher education institutions. On the purpose dimension, analysis showed an intention to strengthen both intrinsic values and extrinsic purposes, mainly in the direction of meeting market demands. Among institutional leadership (see Chapter 7), there are both an openness to society and market, not in the least for financial reasons, and an ambition to protect academic values, as well as a general welcoming attitude to the transfer of decision-making authority from state to institutions. In spite of further internal devolution of responsibilities, the general trend, after much initial uncertainty, must be summarized as a move towards stronger central authority within the institutions.

At the basic level among academic staff and heads of departments, although the general authority devolution from the state was welcomed, the following internal centralized move of authority is usually regretted. It has led to more work and to a decreasing space for collegial decision-making that appears to threaten the influence and authority of the basic units and the freedom of their staff; all this leading to a tendency to dissociation between institutional leadership and faculty. The institutional leaders are sometimes seen as bureaucrats, in some respects closer allied with state authorities than with their own staff, something which might motivate to categorize them as a 'new intermediary body'. This could be seen as if the old conflict-fraught relationship between the state and the higher education institutions is now possibly replicating itself between the institutions and the disciplines.

Although both tradition and new forms of governance, as well as several structural aspects, constitute frames that curtail possible action and initiatives by academic staff, there is still a widened space for action at the basic level, although strongly varied, due not least to economic differences. For example, in all institutions the renewal of courses and programs has been impressive, an indication of great capacity. Some departments with little external funding, however, are regretting that the available space cannot be fully used because of their weak economy. This restriction was particularly criticized since the new freedom for innovation was immediately followed by cuts in the budgets for undergraduate education, although partly concealed behind growing student numbers.

Another indication of a widened space for initiatives within the basic units is evinced in the generally quite enthusiastic attitudes of the heads of departments. In spite of the fact that their tasks have become more demanding and their working situation is often overloaded, no one wants to return to the old system, and they often express a feeling of being able to affect the development of their units. The position of head of department seems to have changed towards a more attractive and meaningful role, requiring a combination of academic leadership and management capabilities, something which might be leading to the emergence of an alternative academic career path.

Concerning the quality issue, we have seen that nearly everybody testifies to the conviction that quality in higher education demands that teaching and research should be kept together both within individuals and institutions, something which has also been strongly claimed by the Swedish University Teachers' Association (SULF). In practice, though, they are often difficult to combine, especially within the colleges considering their lack of staff with doctoral degrees and sparse resources for research. Moreover, the unquenchable status differences between research and teaching make a deeper integration between them difficult to obtain.

The new demands on systematic quality assurance in the institutions are often interpreted as a result of failing confidence in academic staff and as a form of central control. Only a few ordinary faculty members see the relevance and importance of enlarging the traditional implicit control of quality to a more systematic and public self-control. Similarly, few understand the positive implications for the universities and colleges of the Higher Education Agency audits of institutional quality assurance processes, in contrast to the originally intended direct state control of results by means of performance indicators.

Thus, rules and conditions in the 'arena of policy realization' (see Chapter 2) have certainly changed as a consequence of structural and governance shifts during the 1990s. Some of these tendencies are contrary to basic academic values, reducing individual freedom of both staff and students, and are consequently counteracted. Yet new frames, like the resource allocation system and increased legitimate power at institutional level, cannot be ignored by academic staff, since they have direct implications on their daily activities and will lead, as we have seen, to necessary adjustments within these new frames.

Given the stability in academic values that we have noticed, we hypothesize that changes in basic values will occur much slower, if at all. The fact that more academics have had to shoulder management responsibilities and administrative tasks might, however, be leading to an increased feeling among more staff of a collective responsibility. The academic staff usually show a solidarity in taking on new tasks and obligations. This could perhaps lead to a strengthened affiliation to the institution with its new-gained autonomy. Some changes in values, therefore, may occur concurrent with the pressure for new tasks and shifts in the roles for the academics. Even so, under the surface, the basic academic values seem to be as strong as ever.

Part V

The State, Higher Education and Knowledge Formation

Chapter 11

Transforming Universities
Interpretations and Conclusions

Introduction

In the preceding chapters we have described and analyzed change and continuity as Swedish higher education, towards the end of this century, is meeting increasing demands and is going through a major shift in the relationship between the State and the higher education institutions. Our intention with this study (see Chapter 1) is to describe and put forward some explanations, not only of processes and outcomes on each of the three levels – State, institution, individual/academic community – but also of relationships and processes of interaction between them, thereby possibly illuminating the patterns of change and non-change that we have observed.

We developed and differentiated the concept of autonomy – crucial in a decentralizing reform – by relating it to the two dimensions of purpose and distribution of authority in higher education systems (Chapter 4). This framework was used to analyze and draw some conclusions from our empirical data about change that has occurred within Swedish higher education during the past decade.

The great distance between the two major poles of our study – the values and conditions of knowledge formation in the basic units and of policy formation at state level – stimulated an ambition to contribute to the bridging of this gap through our multidisciplinary approach. In the study of the intermediary level of the system (Part III) we noticed that at that level much of the macro policy is interpreted and transformed to conditions and rules for the basic units.

Theoretical interpretations

We shall now analyze the results from the three levels by means of the theoretical models or metaphors of 'frames' and 'arenas'. Then the analysis will be continued in terms of the actors' capacity to use the available 'space of action', and the resulting realization of autonomy and self-regulation in the institutions will be discussed. The special 'case of quality' will be similarly analyzed. Finally, we shall draw some conclusions from our various analyses and discuss the situation of Swedish universities in transition.

Frame factors and arenas

Aware of the fact that 'existing structures have response sets that shape what follows' (See Chapter 1) we want to emphasize that reactions and responses to the H-93 reform cannot be understood without taking into account the framing factors caused by the history of the system. Reactions towards the H-93 reform, as they appear in our empirical data, are dependent on earlier structures and models of governance. Although formally disposed of, earlier system character- istics and earlier reform issues have been almost 'internalized' in the higher education institutions and among individual leaders and staff members. Thus, institutions do not start from scratch when they respond to demands and expectations on 'improvements' – whether imposed from outside or derived from internal initiatives. On the contrary, current structure and models of governance and manage- ment are being shaped on the basis of the impact of earlier reforms and of additional modifications, adjustments and changes (Dahllöf 1984).

Therefore, in order to understand reactions and attitudes towards the H-93 reform, and in order to examine the links between the macro and micro level change processes, one needs an almost 'archaeo- logical' knowledge of the system (which the overview in Chapter 3 is intended to provide) in addition to information about present preconditions.

In our study, for example, measures taken in the 1960s to meet the expansion of higher education at that time, still act as framing factors and influence the values and motivation of today's actors. A prominent example was the establishment of the senior lecturer position entirely for teaching within undergraduate education. An example from the 1970s was the introduction of the concept of decentralization, with reference at that time to ideas of democratization and corporatism. Those ideas have formed preconditions for the understanding of a later reform of decentralization, where, however, the same concept is used with a different meaning of both individual freedom and devolution of authority from the state to the institutions.

Certainly not just historic but also current frame factors have an impact. As has been pointed out by Höltta and Karjalainen (1997), with regard to the rapid expansion of the Finnish higher education system, the sudden transition from accelerating economic growth and almost full employment in the late 1980s to a deep recession and mass unemployment in the early 1990s shocked society at large. In this situation the universities were given a key role in the national efforts for economic and societal recovery, although with reduced funding.

In Sweden, similar ideas about the importance of the universities must have contributed to the positive attitudes that we notice among academic leaders and to the readiness among them to take an active part in the reform. Within the public sector, the higher education system was privileged, compared to the comprehensive schools and the health care sector. This fact probably also motivated the universities to seek more external funding, in order to be able to recruit excellent staff and become attractive for competent students. The institutions had to take care of themselves, and were encouraged to do so in a way that was congruent with their own values and goals. The state could no longer be expected to act as a guardian angel if an institution got into trouble.

Not just the system at large, but also the individual institutions are deeply rooted in their own history. We agree with Bargh *et al.* (1996), when they say that a university is like an archaeological site. Although in our investigation we have not had the possibility to undertake such in-depth studies of the six institutions selected for our study, and although we obtained a strong expression of common academic values, we could also discern differences, not only between universities and colleges, but also between universities with different traditions and history.

In order to deepen the understanding of reform outcomes and to bring out the importance of framing factors for processes and results – and especially of the differences in such frames – for two contexts, Lindensjö and Lundgren (1986) used the metaphor of different arenas for policy formulation and policy realization (see Chapter 2). At the time of that study of Swedish school policy and its implementation, strong central steering was still the dominating model of governance, and the results showed that by then the two arenas were clearly separated and the rift between them wide.

The issue now is whether, in the higher education field, the H-93 reform with its explicit devolution of authority and intended increased institutional autonomy has changed the distribution and contexts of policy formulation and/or policy realization; if rules, conditions and processes within these arenas have shifted and whether, in that case, this has led to a reduction of the rift between them and thereby also changed the conditions for reform.

Time and money are always important framing factors. A special aspect of the time factor for an analysis over the three levels of the system will be attended to here. There is a delay from state to basic level which implies not only less information and participation of the latter at an early stage, but also that the real impact of the reform decisions for those who are supposed to be the major implementers of it appears first after a considerable period when measures have been taken at intermediary level. In the meantime the policy formation goes on at both state and institutional levels and changes some of the conditions and rules that were just about to be reacted on in the basic units. At the same time the feedback mechanisms are often not well developed, and reactions and responses from below do not come through effectively to inform the ongoing policy formation processes.

In the following we shall analyze our data from all three levels through the perspective of change and continuity within the contexts and arenas of policy formulation and policy realization respectively.

The most important shift in the policy formulation arena is revealed by studying the network changes presented in Chapter 5. The change in government with the arrival in the autumn of 1991 of the Conservative Coalition led to the most prominent change in higher education policy since the H-77 reform. With Per Unckel as Minister of Education between 1991 and 1994, the extent and the pace of the policy changes in both process and content signified a break with the previous traditions of Social Democratic policy formulation in higher education. Guided by an ideology rooted in liberalism and the role of the individual in society, the Minister intended to use the favorable political support to carry out a major reform of higher education based on changes that the party had been advocating for quite some time. Thus, the corporatist arrangement for policy-making ended, replaced by a loose group of actors operating more like an 'issue network' than a 'policy community'. Mediation involved academic and business elites, instead of powerful trade unions as in the 1970s.

A clear and successful effort to co-opt the academic elites took place during 1991–1994, substantially mitigating the role of some of the traditionally powerful trade unions. The academics' strong presence on the public investigative commissions (begun by the Social Democrats with Högskoleutredningen in 1989) as well as their participation in a dialogue with the Ministry (evidenced by various meetings, seminars and hearings) was a major change in the policy formulation process compared to the bureaucratic and political hegemony of the early 1970s. Further change in this process was the tremendous speed in the formulation of policy and its passage in the Swedish Parliament. The primary factor for such a quick pace was the fact that the mandate for the government was only three years and there was an ever-present fear that the election could be lost in 1994. Although some academics complained about the lack of 'remiss' procedures (often replaced instead by very quick 'hearings') there was a general understanding and acceptance of the nature of this policy 'game', due to the academics' overall favorable view of the H-93 reform. This shift in procedures also brought the academic leaders close to the policy formulation arena, which made them not only well informed but probably also more comfortable with and dedicated to the reform intentions. The academic elites were certainly also influenced positively by the investment in higher education in terms of increases in both student numbers and in research funds (see Chapters 3 and 6).

However, some policy changes were not just the result of changes in political power. As we described in Chapter 5, there was increased awareness across party lines that society had changed in the 1990s. Starting in the late 1980s, new public management ideas which spread across industrialized nations reached their way to Sweden.

Policies such as the new three-year budget frameworks and the decentralization of decision-making and budget responsibility, clearly demonstrated these new public management ideals, and were enacted throughout the Swedish public sector. The weak Swedish economy was an additional factor, lending support to the view that an internationally competitive higher education system could improve the nation's competitive advantage and thereby contribute to the production of wealth. The new 'knowledge society' of the 1990s required a different view of higher education, one that moved beyond the centralized planning for precise job markets, and instead focused on a new form of education and the process of 'learning to learn'. With the H-93 reform, the higher education system was no longer primarily to be used as a tool for societal reform as it was in the 1970s – with efforts to strengthen democracy and improve social class equality – but rather was to stimulate academic excellence, putting quality first so that the confidence of students, employers, the State and the international academic community would not be lost.

Certainly the largest change in rules has been the retrenchment from strong state steering and the consequent adoption of flexible steering mechanisms which followed with the decentralized, competitive system. Here we see new tasks assigned to the higher education institution's board and an extension of the rector's decision-making duties, such as new responsibilities for internal resource distribution, quality assurance, organizational structure and the general economic condition of the university or college. All this could not be directly implemented but required the development of a 'local' policy formulation in the form of mission statements, institutional proliferation, strategic plans and quality development programs. This meant that the arena of policy formulation was extended, not only through the participation of academics in central policy-making, but just as importantly, through the larger reach and importance of the local policy formation process and outcomes. As we have seen (in Chapters 7 and 8), this extension initially caused great uncertainty and in some institutions, rash measures for far-reaching internal devolution of decision-making, which later had to be adjusted in order for the institution to remain united.

All this brought major changes in conditions on the arena for policy realization, which comprises actors at different levels of the institutions, but ultimately those in the basic units. Also an intermediary body, here the Higher Education Agency, has a part to play in the realization of a reform. What impact have the new policy and policy process involved in the H-93 reform had on this arena?

Our results show quite clearly that rules and conditions within the institutions have undergone considerable change due to the reform and to other concurrent events. In a short-term perspective the single most evident change in rules for institutions and departments, also as expressed in responses by teaching staff, has been the new resource allocation system for undergraduate education. With its radical shift from input-to performance-based resource distribution it has, as intended, led to increased economic considerations in general and for various types of courses, and turned the attention of leaders, managers and staff to the students, their recruitment and the progress of their studies. In combination with the strong growth in student numbers as well as in student categories this change in structure has had considerable impact on the working conditions at basic level. It demands more effort for teaching and examination and for the development of existent and new courses in order to keep up both quantity and quality of undergraduate education, and thereby secure maximal funding; all this at the same time as demands on research, administration and cooperation with the external society have also increased.

From the point of view of the institutional leaders, the overall expectations for expansion during the first years particularly saved them from having to make priorities and decide on selective financial support. The only limit, within a generous frame of study places – initially strongly overdrawn – was the innovation capacity of the staff. However, such undirected expansion also brought about a varied pattern of external connections and funding. This, in turn, caused imbalance between faculties and departments and research groups with different possibilities to develop their own links to external funds. In this respect, the more successful units became more independent of the institution and usually less loyal to other faculties and departments. This is most likely one reason for the increasing centrifugal forces within the institutions, mentioned by almost all institutional leaders we interviewed.

The second most noticeable reform changes in the arena of realization (but probably to become even more important in a wider time perspective) are the various consequences of the devolution of authority and responsibility to higher education institutions and their further distribution within the institutions. The impact varies between institutions, depending on frame factors like the size and economy of institutions and departments and on the different local governance models that have been chosen. It has also varied, already during the short time-span that we can now review, due to initial uncertainty and internal conflicts about the optimal way of organizing the institutions and of distributing authority and responsibility.

The measures taken by the institutional leaders in order to establish conditions for realization of the reform intentions – such as the development of vision statements, strategic plans and quality programs – broke with many expectations of more individual freedom among the academic staff. However, the creation of a more collective leadership through the establishment of vice-rectors and other additional academic leadership positions was intended as a step towards overcoming this gap in trust and expectations.

The kind of change that follows from the strengthening of leadership and management and from internal rules of more self-regulating institutions involves shifts both in influence and in types of decision-making. Departments have taken on increased responsibility and obligations for their staff and economy, yet the scope for collegial decisions appears to be shrinking while instructions from rectors' and deans' offices increase, something that affects conditions and climate within the basic units.

As we have seen, the H-93 reform aimed at raising the level of competition within higher education and thereby, it was reasoned, also the quality. Competition has also risen due to general trends in society and in the international academic world. Such trends, as incentive for status and authority – in a field already characterized by strong competitiveness and aspirations for excellence – have certainly had an impact on the institutional conditions. There is increased competition for funding and positions, for student places and for students; internal competition between faculties, departments, research groups and individuals; external competition among colleges to become universities and between universities both nationally and internationally; competition with a growing number of other types of organizations providing research and post-secondary education. All of it contributes to rising pressure on the higher education institutions, and consequently on the working conditions of staff and leadership with the consequences for the quality of higher education not at all obvious, and most likely not solely positive.

Several respondents comment that there is now more need for cooperation than for competition.

The Higher Education Agency, the latest intermediary body between government and institutions, acts on both the policy formulation and realization arenas, primarily by means of its tasks concerning quality in higher education. These tasks imply both assessment of academic standards and the scrutiny of the internal quality assurance undertakings. In the way the agency has interpreted the government's instructions and carries out its quality assurance activities it has taken on both a controlling and a promoting function. Its own strategy is to stimulate the development of Swedish universities and colleges to become truly self-regulating institutions. The major instrument for that purpose during the first period has been the auditing of local quality assurance and development programs.

The Agency can be looked upon as a coupling station and a buffer between the State and the institutions. It is part of central policy formation in that it interprets the government's commission to it in terms closer to the higher education institutions. The Agency contributes to the realization of central policy by challenging the institutions to take on their new responsibilities. By relevant feedback it keeps the state authorities informed about the progress of the institutions. Compared to the action by similar bodies in some other countries, it is a quality control done with 'kid-gloves' and with the major aim of providing support. The audits that the Agency has carried through are actually a judgment of how the new model of self-regulation has been implemented, a strategy which has been successful in activating the institutions in this respect.

The framing factors that we have here pointed to (and certainly many others) restrict the possibilities and alternatives for the actors – both those involved in policy formulation at central and at local levels – but even more so for those expected to realize the policy intentions. What is left of the intended room for initiatives and enterprise after these frame factor restrictions have been considered we have termed the 'space of action'. How this space is distributed and used within the institutions will be the topic for the next section.

Capacity to use 'space of action', realized autonomy and self-regulation

As indicated in Figure 4.1 the shift in state governance of higher education in Sweden has been from a highly centralized, utilitarian type 'social goals' to a decentralized, more market dependent type 'invisible hand'. With this movement of responsibility and authority from the state, a requirement is placed on the universities and colleges to develop their own self-regulation. The increasing dependence on market forces requires that the institutions become strategic actors on this market, again presuming a strong institutional self-regulation. Thus, the new space of action granted to the institutions must be used to develop their internal governance. In doing so they have to rely on their own capacity.

The actor/structure model for realizing autonomy through capacity to use the available space of action (see Chapter 2) helps us illuminate an aspect of the self-regulating university which is often overlooked – the capacity of the academics and the institutional leaders to fulfill the responsibilities which have been transferred to them during the change from a 'state control' model to a 'state supervision' model (see Chapter 1). Thus, judgments on the extent of university autonomy, i.e. what we call 'realized autonomy', should also include an analysis of these actors' capacities, including motivation and readiness to act. This model also raises the awareness of the fact that the available space of action is not equally distributed within an institution. As mentioned earlier, faculties, departments and research groups vary in what they can offer to the society and the market, and thereby also in their opportunities to establish networks and obtain external funding.

Two examples from our study can be used to exemplify the variation in space of action and capacity, and the consequential degrees of realized autonomy achieved: the creation of new courses and the establishing of a quality assurance system.

In the first case, through the H-93 reform the centrally regulated study-lines were to be replaced by locally formed courses and programs, i.e. the intended space of action was considerably widened. Although several structural forces had a restricting impact on it this space was still large. As we noted (Chapter 6) there has been an impressive creation of new courses, often courses that are multidisciplinary in their nature. This abundance clearly indicates that the capacity within the institutions (both competence and motivation) for innovation was high and the available space was used effectively, leading to a high degree of realized autonomy for the institutions in this respect.

In the second case, concerning quality, the devolution of authority to the institutions was also large. The institutions were granted freedom in forming their own systems for quality assurance and programs for quality enhancement, i.e. the space of action is wide. In this case, however, the readiness of the leadership and the motivation of the staff were in general comparatively low. Since these kinds of demands for systematic quality measures were entirely new, there was also a lack of competence and experience with methods for quality assurance. Therefore, as regards the case of quality, we believe it is fair to conclude that the institutions did not have the capacity – neither motivation nor competence – to match the space granted.

The case of the quality issue

The quality issue was chosen as a special theme because it may involve change in both values, mission and distribution of responsibility (see Chapter 1). It also reflects challenges of an expanding higher education system and new forms of resource allocation.

In Sweden, even more pronounced than in many other European countries, the strategy of 'freedom for quality' was hopefully regarded as the solution to the problems ensuing from the tendency towards mass higher education and declining resources. The government was outspoken in its H-93 reform policy with its intentions to raise quality and efficiency by providing universities and colleges with increased responsibility and a wider space of action. As a direct consequence of the major shift to more autonomous institutions, the rules on the policy realization arena changed, meaning that the already existing responsibility for quality of teaching and research was reinforced, greater obligations were laid on the institutional leadership and requirements were added for accountability.

It follows from this that responsibility for quality in higher education could no longer be a concern solely for the individual teacher, or even for small groups of teachers. There was a marked shift towards the need for united responsibility and a recognition that some must undertake the tasks. Without reducing the responsibility of the individuals, the demands on the leadership on all institutional levels have become pronounced. This shift can be followed in the way the focus of quality measures has changed: from developing teaching methods to increasing teacher qualifications, thereafter emphasizing evaluations, and, recently, to empowering institutions to develop their quality assurance undertaking.

The prescribed institutional programs for quality development and the accountability demands required some system for quality assurance and reporting of results within institutions, something which entailed new regulation, centrally initiated, as well as more administrative forms of quality assurance than before. As we have seen, most of our respondents did not appreciate this kind of change and doubted its effectiveness. In the realization arena common rules for quality assurance are often seen as encroaching on individual freedom, and may as much be looked upon as control of the teachers as of the results. A striking example is the difficulty of faculty to comprehend the obligations and necessary rules of self-regulating institutions and to see any benefits of internal self-control, since the immediate effects appear to run contrary to their basic values. As we exemplified above concerning the quality case, the available space for realizing autonomy was not effectively used. Although the future in this respect looks more promising, this past inability might have weakened the state authorities' confidence in the institutions on this issue. (The recent national legislation on effective quality assurance measures for graduate students may be a possible example of such lack of trust.)

The initial reform document was quite radical in its policy formulation of the quality issue, while the governments, afterwards, have shown much hesitation in how to handle it. By their indecision there has been a lengthy process and much scope was transferred to the intermediary bodies to form the procedures of quality control, delegating to them an influential part to play on the borderline of the two arenas. A manifest example of this shift in the policy formulation arena is the case when the University Chancellor managed to influence the public investigative commission in charge of establishing a quality system connected to resource allocation. By doing this he helped to prevent the introduction of the governments' system for general quality indicators in exchange for the development of local quality assurance systems. This has resulted in a model that is well suited to the responsibilities of self-governing institutions, while the national agencies have been more restrained in undertaking direct quality assessments. This is a policy meant to constitute a challenge to the institutions to take on as much as possible of the responsibility for quality by internal assurance and control in their own arrangement. However, not all institutions, and certainly not all academic staff, have understood the crucial difference in object between evaluation of academic standards and of internal quality assurance measures.

The declining ambitions and commitment by the governments concerning these matters also seem to have reduced the expected impact, however. Although the H-93 reform proposal can be read as a textbook example of transition to self-regulating institutions and a supervising state (Bauer 1996), the governments themselves have not always acted according to this governance model and its crucial principle of relevant feedback. One could claim that, compared to several other countries, Swedish universities and colleges have been less subject to pressure for accountability and quality control, and instead mildly encouraged and supported to develop their own systems and processes for it (Askling, Bauer and Marton 1998).

In perspective of the two arenas, one could say that the trend entails a widening of the formulation arena. There is scope for policy formulation concerning quality also within the basic units in that no specific model or procedure for quality assurance is prescribed (as it is in several other countries), but is left to the institutions and their basic units to form according to their own characteristics. However, it is on the intermediary level, through the overlapping responsibilities for policy formulation and realization, that most authority has been placed. Yet, it might take some time before this new situation is fully realized and dealt with in the institutions, and that the importance of self-regulation in this respect is fully comprehended by the staff.

As shown by our interviews with academic staff members the quality concept itself is problematic. By tradition in the universities it has meant excellence (not much further elaborated, but heavily loaded with associations to research). With the trend of mass higher education and the decline in support per student, there appears to be a problem with such a definition of quality: 'Means for achieving efficiency while sustaining quality in universities will be a universal concern', state Dill and Sporn (1995b, p.4) in their overview of implications of a post-industrial environment for the university. Such concern is also expressed by our respondents, but the consequences of it for the quality concept and the measures for assuring quality were not yet developed at the time of our interviews, although heads of departments and directors of undergraduate studies especially quite often mentioned the reform impact of stimulating and vitalizing discussions on the quality issue.

Although several of our respondents talk very hesitatingly about quality matters, there is an overwhelming homogeneity in one respect: quality implies that the two core activities, teaching and research, should be held together and be integrated in the teacher/researcher profession. This is a very strong statement in times when generic forces are fragmenting the relationship between teaching and research, and in several countries there are tendencies at differentiation with the academic profession. We have already interpreted this strong united opinion regarding the integration of teaching and research by Swedish academics partly as a consequence of the long period of separation between the two in Swedish higher education, an opinion further reinforced by the long and intensive battle for their integration by the Swedish Association of University Lecturers (SULF). This tendency is most clearly shown in the ambition of all institutions to raise the proportion of teachers with doctoral degrees, and in the colleges in their continuous struggle for permanent funding for research. However, a rather simple idea generally prevails concerning the interaction between teaching and research: The best way of improving the quality of teaching is considered to be deepening of the disciplinary or specialist knowledge of the teachers. This indicates that there is no profound professional inquiry and elucidation of the connection between research and teaching/learning behind this general statement. Rolf (1997) has pointed to the remarkable way in which the interest group organizations (in this case SULF) have sometimes taken over the argumentation. He suggests that the professionals and their institutions should develop 'more imagination in the caring for the knowledge they are claiming' (p.80, our translation). An interesting attempt in this direction is the theory of knowledge formation processes of learning and research that has recently been developed by Bowden and Marton (1998).

There is also this well-known and problematic bias or one-sidedness in the views on the two core activities. While the 'teaching burden' is a common expression, research is mentioned in terms of opportunity and reward. That research is provided with extensive quality assurance mechanisms is generally accepted, even appreciated, while similar procedures for teaching and learning are often looked upon as unnecessary bureaucracy. In research, quality is collegially maintained, 'the responsibility for course quality resides largely within the individual tutor alone, operating within a culture of private enterprise and professional judgment' as a foreign evaluation team of a Swedish program expressed it (Worcester College 1994, p.9). Rolf (1993), in an article on professionality and quality maintenance, states that the teacher role in many ways is parasitic on research, i.e. the professionally more established role of researcher lends status to the older but less developed teacher role. So, if the core of quality in higher education is primarily dependent on the combination and integration of teaching and learning with research, more attention should be conferred on the teaching/learning perspective.

The development of intrinsic professional concepts and criteria of quality in higher education is very important now, when competing interests, be they articulated by state authorities or by different actors on the market, are ready to apply their own criteria of quality to higher education and research. Such extrinsic concepts of quality are certainly also legitimate, but if they are not balanced with well-reasoned, explicit professional quality criteria there is a risk for what Elzinga has termed 'epistemic drift', and thereby for the universities to lose more and more of their specific mission, the development not only of the knowledge but of knowledge formation processes:

> At one level epistemic drift refers to shift of focus from internal quality control criteria – e.g. peer review – to external relevance criteria. At another level it refers to a corresponding shift of focus from the logic and problem sets and research agendas determined by the development of theory to those generated by mission-objectives and utilitarian goals formulated outside research. (Elzinga 1993, p.232)

This is valid not only for research but also for the formation of teaching and learning in order to balance the intrinsic and extrinsic values and requirements. Our respondents in this study also expressed predominantly academic or professional aspects and criteria for quality in higher education.

A problem is that the principal instrument for professional quality control – the peer review – has become questioned recently for several reasons (see, for example, Henkel 1997c, Newby 1997). The academic quality concept, criteria and methods may need a thorough survey and development in order to come up to the increasing and more complex demands on higher education and research that are emerging.

Hardly any of the respondents among the academic staff members mentioned more administrative quality aspects, for instance a well-functioning and well-managed institution or department. This is a sign of a predominantly individualistic view on quality, but it also reflects an unawareness, and perhaps ignorance, about the requirements of self-regulation. There are some considerations about extrinsic values and tasks, but little concern, if any, expressed about whether commissioned research or education ought to be subject to more rigorous quality control, apart from the market mechanisms. Higher consciousness among academic staff about these various quality perspectives and criteria seems to be needed, especially as more and more of the funding is to be obtained on the market and as the demands from the 'knowledge society' become more varied.

A primary group to pay attention to besides the professionals are, of course, the students. Opportunities for the students to affect development of quality according to their criteria may have decreased in that student representation in boards and delegations has been reduced lately. The reform goal that students should affect quality enhancement through 'voting by their feet', i.e. in free selection of courses and institutions, has also been thwarted through the restrictions on the number of students admitted into higher education. The major instrument for students to influence their education and training is now the course evaluations that are everywhere part of the institutional quality assurance systems. However, these evaluations are not always well designed (Toshach Gustafsson 1996), and even when they are students often complain that they do not lead to enough change. Part of an explanation for this may be that student and teacher considerations of what is essential in a course do not agree, but this would offer an excellent opportunity for a discussion of different aspects of quality and the possibilities for their combination. Although our data support the idea that market models of quality are usually alien to faculty, these models constitute a challenge that cannot be ignored. For example, debates about students as customers raise salient questions about the balance of responsibilities between students and staff and about what roles students should have in defining and assessing quality (Bauer and Henkel 1997).

'The students at the universities should meet a milieu where there is a well-reasoned and contemplated attitude to knowledge' writes Olausson (1995, p.33), and adds that it is not enough with more and better knowledge but that the students when they leave the university:

> shall have been offered the possibility to reflect on and acquire a critical ethical or moral attitude as to the use of the knowledge which they are carrying, ... something which demands a vital and intensive debate about this with teachers and with co-students during the time at the university. (Olausson 1995, p.35, our translation)

This view seems related to Barnett's (1997), expounding on levels of critical thinking as an essence of higher education.

These kinds of quality aspects in higher education could probably be agreed on by many university teachers since they correspond to ideal academic values, but what are the prerequisites for their realization? Both increasing student numbers and tougher demands on students' quantitative performance imply a more difficult situation for the universities and their missions. Here we meet with the restricting impact of various frame factors in the system. Concerning the H-93 reform we have already emphasized the potential effects of the new performance-based resource allocation system and its double perspective on quality: the risk that in the short-term the quality level will be lowered just to get students to pass, but in the long run the chance that the quality level will increase (due to increased attention to the students and their study results in order to improve the institution's reputation), both done in order to reach the goal of obtaining maximal resources. In a recent study of examination in Swedish universities (Högskoleverket 1997a), a similar picture is drawn of a quality conflict between ambitions to attain and reflect in the examination the goals of critical thinking and problem-solving competence (laid down in the Higher Education Ordinance) and to handle the growing student numbers and the pressed schedules of both teachers and of students (especially students who must meet the strict requirements of the state sponsored financial aid/loan system). The intentions and goals expressed in central policy and the ambitions and aims of many teachers and students in reality become severely curtailed by system factors and prevailing conditions.

New courses and more students render new resources. Efforts to uphold and enhance quality require resources. That the new demands for systematic quality assurance and accountability have met with some difficulties and resistance among academic staff is logical. There was, for instance, a clear change in interest when the first intended five percent of the undergraduate funding to be distributed according to quality criteria, was abolished. Not only is the economic compensation for high quality teaching non-existent, neither is there much individual reward for it in the form of meriting qualification, and nor does the Swedish national quality audit system reward high quality by contributing to clear status enhancement of well-qualified universities and colleges.

The existence of internal systematic quality assurance and self-evaluation are decisive characteristics of self-regulating institutions (Kells 1992). Our data illustrate that there is yet much to be attended to and accomplished in this respect in Swedish universities.

Conclusions and discussion

Let us now return to our point of departure in Chapter 1, the two poles of our study: the values and prerequisites for the knowledge formation processes at basic level, and the policy formulation process and reform decisions at state level. The comprehensive H-93 reform with its crucial change in the relationship between the state and the institutions has provided opportunity to catch sight of change processes otherwise buried within the system.

A general conclusion from our 'arena'-analysis is that the shift since the 1970s has involved a widening and overlapping of the contexts of policy formulation and policy realization, implying a strongly increasing significance of the intermediary level: the national agencies and the higher education institutions and their mediating roles between the two poles.

Thus in the 1970s the development of policy took place at state level. In strong contrast to this situation, the process of change during the late 1980s, further codified and expanded in the H-93 reform, entailed a strong movement of authority to the intermediary level, from the macro as well as from the micro level. Large responsibility for local policy formulation was placed on the institutions and their leadership, and the national agencies were used more as interpreters and buffers than as executive authorities. Also, in the process of implementing policy, the institutional leadership has now got a larger claim and influence on the rules and conditions.

Thus the earlier marked rift between the two policy contexts has been overarched. As we have seen, however, this change does not necessarily imply that the conditions for a successful reform implementation have improved. It implies a strengthening of the institutional axis versus that of the disciplines or schools, something that may appear opposite to academic goals. Therefore, conflicting motives and aims have moved closer – from a uniting criticism of external central policy and decision-making and of national bureau-cracy to more polarization and competition within institutions. As pointed to in the Conclusion of Part IV, there are indications that the clash of interests between the State and the universities, in some institutions is about to replicate itself between the institutional leadership and the academic staff, or to put it another way, between the institution and the disciplines.

However, reforms such as the H-93 reform, that significantly increase the space of action for the higher education institutions, i.e. intend to widen and deepen institutional autonomy, also presuppose the development of self-regulation within the institutions. This requirement is reinforced by the simultaneous shift in purpose towards more market relevance of research and education. Such reform – transferring responsibilities to local units – must build on a mutual trust between the levels. It requires greater correspondence between policy and values to become functional.

Underneath all the visible types of change in conditions that we can observe prevail the values on which activities are based and the goals towards which they are aimed. From our earlier analysis we learnt that in central policy making a considerable change in values has occurred since the H-77 reform, from strong social values and equality goals to emphasis on both intrinsic academic values and market principles with the common goal of raising quality. Among our academic staff respondents, traditional academic values are as preponderant as those that were expressed in the criticism by academic oligarchy at the time of the decision on the H-77 reform; and hardly anybody considers changes that occurred lately to be reason enough for any major shift in this respect. As has been frequently noted, the academics' formulation of values and ideals for the university are extremely stable.

If we try to characterize the general position of academic respondents in the purpose/authority scheme (Figure 4.1), in 1977 (according to the general criticism of the H-77 reform) they would have been placed in the 'security guard' quadrant with the typical 'Humboldtian' view. The movement taking place that we can discern (our interviews are not detailed enough to record minor changes) is in the direction of decentralized authority, while there are few signs of increasing interest for extrinsic values *per se*. Academics holding leadership and management positions, on the other hand, although giving evidence of maintaining the same value basis as the rest of the faculty, tend to show more readiness to pay regard also to utilitarian values and purposes, even if often motivated primarily by economic necessity.

Our interviews with academic leaders and staff provide ample support for the conclusion that, at the time of our study, the correspondence between policy and basic values was far from being reached. It seems as if traditional academic values include a concept of individual autonomy and freedom that becomes threatened by the increasing requirements of a strengthened institutional autonomy, i.e. the replacement of parts of state regulation with a developed self-regulation. In times of such value-loaded shifts there is a tendency to hold on to the old system (even though that had been thoroughly criticized) and, in this case, to prefer a steering and regulating authority at a distance, to a growing internal regulation and control.

Our study shows that motivation among academic staff to understand and accept the demands of self-regulation in order to keep and realize the autonomy now granted to the universities and colleges seemed rather low, but that among the institutional leaders, on the other hand, the insight about this has usually been high. Although several of their measures concerning reorganization, internal distribution of authority and new regulation have caused a widening of the rift between leaders and academic staff in some establishments, there are indications of an initial understanding of the necessity to strengthen the higher education institutions, even at the cost of individual and group interests. Such insight among academic staff is also promoted as the decreasing funds and limited ability of the State to act as a 'security guard' become more and more apparent, at the same time as competition from other institutions and organizations grows. Given such an exposed and vulnerable position in a changing and demanding environment, several of our respondents reflected upon the benefits of 'the Humboldtian university'.

Concerning the quality issue, our data provide evidence that internal quality assurance and control as an essential function in a self-regulating institution has not been satisfactorily emphasized. Focus has been mainly on methods, while many leaders have underestimated the significance of quality assurance and assessment as instruments for leadership and improved management.

Not only are universities important agents of change in society, universities have also been able to transform themselves as the societies in which they are integrated changed. This is confirmed and exemplified also in our empirical results. Major changes in structure and values of the post-industrial society, however, are now confronting higher education and research with unprecedented challenges. In his recent study of 'the Entrepreneurial University' Clark (1998a) claims that 'demands now mount upon universities more comprehensively and faster than they can handle – unless they take steps to alter their character' (pp.5–6).

To enhance the capacity of the universities to meet these challenges, all over the world the higher education systems have been subject to extensive governmental reform movements during recent decades. We have here reported on the 'Swedish case'. The question now is: Do Swedish universities – with their long tradition of extensive state regulation, combined with an internal 'culture of private enterprise' and strong individualization – have capacity and motivation to match the new space of action and to realize maximal autonomy? As we have emphasized, widened institutional autonomy under the H-93 reform does not primarily mean more freedom for the individual, but instead increased collective responsibility and necessary institutional regulation to establish the frames within which academic freedom can be practiced, while extreme individualism can be limited. As academic staff often do not experience as much new space for initiatives as they had expected, they often see the changes within their institutions as threats to their influence and interests.

In order for universities and colleges to meet the challenges placed on well-functioning, self-regulating institutions, it is important for them to develop the knowledge among all staff of their own system and organization, and to increase the understanding of the new conditions and environment that universities and colleges are facing today. If not, there is a risk that the new-gained space of action could be overtaken by other public authorities, become reduced through simultaneous structural change and concurrent government policy or get lost to market forces. There is also a risk that the opportunity for the realization of increased institutional autonomy could become totally dispersed, or reduced by prevalent attitudes and values within the institutions. In this context, Kerr's observation is well worth considering. He sees a tendency among academic staff to place:

> more emphasis on individual and group advantages and concerns and less on the overall welfare of the college and university as a self-governing community concentrated on advancing knowledge. (Kerr 1994a, p.132)

He continues:

> Historically, higher education has mostly been threatened from without, particularly its autonomy and its academic freedom; and it has been oriented towards defense against external intrusions. Now the greater threats may be coming from within, and higher education is not oriented so much toward internal introspection. (Kerr 1994a, p.135)

Seen in the historical perspective of Swedish higher education, it becomes obvious that the H-93 reform signifies a crucial change in the relationship between the state and the universities. It is essential then, if the change to a decentralized system is to be maintained, that state authorities play their new role strictly, allowing time for the institutions to take on these new responsibilities and reward them for doing so.

As we have exemplified, governments have not been able fully to keep the new contract with the institutions. They too, of course, are dependent on changes in society and must be able to react on trends in, for instance, economy, labor market and regional development, which more and more are affected by and affecting higher education and research as the importance of the universities for society has grown. Yet, if they really want to see universities and colleges take more responsibility under a self-regulating system, governments should be more aware of the balance needed between societal demands and prerequisites for knowledge formation. Constantly shifting frames and rules can be harmful to the development of self-regulating universities.

If self-regulation is to continue to be supported, transformation of the universities could now come from within. Considering the increasing requirements on the tasks and roles to be fulfilled by universities and colleges in the developing knowledge society (see, for example, Scott 1997) it is unrealistic that each higher education institution could handle them all, much less so with high quality. Clark (1998a, pp.5–6) talks about 'a demand-response imbalance in the environment-university relationship' in which '*demands on universities outrun their capacity to respond.*' Kerr (1994b) discusses what he calls the 'convergence model' of higher education, as in his opinion the best response, both to the new requirements for a more highly trained labor force and to the demands of young citizens for greater opportunity and equality. The convergence model effects this through the differentiation of functions among higher education institutions.

The new frames of the Swedish higher education system will probably stimulate a differentiation of universities and colleges. Institutions may, to a much greater extent than earlier, form their own mission, goals, governance and profile, so that together they can meet the growing demands on them, while protecting and enhancing the quality of their own delineated mission.

With this book, we hope to have contributed to a better understanding of the Swedish higher education system and to the possibilities for realizing autonomy in the universities and colleges at a time when they are 'to take steps to alter their character' and to form their own profiles and missions. The demands upon them are growing fast and will most likely continue to do so in the future. By taking a look at the past, we may have contributed some insights into the future.

Epilogue

We have discussed recent changes in higher education in Sweden, covering political decisions, their institutional mediation and the ways in which they were perceived by actors within the system. We have examined how political decisions affect institutional structures and how institutional adaptations affect the people in the institutions. This was presented against the background of the university in a period of change, in a period where the traditional university is facing serious challenges and doubts to its ability to survive in the new 'knowledge society' (Scott 1997). Our focus has been on reform of the university in Sweden, and our evidence supports Teichler's (1988, p.99) statement that although reforms may have far-reaching political, social and economic goals, it is very rare that they focus on 'to what extent learning in higher education is most successfully promoted'.

Thus, in this epilogue, we would like to comment on learning in higher education for a knowledge society by reversing our perspective from system to activities and outcomes and also making a conditional, normative turn.

So far, we have approached our main issue, change, by focusing on purpose, models of governance and main structures from the point of view of politicians, institutional leaders and academics. We have used the recent higher education reform for analyzing preconditions for and experiences of change but we have concentrated on system changes and not raised the question whether one kind of change would be better or worse than another kind of change, nor have we made judgment on what kind of changes will affect the basic activities of the institutions positively or negatively. We have used an actor/structure perspective and given voice to the more permanent actors in the system and their own perceptions of purpose, autonomy and their own space of action in the higher education system.

The turn we now will take is normative because we take our point of departure in a particular view of a better university, in some specific ideas about what kind of outcomes the university should achieve in terms of student capabilities. It is conditional because this particular view, these particular ideas, are used to exemplify the line of reasoning that derives from taking a certain view, certain ideas, and certain values as the point of departure. One could have chosen another view, other ideas, other values, and the structure of the reasoning would still remain the same: one starts with some reasonably explicit statements about what the university should achieve, and then one advances conjectures about what conditions might be conducive to the aims thus stated.

So, the following is an illustration of what taking a particular view of a better university, with some specific ideas about better outcomes achieved by the university, might imply for policies in higher education.

Teaching and research

To begin with we ask the question 'Is there anything said in the previous chapters about a better university?' Quite a bit is said about 'quality' and about the participants' thoughts about quality. If we use 'high quality in the university context' and 'a better university' as synonyms then we can conclude that most of those interviewed in our study claim that in a better university there is a strong connection between teaching and research (see above, for instance, pp.174–175, p.214, p.220, p.246). Contemplating the nature of this relationship strikes us as a reasonable way of embarking upon the normative turn. So how are teaching and research related, or – in the normative spirit of the present chapter – how should they be related?

Research

Let us consider research first. The idea of research is formation of knowledge which is new in an absolute sense. It is supposed to extend what is known, and when this happens, not only does the individual researcher learn, but also humanity learns. Because what human beings know together is widened. Important results change our way of seeing, our way of understanding, the phenomena studied. Seeing something in a new way amounts to discerning and taking into consideration other aspects of the phenomenon than we had previously discerned and taken into consideration. Not all research yields such results. In fact, most does not. But important findings are, however, always of this kind.

Teaching

One of the main tasks of the university is teaching. Yet we ask: Why teaching? The university surely wants its students to learn and teaching is surely considered as a way of bringing about learning. But this is certainly not the only way. Nor is this a necessary way, or even necessarily a predominant way. So instead of focusing on the relationship between teaching and research, we should focus instead on the relationship between learning and research. We have dealt with research very, very briefly in the previous section. Let us now look at learning at the university – what it is like, what it should be like.

Learning

So called natural learning is a by-product of the learners' partici-pation in social practices. These social practices do not thus have learning as their aim. Their aim might be the production of goods or services, or simply having fun. By trying to contribute to work or entertainment, for example, people become better at work or at entertaining each other. Such forms of learning are frequent in pre-industrial societies. Recently they have become objects of attention in the educational research community and have been referred to as instances of authentic learning (see, for instance, Brown, Collins and Duguid 1989).

Institutional forms of learning – and the university is certainly an institution – have in common that they are supposed to equip the learners for coping with situations in the future, outside those institutions.

All forms of institutional learning suffer from one, big dilemma, as old as institutional learning itself. While the aims of so-called authentic practices are very much located within those practices, when it comes to 'less authentic practices' their aims are outside themselves, so to speak. The existence of schools and universities is justified by reference to the fact – or rather to the hope – that they are enabling the students to handle situations other than the ones in which they are 'getting enabled'.

The higher the rate of change in society, however, the less we can say about the situations that the students of today are going to face tomorrow. The greater the dynamics of the working place, the greater our ignorance of what it is going to be like in the years ahead.

We can express the same idea in yet another way. The future is necessarily always unknown. But there are degrees of uncertainty.

And we would like to argue that the future we are preparing our students for is becoming less and less transparent. Or more and more unknown. Yet, what are the tools we can use in the face of the unknown? It is our knowledge, it is what we know. It is what is known. Thus, we are trying to prepare our students for the unknown by using what is known. As a result, the key question becomes: 'How can this be done?'

How can the learners develop capabilities which make them prepared to deal with the varying situations of their working life (and to a certain extent their civic life, as well)? Here we build on a developing theory of learning (Marton and Booth 1997; Marton 1998; Marton and Fazey (manuscript)). One of the theory's points of departure is that people do not act in relation to the situations they encounter, as such, i.e. in relation to them in an objective sense. Rather, people experience and understand situations differently and people's ways of acting in a situation are contingent on their ways of experiencing and understanding that situation. So the extent to which we can draw on what we have learned previously is a function of what in our past appears relevant from the point of view of the particular situation. Now, the reason why we understand the same situation differently is that we see each situation through our past, through our previous experiences, through our differing biographies. We see a situation from the point of view of what preceded it and we see what preceded it from the point of view of the situation. The core of the argument is that acts spring from the situations as they are experienced, hence we are arguing for the primacy of people's ways of experiencing the world. Thus, the most important form of learning is to learn to experience certain classes of phenomenon around us in particular ways. Engineers develop particular ways of seeing electronic phenomena, economists develop their particular ways of seeing their professional world, and so do doctors and nurses, lawyers and social workers, etc.

Developing a particular way of seeing amounts to becoming capable of discerning and simultaneously taking into consideration certain aspects of the phenomena in question, those aspects that are critical in relation to the particular perspective adopted. And the capability for discerning a particular aspect springs from having experienced variation in that particular aspect. If the students keep getting problems which are of the same kind but where the actual parameters vary they learn to use different parameters given that they recognise the kind of problem they are dealing with. If the students, on the other hand, keep getting problems which they have to formulate, define, and structure, the likelihood is much greater for developing capabilities for formulating, defining or structuring novel problems.

Thus, we would suggest that if you expect variation in working life, you should make use of variation in the educational setting. Students can only be prepared for variation among situations in the future by experiencing variation here and now.

An important point is that we may not be able to develop exact procedures for dealing with the situations embedded in the unknown future. We can not do so exactly because we do not know what those situations are going to be. But we can develop the eyes through which those who are currently our students are going to see varying situations in their future professional life. And we have to make sure that they are going to see those situations in such ways which will enable them as professionals to handle them (the situations) in powerful ways – by drawing on what they have learned long before anybody could even imagine those situations.

The main point is that the capability to see, the capability to experience, can be developed even if that which is going to be seen, that which is going to be experienced is, as yet, unknown. This has direct relevance for the knowledge formation process.

Knowledge formation

In research, entirely new knowledge is formed. This is the idea at least. When learning, the students form knowledge which is new for them, but not new for others – for example, it is not new for their teachers.

The most important research results enable humanity to see certain phenomena or certain classes of situations in new and in more efficient ways. The most important forms of learning enable the learners to see certain phenomena or certain classes of situations in new and in more efficient ways. And it is exactly here that the link between research and learning is to be found. The connection between the two rests with the similarity in the qualities that characterize their most fundamental forms.

The university could then be reasonably judged in terms of the extent to which it brings about such qualities. A better university would then be expected to be very good in bringing about capabilities (learning outcomes) and findings, discoveries (research outcomes) of the kind described above. This is what we believe the recent 'quality' debates should be focused on, but as Barnett (1992) mentions, the modern debates about quality have mostly taken place in a conceptual void.

In the following we attempt to partly fill this void, but we will restrict our presentation to the capabilities that the graduates develop. This does not mean that we consider the two other tasks of the university – research and service to society – to be less important. The restriction derives from the fact that the 1993 reform in Sweden (the main study object of this book) was largely motivated by, and focused on, improving quality in undergraduate education.

Individual and collective capabilities

According to the above line of reasoning, 'better learning' is more efficient in making the students capable of handling undefinable and varying situations in their working life. This sounds fair enough if we think in terms of individual capabilities. But what about the collective capabilities, that is to say, the capabilities of organizations, of a society, of the nation? Quite obviously, not only individuals, but also organizations, societies and nations have to deal with, cope with and master the diversity of an unknown future. It seems to us very reasonable to talk about the capabilities of units larger than – occasionally much larger than – the individual. And we believe that universities should be judged in terms of their contributions to better learning not only in terms of the outcomes of the individual, but also on what we will call the 'collective level'. Hence we are going to discuss the qualities of – and the possible paths to – better learning both on the individual and collective level.

Developing individual capabilities

We have declared above that in accordance with the particular view of learning taken as the point of departure in this epilogue, a core task of the university is to enable the students to engage in effective action in novel situations in the future. And the capability to engage in effective action is assumed to spring from being capable of effective ways of seeing.

This means that in different subjects, and in different parts of different subjects, we have to try to clarify what ways of seeing, of experiencing, we are trying to bring about. Now, as ways of seeing, ways of experiencing, are taken for granted as aspects of the experts' ways of relating to the world, they have to be found, discovered – or rather rediscovered. The teacher has to listen to the students, the teacher has to learn from the students, in order to reveal what is taken for granted by the students, but which should not be taken for granted – their preconceived ideas. And the teachers have to reflect on their own ways of reasoning in order to reveal what is taken for granted by themselves, but which should not be taken for granted – their habitual ways of making sense of the world which make them experts in the field.

In every field of knowledge, we can define the ways of under-standing phenomena – in terms of aspects of one's professional world discerned and focused on simultaneously – which underlie powerful ways of acting. And these ways of understanding can be developed through bringing about particular conditions of learning. On the other hand there are no logical, systematic relationships between general modes of teaching and the kind of learning aimed for. And of course, there can never be. The precise meaning of every teaching method has to be found in relation to different contents, and the kind of learning aimed for can never be derived from the teaching method. No, we have to turn the whole question around. We have to specify what 'better learning' means in different subjects and in parts of different subjects and examine the potential of different teaching methods – or entirely different arrangements – in terms of their potential to bring about the conditions from which the desired learning springs.

Achieving this is by no means a trivial undertaking. Who can identify and/or discover the ways of seeing that should be developed in the students? Who can find the way in which teaching can contribute to making this happen? And who can assess the extent to which it has actually happened? It has to be a staff with a very good understanding of the field of knowledge, parallelled with a great interest for and deep insights into the acts and processes through which knowledge comes into being within their particular field. It has to be a staff combining the mastery of the subject matter with the mastery of questions of knowledge formation within one's domain of expertise. But through history, knowledge and the acts of knowing have become separated. In most disciplines, the focus is on knowledge itself in a particular field of knowledge (such as mathematics, economics, law etc.) and not on how knowledge is formed (individually or socially) within those fields. On the other hand there are disciplines where we can find an interest for how knowledge is formed individually (for example, psychology, pedagogy) or socially (for example, philosophy of science, history of ideas). But these disciplines have an interest in questions of knowledge formation in the general sense. What we would need is specialization on the questions of knowledge formation within various fields and domains. To achieve this you have to carry out a partial rearrangement of the way in which knowledge is structured at universities, and developing questions about knowledge formation in different specific subjects into legitimate specializations within those subjects. (This argument is more fully developed by Bowden and Marton 1998.) This means that questions about learning and teaching would be dealt with in terms of the specific content of each subject.

Developing collective capabilities

In the section above we developed a line of argument about how capabilities characterizing better learning in our sense of the expression can be fostered in the students. But 'better learning' must be better learning also in relation to organizations, industry, society and the nation. Where do we begin in order to bring about 'better learning'?

First, one is tempted to believe that the higher the number of capable individuals within an organization or within a nation, then the more capable the organization or the nation is. However, this is not necessarily true. Once again, the whole is more than the sum of its parts. The capability of a collective is not only – or perhaps not even mainly – a function of the capabilities of the individual members of that collective, but of the particular pattern or mix of capabilities represented by them.

The capability of the collective – the work force of a nation, for instance – (has to be judged in terms of the level and range of individual capabilities and in terms of the variation and differentiation of capabilities within the collective.

Some frequently used measures of a nation's collective capabilities are the proportion of the population or percentage of age cohorts with completed education on different levels (primary, secondary, tertiary). As far as the quality or standards within levels are concerned, international comparisons are often carried out using standardized tests of achievement. What can be concluded from such studies is that, on the average, students from one country are doing better than students from another country in algebra, reading comprehension, English, etc. (as measured by the particular tests used).

What is captured neither by statistics about completion rates at different levels of the educational system nor by average test results from international comparisons is the multitude of capabilities in different countries, the complex of all the different competencies that are present in the population, in terms of differentiation, range and extent.

Not only individuals, but also collectives are facing an increasingly unpredictable future. How can, for example, a nation prepare for dynamic changes, diversity and variation in circumstances, conditions and demands? The fact is that greater variation in the capabilities of the work force enhances the likelihood of the match between varying demands and individual capabilities. In times of dynamic changes stability can only be achieved through variation.

The space of action

Throughout this book we have referred to the idea that the structure constituted on one level does not determine but constrains what the actors might do on the next level. On the level of policy, constraints are set up for what the institutions can possibly do, on the institutional level constraints are set up for what the actors within the institutions can possibly do. The political scientist points to the structure that delineates the actors' options and to the actors who may or may not make use of the options available (see pp.252–257). The educational theorist points to the frames that constrain what can be done – and to some extent what can be thought – within the institution and how much space of action there is left to the participants and to what extent they make use of that space (see pp.258–266).

Space of action and individual capabilities

The notion of space of action is interesting also in another way than just pointing to the boundary conditions for alternative deeds. To the extent the space of action is used and alternative courses of action are considered, the participants become aware of that which varies. To the extent different options are available for setting the goals for a professional education, for example, the participants become aware of the issue of educational aims. As Bowden and Marton (1998) point out: that which varies is likely to be discerned. So by widening the space of action the possibility for adjustment to local conditions is greater, increasing not only the participants' responsibility, but more importantly, increasing their awareness (since they can now consider more options). As mentioned in Chapter 1, Teichler (1988), in studying changes in governance of the higher education system towards reduced government control and devolved authority, has also found that such a change stimulated institutional initiatives and promoted diversity.

The space of action and collective capabilities

On the national level, the question now becomes how to create a space of action for the higher education institutions which allows for collective variation. As previously emphasized, the capabilities of the collective are not only a function of the competence of the individual members of that collective, but also of the particular pattern or mix of competencies represented by them. For example, it does not benefit the nation if there are hundreds of Nobel prize-winners in chemistry but no talented researchers in physics. In teaching, it does not benefit the nation if all universities adopt one type of teaching method (problem-based learning for example), thus neglecting all other types (varieties) of teaching methods. Therefore, it is not a singular excellence (competence) which is required, but rather a range of competencies which is crucial. It is not only variety in the same dimension which is important, but variety between dimensions as well. With a greater variation in the capabilities of the work force, the likelihood of a match between individual competencies and the varying demands on the nation is more pronounced. We have found in our research for this book that as early as 1974 one university was arguing along such lines (although their argument went unheeded). Criticizing the work of the U68 Commission (which was to prepare the groundwork for the major 1977 Reform), Uppsala university wrote that they have not:

> discussed what relationship exists between the nationally uniform Swedish university education and the difficult job market for academics. As the education is now organized, the repercussions are very severe if an oversupply of a certain type of career arises, due to [the fact that] all universities educate for precisely the same types of work [careers]. If one had allowed the university itself to profile

its education, it might have been an advantage for the national job market. (Remiss: Uppsala University, 27 November 1974, p.12)

Institutional autonomy, space of action, and variation

In this book we have mentioned the international trend towards greater degrees of self-regulation in universities and we have argued that this development is very much present on the Swedish scene as well. The transition to a self-regulating university can be seen as a widening of the space of action: with a higher degree of autonomy granted by the State and increased self-governance on the part of the university.

We also recognize the importance of understanding the space of action in terms of how much of the space is used by the actors (Lundqvist 1987), what we here call 'realized autonomy' (see Chapter 2, pp.34–35). The conclusion one can draw from this type of understanding of the space of action is that the extent to which a university is 'self-regulating' or the extent to which a higher education system has adopted self-regulation is an empirical issue based on the institutions' handling of the available space of action.

We would also like to stress that bringing about a larger space of action is not simply an issue of greater decentralization of state powers to the institutions. It is also a question of the purpose of higher education and its perceived role in society. In combining shifts in authority with shifts in purpose (Table 4.1), different aspects of institutional autonomy are impacted differently in the four models. Our summary of the Swedish case in Part II describes the shift in models from that of 'social goals' in the 1970s to an 'invisible hand' model in the 1990s, reflecting changes in both the distribution of authority and in the purpose of higher education. In Chapter 11, we discussed the implications of such a shift on the universities' space of action and how their realized autonomy has increased.

What Table 4.1 has not yet taken into consideration however, is how the four governing models (see Figure 4.1) support or hinder national variation. Now if we continue our line of reasoning that the unknown needs of the future can only be met by a population of diversely educated citizens, then it becomes quite crucial to widen the range of our theoretical tools. We would like to go beyond the debates on institutional autonomy, or at least combine such debates with our theory of 'better learning'. This would imply an evaluation of the role of the state in contributing to a higher education system which could foster national diversity, that is to say, increasing the nation's collective capabilities.

In various sections of this book we have referred to how the expectations of national uniformity were reflected in the Swedish higher education system, (for example, see pp.88–89, pp.162–164), which runs in contrast to our view of collective capabilities presented here. Recently, we have seen how the state has retrenched somewhat from the Swedish political principle of 'high and equal quality' (see pp.90–91) within all of the nation's higher education institutions in the face of pluralistic developments in society (see p.122–123) combined with a more diversified student body and increased demands from external interests (such as businesses). Yet emphasis should be placed on the word 'somewhat', as the principle of equivalence (see p.55) still remains strong, especially in respect of degrees awarded from the different higher education institutions. Thus, a complete turn towards increasing the nation's collective capabilities is not yet evidenced.

As for increasing individual capabilities, our study reveals that the space of action for this has dramatically increased. The capacity for individual academics to more freely plan their course curriculum and for the departments to more freely establish academic courses, often multidisciplinary in their nature, has led to more concern for teaching, learning and examination (see Chapter 10). However, this flourish of new 'activity' is somewhat misleading if one follows our line of reasoning for 'better learning'. While there is much discussion of quality education as one which increases the student's ability to solve problems and use critical thinking (which are goals outlined in the Higher Education Law), there is rarely an understanding or advocation for 'better learning' as we would describe it, with a focus on the knowledge formation process within the subjects, within the disciplines (see this epilogue, section 'Developing individual capabilities'). There is instead a general hesitancy for academics to discuss these issues at a deeper level, that is to say, to discuss their 'ideology' of higher education and research (see p.212). One exception was, however, given by a lecturer of physics quoted earlier who stated:

> The most important thing I try to do is to provide a different way for teaching physics, a way that provides more opportunities for the student to make his own discoveries. I would like to achieve

that physics could be made simpler. Behind it all are really very basic thoughts – this is where we should start teaching, not really on the forms, but on these basic thoughts that are more persevering, that help you to understand the world around. (p.221)

Transforming universities

In closing, we would like to go one step further. The model referred to in the previous section (Figure 4.1) depicts four different types of state governing models in terms of two orthogonal dimensions: purpose and authority. Now, this model suggests that 'cultural' and 'utilitarian' purposes are rival options. And so are the two kinds of authorities: 'centralized' and 'decentralized' with the associated driving forces 'social goals' and 'market demands'.

The question is whether the tensions in the model are apparent or inherent. Could we envisage a way to transcend the four types of state governing models, thus doing away with the scaffolding once our building (this book) has been completed? Could we envisage that on a deeper level the mission of the university (as far as undergraduate education is concerned) is to equip the students with the most powerful cultural tools humanity has produced in order to enable them to see and handle the world around them in the most powerful ways to the benefit of humanity? Is it possible to label such goals external or internal? Do they correspond to social goals or market demands?

We would like to argue that the development of capabilities on the individual level and on the collective level takes a fair amount of space of action – to allow for the necessary variation within institutions and between institutions. But 'better learning' of the kind hinted at in this epilogue will not come by itself. As we pointed out it takes the development of certain interests and certain insights. Such interests and insights are likely to grow given that there is a space for growth and incentives for growing. We would like to suggest that it takes the state acting as an illuminated and vicarious customer. A customer who knows and honors the value of better and more varied learning (as well as more varied types of learning) and one who acts on behalf of present and future generations. A customer who is able to appreciate the importance of mixing governing models so that various driving forces (from academics, from markets, from society) have the possibility of being met, without one force having a dominant role.

Thus, we would argue that no area of Clark's 1983 triangle (state, market, academic oligarchy) or the quadrilateral created by Becher and Kogan's 1992 extension (to include interests representing the public/social utility) should have a dominant role. Rather, it is the balancing of these forces which creates the best conditions for variation. According to our observations for the Swedish case, a profoundly successful 'transforming of universities' has not yet taken place, at least not when the reforms are seen from our normative perspective. Transforming society's expectations of universities in a deeper sense takes a greater awareness of what they are transformed from, and to, and why.

Appendix 1 Number of Full Time Equivalents (FTE) of academic staff at a selection of university faculties 1995/96

Faculty	Title		Women					Men					Total
			<34	35–44	45–54	55–59	>60	<34	35–44	45–54	55–59	>60	
Humanities	Lecturer	FTE	12	30	45	15	9	10	28	34	12	3	198
		FTE of which Ph.D.	2	2	4	2	0	1	2	1	2	0	16
	Assistant Prof.	FTE	2	36	22	4	0	9	46	16	2	0	137
		FTE of which Ph.D.	2	35	22	4	0	7	45	16	2	0	133
	Sr. Lecturer	FTE	1	47	103	47	33	13	79	183	44	42	592
		FTE of which Ph.D.	1	38	95	43	29	9	66	168	42	36	527
	Professor	FTE	0	2	12	3	8	1	13	58	38	38	173
		FTE of which Ph.D.	0	2	12	3	5	1	13	58	33	34	161
Natural Sciences	Lecturer	FTE	14	13	9	3	0	25	27	39	7	2	139
		FTE of which Ph.D.	1	2	1	1	0	3	4	3	4	0	19
	Assistant Prof.	FTE	14	29	4	0	0	60	102	10	0	0	219
		FTE of which Ph.D.	12	29	4	0	0	55	101	10	0	0	211
	Sr. Lecturer	FTE	7	28	40	15	10	26	174	210	67	36	613
		FTE of which Ph.D.	6	27	38	13	9	25	173	202	60	32	585
	Professor	FTE	0	2	7	1	1	1	22	79	42	30	185
		FTE of which Ph.D.	0	2	7	1	1	1	22	77	42	28	181
Social Sciences	Lecturer	FTE	34	70	172	68	32	51	89	167	41	19	743
		FTE of which Ph.D.	0	3	4	1	0	0	4	2	2	1	17
	Assistant Prof.	FTE	5	10	11	1	1	9	55	23	0	0	115
		FTE of which Ph.D.	3	8	11	1	1	9	53	23	0	0	109
	Sr. Lecturer	FTE	8	66	144	37	19	33	163	367	132	59	1028
		FTE of which Ph.D.	7	48	115	26	14	24	134	307	95	38	808
	Professor	FTE	0	0	16	2	3	0	24	132	51	25	253
		FTE of which Ph.D.	0	0	16	2	3	0	24	127	47	21	240
	Total FTE		97	333	585	196	116	238	822	1318	436	254	4395

Source: Högskoleverket (1998d)

Number of Full Time Equivalents (FTE) of academic staff at the colleges 1995/96

Title		Women					Men					Total
		<34	35–44	45–54	55–59	>60	<34	35–44	45–54	55–59	>60	
Lecturer	FTE	62	198	406	133	75	156	278	395	123	53	1879
	FTE of which Ph.D.	1	0	2	0	2	2	7	8	1	0	23
Asst. Prof.	FTE	0	1	0	1	0	0	2	1	1	0	6
	FTE of which Ph.D.	0	1	0	1	0	0	2	1	0	0	5
Sr. Lecturer	FTE	14	37	85	42	24	33	159	318	102	63	877
	FTE of which Ph.D.	7	31	68	29	22	22	136	213	57	29	614
Professor	FTE	0	0	0	2	0	0	1	10	3	3	19
	FTE of which Ph.D.	0	0	0	2	0	0	1	9	3	3	18
Total FTE		76	236	491	178	99	189	440	724	229	119	**2781**

Source: Högskoleverket (1998d)

Appendix 2 Facts about the Higher Education Sector in 1997

Students	Academic year 1996/97	Change from 1995/96	Proportion of women 1996/97
New higher education students	65,700	-1%	57%
Registered undergraduates	300,380	+5%	58%
Undergraduate degrees	35,000	+9%	60%
New postgraduate students	3,390	+9%	44%
Active research students	16,550	+6%	39%
Doctoral degrees	1,720	+8%	33%
Licentiate degrees	840	+3%	33%
	Fiscal year 1997		
Total full-time equivalent students of whom	249,750	+7%	56%
Universities and specialized professional institutions of higher education	160,610	+6%	51%
University colleges (excluding fine arts and health sciences)	69,950	+12%	57%
University colleges of fine arts	2,070	+4%	59%
University colleges of health sciences	17,120	+1%	88%
Total annual performance equivalents of which	206,230	+6%	57%
Universities and specialized professional institutions of higher education	130,900	+5%	52%
University colleges (excluding fine arts and health sciences	57,680	+12%	59%
University colleges of fine arts	1,970	+2%	58%
University colleges of health sciences	15,680	+0.5%	89%
Staff (FTE) at state, regional authority and private universities and university colleges of which	44,750	+1%	47%
all teaching personnel	21,060	0%	34%
Proportion of professors, senior lecturers, junior lecturers and postdoctoral fellows with doctoral degree	53%	+2%	31%

Appendix 2 Facts about the Higher Education Sector in 1997 (continued)

Costs, Million Swedish Kronor	*Fiscal year 1997*
Total higher education cost	37,600
of which	
State universities and institutions of higher education	26,800
University colleges of health sciences	1,100
Private universities and university colleges	2,300
Student financial support	7,200
Other	200
Net operational cost of state universities and institutions of higher education	26,800
of which	
Universities and specialized professional institutions of higher education	22,500
University colleges (excluding fine arts)	4,100
University colleges of fine arts	380

Source: Source: Högskoleverket (1998b)

Appendix 3 GDP per capita, percent of OECD average
Current PPP (Purchasing Power Parity)

1970		1990		1995	
Rank	Index	Rank	Index	Rank	Index
Switzerland	154	Luxembourg	143	Luxembourg	159
United States	148	United States	137	United States	138
Luxembourg	131	Switzerland	133	Switzerland	127
Sweden	**115**	Canada	114	Norway	121
Canada	108	Japan	110	Denmark	112
Denmark	106	Norway	109	Japan	110
France	106	France	108	Canada	109
Australia	104	Iceland	108	Austria	109
Netherlands	104	**Sweden**	**106**	Belgium	108
New Zealand	101	Austria	104	Germany	106
United Kingdom	98	Denmark	103	Iceland	104
Belgium	95	Belgium	102	France	104
Germany	95	Italy	102	Italy	102
Austria	91	Finland	101	Netherlands	101
Italy	89	Germany	100	Australia	99
Norway	89	Netherlands	100	**Sweden**	**95**
Finland	86	Australia	100	United Kingdom	95
Japan	85	United Kingdom	99	Finland	89
Iceland	83	New Zealand	84	New Zealand	87
Spain	67	Spain	74	Ireland	85
Ireland	56	Ireland	70	Spain	74
Greece	53	Portugal	59	Portugal	67
Portugal	47	Greece	57	Greece	61
Mexico	37	Mexico	32	Mexico	35
Turkey	28	Turkey	29	Turkey	29

Source: Lindlbeck 1997, based on OECD National Accounts and Main Economic Indicators.

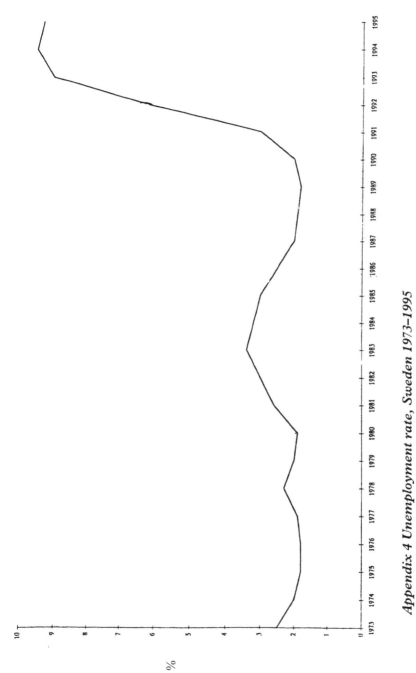

Appendix 4 Unemployment rate, Sweden 1973–1995

Source: OECD Economic Outlook 1995

Appendix 5 Budget deficit as percent of GDP, Sweden, 1968–1996

Source: Ekonomifakta, and Andersson and Elsässer (1997)

Appendix 6 State expenditures for higher education and research 1977/78–1983/84 (in billions of 1980 Swedish kronor)

Year	Teaching	Research	Other	Total
1977/78	1.937	1.477	0.417	3.832
Change from previous year	N/A	N/A	N/A	N/A
1978/79	2.161	1.635	0.191	3.987
Change from previous year	+11.6%	+10.7%	-54.2%	+4.0%
1979/80	2.237	1.691	0.180	4.110
Change from previous year	+3.5%	+3.4%	-5.8%	+3.1%
1980/81	2.289	1.710	0.172	4.172
Change from previous year	+2.3%	+1.1%	-4.4%	+1.5%
1981/82	2.271	1.748	0.171	4.190
Change from previous year	-0.8%	+2.2%	-0.6%	+0.4%
1982/83	2.242	1.800	0.170	4.212
Change from previous year	-1.3%	+3.0	-0.6%	+0.5%
1983/84	2.159	1.848	0.173	4.178
Change from previous year	-3.7%	+2.7%	+0.69%	-0.8%

Source: Universitets och Högskoleämbetet (UHÄ) (1985)

Appendix 6 State expenditure for higher education and research 1984/85–1992/93
(in billions of 92/93 Swedish kronor)

Funds Type	1984/85	1985/86	1986/87	1987/88	1988/89	1989/90	1990/91	1991/92	1992/93
Undergraduate education	4.731	4.898	4.965	5.060	5.020	4.995	5.011	5.229	5.716
Faculty funds	3.063	3.305	3.361	3.688	3.779	3.794	3.856	3.874	4.068
Other funds	2.458	2.604	2.360	2.368	2.203	2.203	2.306	2.578	2.732
Total for Higher education	**10.252**	**10.807**	**10.686**	**11.116**	**11.002**	**10.992**	**11.173**	**11.681**	**12.516**
Change from previous year		5.4%	-1.1%	4.0%	-1.0%	-0.1%	1.6%	4.5%	7.2%
State funds	2.536	2.598	2.736	3.118	3.408	3.519	3.144	3.401	3.219
External funds	0.877	1.022	1.199	1.417	1.630	1.706	1.663	1.621	1.937
Contract education	0.074	0.102	0.138	0.178	0.208	0.189	0.245	0.241	0.235
Total for external funds	**3.487**	**3.722**	**4.073**	**4.713**	**5.247**	**5.414**	**5.052**	**5.263**	**5.391**
Change from previous year		6.7%	9.4%	15.7%	11.3%	3.2%	-6.7%	4.2%	2.4%
Donations	0.189	0.239	0.294	0.218	0.237	0.217	0.321	0.445	0.378
Total funds	**13.928**	**14.768**	**15.053**	**16.047**	**16.486**	**16.623**	**16.546**	**17.389**	**18.284**
Change from previous year		6.0%	1.9%	6.6%	2.7%	0.8%	-0.5%	5.1%	5.2%

Source: Verket för Högskoleservice (VHS) (1994)

Appendix 7 Number of Full Time Equivalent students* in undergraduate education 1988/89–1997 (except for contract teaching)

	1988/89	1989/90	1990/91	1991/92	1992/93	1993/94	1994/95	1995/96	1996	1997
Uppsala University	11,633	12,202	12,799	14,343	16,013	17,430	18,936,	19,340	19,734	18,970
Lund University	17,792	18,184	19,438	20,668	22,986	25,586	26,476	27,575	28,286	28,532
Göteborg University	13,985	13,862	14,519	16,137	18,346	20,456	21,394	22,196	22,358	22,518
Stockholm University	15,337	15,386	16,026	17,689	19,090	20,589	20,762	20,763	21,684	23,932
Umeå University	6,345	6,448	7,104	8,168	9,794	11,312	12,596	14,218	14,619	14,487
Linköping University	6,887	6,843	7,269	8,024	9,254	10,358	10,832	12,070	13,019	14,124
Karolinska Institute	2,260	2,176	2,296	2,363	2,495	2,615	2,845	2,566	2,973	2,984
Royal Institute of Technology	5,033	5,885	6,264	6,696	7,220	8,467	9,056	9,498	9,447	10,044
Luleå University of Technology	3,035	3,129	3,382	3,682	4,191	5,404	5,345	5,918	6,357	6,590
The Swedish University of Agricultural Sciences				1,923	2,036	1,780	2,058	2,354	2,465	2,877
Chalmers University of Technology	4,698	4,951	5,096	5,424	6,098	6,780	6,747	6,911	7,104	7,278
Stockholm School of Economics						1,125	1,421	1,477	1,472	1,383
University College of Jönköping	1,368	1,464	1,679	2,026	2,338	2,960	3,005	3,418	3,707	4,034
University College of Borås	1,093	1,168	1,363	1,647	2,034	2,302	2,499	2,914	2,838	2,961
Dalarna University College	1,156	1,336	1,714	1,883	2,416	2,767	2,880	3,514	3,845	3,729
Gotland College of Higher Education			(101)	(231)	(300)	(394)	(468)	(378)	(724)	(626)
University College of Gävle/Sandviken	1,225	1,364	1,478	1,749	2,149	2,690	3,017	3,352	3,457	3,520
University College of Halmstad	755	868	1,027	1,271	1,519	2,007	2,297	2,668	3,046	2,954
University College of Kalmar	1,404	1,659	1,807	2,031	2,260	2,611	2,818	2,987	3,207	3,644

Appendix 7 continued

	1988/89	1989/90	1990/91	1991/92	1992/93	1993/94	1994/95	1995/96	1996	1997
University College of Karlskrona/Ronneby	211	558	654	952	1,130	1,332	1,435	1,623	1,725	2,201
University College of Karlstad	2,570	2,902	3,282	4,055	5,022	6,136	6,240	6,449	6,571	6,791
Kristianstad University College	1,037	1,098	1,278	1,666	1,870	2,087	2,299	2,615	2,774	2,956
University College of Skövde	617	700	842	992	1,209	1,609	1,890	2,434	2,660	2,522
University College of Trollhättan/Uddevalla			449	691	914	1,276	1,397	1,520	1,648	1,892
University College of Växjö	2,774	3,063	3,303	3,858	4,499	5,150	5,039	5,263	5,521	5,659
University College of Örebro	3,257	3,151	3,533	3,790	4,230	4,919	5,788	5,862	7,045	7,160
Stockholm University College of Physical Education and Sports					250	417	484	370	438	453
Stockholm Institute of Education	3,575	3,306	3,497	4,471	4,718	5,524	4,874	5,867	4,654	4,693
Malmö University College										(222)
Mid-Sweden University College**	2,852	3,164	3,592	4,519	5,218	6,846	7,119	7,079	8,677	9,299
University College of Mälardalen***	1,458	1,581	1,844	2,227	2,645	3,320	3,522	3,918	5,610	6,177
Södertörn University College										1,287
Erica Foundation						35	33	43	39	35
Gammelkroppa School of Forestry						16	30	18	18	18
Johannelunds Theological Institute								32	43	56
Stora Sköndal Foundation						157	167	177	180	211
Stockholm School of Theology						38	80	78	102	142
Örebro Theological Seminary						23	45	52	75	84
University Colleges of Arts in Stockholm	1,598	1,575	1,662	1,633	1,648					
University College of Dance						92	105	101	107	109
University College of Film, Radio, Television, and Theatre						125	137	112	121	138

Appendix 7 continued

	1988/89	1989/90	1990/91	1991/92	1992/93	1993/94	1994/95	1995/96	1996	1997
University College of Management in Graphic Production						165				
University College of Arts, Craft and Design						612	600	533	572	623
Royal University College of Fine Arts						189	191	220	218	211
Royal University College of Music in Stockholm						557	569	539	557	610
Stockholm University College of Opera						47	47	39	39	37
Stockholm University College of Acting						69	73	76	75	69
Ingesund College of Music						115	144	138	160	155
University College of Music Education in Stockholm							107	116	121	122
University Colleges for Health Sciences	14,586	15,386	15,655	16,185	17,291	17,325	17,651	15,159	15,269	15,927
Total	128,541	133,409	142,852	160,763	180,883	205,420	215,050	224,172	234,637	244,198

*The term full time equivalent student is new from 1993/94. It corresponds to the earlier term full time equivalent study place
** Before 1993/94: University College of Sundsvall/Härnösand och University College of Östersund
*** Before 1993/94: Högskolan i Eskilstuna/Västerås.
Source: Högskoleverket (1998c)

Appendix 8 Students and some categories of higher education staff in Sweden, 1985–1995[1]

Year		Academic staff			
	Students[2]	Professors	Other academic staff	Technical admin. staff	Total
1985/86	185,000	1,484	13,569	14,821	32,693
1986/87	180,700	1,547	13,225	14,878	32,535
1987/88	185,700	1,597	13,519	14,524	32,902
1988/89	188,400	1,666	13,272	14,649	33,180
1989/90	193,200	1,708	13,423	14,563	33,603
1990/91	203,200	1,803	13,345	14,235	33,365
1991/92	221,900	1,858	14,043	14,670	35,194
1992/93	241,900	1,879	13,718	15,034	35,958
1993/94	256,400	1,914	13,794	15,322	37,385
1994/95	269,800	2,002	15,524	15,355	38,722
1995/96	285,817	1,990	15,256	15,294	39,468
Changes 1985–1995	+54,4%	+34,1%	+12,4%	+20,1%	+20,7%

Source: Statistiska Centralbyrån (1996c)

1   Some categories of staff included in the total are omitted in the table
2   Number of students registered

References

af Trolle, U. (1990) *Mot en Internationellt Konkurrenskraftig Akademisk Utbildning.* Lund: Studentlitteratur.

Andersson, J. (1997) 'Den frihet väl kan bära.' In Acta Universitatis Upsaliensis *Uppsala Universitet Inför 2000-talet.* Uppsala: Uppsala universitet.

Andersson, P. and Elsässer, B. (1997) *Svensk Samhällsekonomi.* Stockholm: SNS.

Andrén, C-G. (1996) 'Examensrättsprövningar och deras effekter – ett fyraårigt perspectiv.' In Högskoleverket 1993 *Års Reform. Vad Blev Det Av Den? Sju Vittnesmål Efter Tre År.* Stockholm: Högskoleverkets skriftserie 1996:6S.

Ashby, E. and Anderson, M. (1966) *Universities: British, Indian, African. A Study in the Ecology of Higher Education.* London: Weidenfeld & Nicolson.

Askling, B. (1983) *Utbildningsplanering I En Lärarutbildning.* Studies in Curriculum Theory and Cultural Reproduction nr 7. Lund: Liber.

Askling, B. (1994) 'Institutional responses in Sweden.' In D. Westerheijden, J. Brennan and P. Maassen (eds) *Changing Contexts of Quality Assessment. Recent Trends in West European Higher Education.* Utrecht: Lemma.

Askling, B. (1997) 'Quality monitoring as an institutional enterprise.' *Quality in Higher Education 3*, 1, 17–26.

Askling, B. (1998a) 'Utvärdering för självkännedom.' In L. Åberg (ed) *Utvärdering – Ett Medel För att Säkra Eller Utveckla Kvalitet.* Stockholm: Forskningsrådsnämnden, Rapport 98:1.

Askling, B. (1998b) 'Sweden: Professional diversity in an egalitarian system.' In D. Farmham (ed) *Managing the Academic Profession.* London: Open University Press.

Askling, B. (1998c) *Institutional Governance and Management in a Context of Policy and System Change.* Report from Department of Education and Educational Research. Nr 1998:2. Göteborg University.

Askling, B. and Almén, E. (1997) '"From participation to competition." Changes in the notion of decentralization in Swedish higher education policy.' *Tertiary Education and Management 3*, 3, 199–210.

Askling, B., Almén, E. and Karlsson, C. (1995) 'From a hierarchical line to a vertical triangle. A new model for institutional governance at Linköping University.' Paper presented at the 17th EAIR Annual Forum, Zürich, August 1995.

Askling, B. and Bauer, M. (1997) 'The role, functions and impact of a National Agency in the evaluation of a decentralised higher education system.' Paper presented at the CHER conference in Alicante, 19–20 September 1997.

Askling, B., Bauer, M., and Marton, S. (1998) 'Swedish universities towards self-regulation – a new look at institutional autonomy.' Paper presented at the EAIR Forum in San Sebastian, 9–12 September 1998.

Askling, B. and El-Khawas, E. (1997) 'The academic profession: Evolving roles in diverse contexts.' Paper presented at the ASHE Annual Conference, 5–9 November 1997.

Askling, B., Karlsson, C. and Rydberg, L. (1997) 'Towards a diversification of academic tasks and the prospects of a multiplicity of academic professions.' Paper presented at the 19th EAIR Forum, Warwick University, 26–30 August 1997.

Atkinson, M.M. and Coleman, W.D. (1992) 'Policy network, policy communities and the problems of governance'. *Governance 5*, 2, 154–180.

Bargh, C., Scott, P. and Smith, D. (1996) *Governing Universities. Changing the Culture?* London: Open University Press.

Barnett, R. (1992) *Improving Higher Education. Total Quality Care.* Buckingham: SRHE and Open University Press.

Barnett, R. (1997) *Higher Education: A Critical Business.* Buckingham: SRHE and Open University Press.

Bauer, M. (1994) 'Changing context of quality assessment in Sweden.' In D.Westerheijden, J. Brennan and P. Maassen (eds) *Changing Contexts of Quality Assessment. Recent Trends in West European Higher Education.* Utrecht: Lemma.

Bauer, M. (1996) 'Quality as expressed in a Swedish reform of higher education and as viewed by university teachers and leadership.' *Tertiary Education and Management 2,* 1, 76–85.

Bauer, M. and Henkel, M. (1997) 'Responses of academe to quality reforms in higher education. A comparative study of England and Sweden.' *Tertiary Education and Management 3,* 3, 211–228.

Bauer, M. and Kogan, M. (1997) 'Evaluation systems in the UK and Sweden: Successes and difficulties.' *European Journal of Education 32,* 2, 129–143.

Becher, T. (1989) *Academic Tribes and Territories. Intellectual Enquiry and the Cultures of Disciplines.* Bury St Edmunds: SRHE and Open University Press.

Becher, T. (1997) Traditional and modern concepts of institutional quality. In Högskloleverket *Kvalitet-och Förbättringsarbete Vid Universitet och Högskolor.* Lecture given in conference in Uppsala 9–10 January 1997. Högskoleverkets skriftserie 1997:4 S. Stockholm.

Becher, T., Henkel, M. and Kogan, M. (1994) *Graduate Education in Britain.* London: Jessica Kingsley Publishers.

Becher, T. and Kogan, M. (1992) *Process and Structure in Higher Education.* Second edition. London: Routledge.

Ben-David, J. (1991) *Scientific Growth. Essays on the Social Organization and Ethos of Science.* Berkeley: University of California Press.

Bennich-Björkman, L. (1997a) 'Why universities need leaders. The importance of departmental leadership.' Paper presented at the conference "What Kind of a University?", London, 18–20 June 1997.

Bennich-Björkman, L. (1997b). *Organising Innovative Research. The Inner Life of University Departments.* Guildford: Pergamon.

Berdahl, R. (1990) 'Academic freedom, autonomy and accountability in British universities.' *Studies in Higher Education 15,* 2, 169–180.

Berg, B. and Östergren, B. (1977) *Innovations and Innovation Processes in Higher Education.* Stockholm: UHÄ.

Bergendal, G. (ed) (1990) *Praktikgrundad kunskap.* Lund: Studentlitteratur.

Bernstein, B. (1971) 'On the classification and framing of educational knowledge.' In M. Young (ed) *Knowledge and Control. New Directions for the Sociology of Education.* London: Collier-MacMillan Publishers.

Bernstein, B. (1977) *Class, Codes and Control. vol.3 Towards a Theory of Educational Transmission.* London: Routledge and Kegan.

Björklund, S. (1996) *En Författning för Disputationen.* Acta Universitatis Upsaliensis. Stockholm: Almqvist and Wiksell International.

Bladh, A. (1987) *Decentraliserad Förvaltning.* Lund: Studentlitteratur.

Blau, P. (1964) *Exchange and Power in Social Life.* New York: John Wiley and Sons.

Bleiklie, I. (1993) 'Lederrollen ved universitetene.' Bergen: LOS-centre Notat 9343.

Bleiklie, I. (1994a) *The new public management and the pursuit of knowledge*. Bergen: LOS-centre, Notat 9411.

Bleiklie, I. (1994b) 'The politics of university governance. Scandinavian experiences.' Paper presented at the CHER Conference, Enschede, 5–7 October 1994.

Bleiklie, I. (1996a) (ed) *Kunnskap og Makt. Norsk Høyere Utdanning i Endring*. Otta: Tano Aschehoug.

Bleiklie, I. (1996b) 'Rendering unto Caesar ... On implementation strategies in academia.' Paper presented at CHER Conference, 27–30 June 1996, Turku.

Bleiklie, I. (1997) 'Justifying the evaluative state – new public management ideals in higher education.' Paper presented at CHER Conference, Alicante, 18–20 September 1997.

Bleiklie, I. and Marton, S. (1998) *Linking Institutional Design with Policy Design – A Dynamic Network Approach*. Bergen: LOS-centre Notat 9810.

Bleiklie, I., Marton, S. and Hanney, S. (1997) 'Policy regimes and policy design – a dynamic network approach. The cases of higher education in England, Sweden and Norway.' Paper presented at the European Consortium of Political Research, Bern, 27 February–4 March 1997.

Blomqvist, G. (1992) *Elfenbenstorn eller Statsskepp? Stat, Universitet och Akademisk Frihet i Vardag och Vision från Agardh till Schuck*. Lund: Lund University Press.

Blomqvist, G. (1994) 'Förädlingsverk eller kraftcentrum? Det svenska universitetets väg från bildning till forskning.' *Tvärsnitt 16*, 3–4, 10–19.

Bohlin, I. (1998) *Sken och Verklighet. Kvalitet inom Universitetsvärlden i Relativistisk Belysning*. BVN rapport 1998:1. Stockholm: Byggforskningsrådets vetenskapliga nämnd.

Bohlin, I. and Elzinga, A. (1998) 'Rationalistiska och relativistiska perspektiv på kvalitet och kvalitetssäkring.' In L. Åberg (ed) *Utvärdering – ett Medel för att Säkra Eller Utveckla Kvalitet*. Stockholm: Forskningsrådsnämnden, Rapport 98:1.

Bourdieu, P. (1977) *Outline of a Theory of Practice*. Cambridge: Cambridge University Press.

Bowden, J. and Marton, F. (1998) *The University of Learning*. London: Kogan Page.

Braybrooke, D. and Lindblom, C. (1970) *A Strategy of Decision, Policy Evaluation as a Social Process*. New York: Free Press.

Brennan, J. (1995) 'Authority, legitimacy and change: The rise of quality assessment in higher education.' Paper presented at the CERI/IMHE Conference in Paris, December 1995.

Brobrow, D.B. and Dryzek, J.S. (1987) *Policy Analysis by Design*. Pittsburgh: University of Pittsburgh Press.

Brown, J.S., Collins, A. and Duguid, P. (1989) 'Situated cognition and the culture of learning.' *Educational Researcher, 18*, 32–42.

Callon, M. and Latour, B. (1981) 'Unscrewing the big Leviathan: How actors macrostructure reality and sociologists help them to do so.' In K.D. Knorr-Cetina and B.A. Cicourel (eds) *Advances in Social Theory and Methodology: Toward an Integration of Micro- and Macro- Sociologies*. London: Routledge & Kegan Paul.

Castles, F. (1989) *The History of Public Policy*. London: Polity Press.

Cerych, L. (1985) 'Collaboration between higher education and industry: An overview.' *European Journal of Education 20*, 2, 7–18.

Chin, R. and Benne, K. (1969) 'General strategies for effecting changes in human systems.' In W. Bennis, K. Benne and R. Chin (eds) *The Planning of Change*. New York: Holt, Rinehart and Winston.

Clark, B. (1983) *The Higher Education System. Academic Organization in Cross-National Perspective*. Berkeley and Los Angeles: University of California Press.

Clark, B. (1995a) 'Case studies of innovative universities: A progess report.' Paper presented at the Annual Forum of the European Association for Institutional Research (EAIR), Zürich, August 1995.

Clark, B. (1995b) 'Leadership and innovation in universities. From theory to practice.' *Tertiary Education and Management 1*, 1, 7–11.

Clark, B. (1995c) *Places of Inquiry. Research and Advanced Education in Modern Universities.* Berkeley and Los Angeles: University of California Press.

Clark, B. (1996a) 'Case studies of innovative universities.' *Tertiary Education and Management 2*, 1, 52–61.

Clark, B. (1996b) 'Substantive growth and innovative organisations. New categories for higher education research.' *Higher Education 32*, 4, 417–430.

Clark, B. (1997) 'Higher education as a self-guiding society.' *Tertiary Education and Management 3*, 2, 91–100.

Clark, B. (1998a) 'The entrepreneurial university: Demand and response.' *Tertiary Education and Management 4*, 1, 5–16.

Clark, B. (1998b) *Creating Entrepreneurial Universities. Organizational Pathways of Transformation.* New York: Pergamon.

Cyert, R. and March, J. (1963) *A Behavioral Theory of the Firm.* Englewood Cliffs, NJ: Prentice-Hall.

Dahl, S. (1997) *Grundläggande Högskoleutbildning.* Stockholm: Sveriges Riksdag.

Dahllöf, U. (1967) *Skoldifferentiering och Undervisningsförlopp.* Stockholm: Almqvist and Wiksell.

Dahllöf, U. (1971) *Ability Grouping, Content Validity and Curriculum Process Analysis.* New York: Teacher College Press.

Dahllöf, U. (1977) *Reforming Higher Education and External Studies in Sweden and Australia.* Stockholm: Almqvist and Wiksell.

Dahllöf, U. (1984) An educational magpie: Student flow analysis and target groups for higher education reforms in Sweden. In R. Premfors (ed) *Higher Education Organization. Conditions for Policy Implementation.* Stockholm: Almqvist and Wiksell International.

Dahllöf, U. (1991) 'Towards a new model for the evaluation of teaching: An interactive process-centered approach.' In U. Dahllöf, J. Harris, M. Shattock, A. Staropoli and R. in't Veld (eds) *Discussion of Education in Higher Education.* London: Jessica Kingsley Publishers.

Dahllöf, U. (1999) Det tidiga ramfoaktorteoretiska tänkarde. *Pedagogisk Forskning 4*, 1, 5–29.

Demker, M. and Bjereld, U. (1996) 'En decentraliserad forskning äventyrar kvaliteten: Bättre ge studenter ökade möjligheter till grundutbildning vid de regionala högskolorna.' In *Svenska Dagbladet.* 24 October 1996. Stockholm.

Departementsserie (Ds.1992:1) *Fria Universitet och Högskolor.* Stockholm: Allmänna Förlaget.

Departementsserie (Ds.1993:9) *Hearing om Resursberedningens Betänkande (SOU 1993:3).* Stockholm: Allmänna Förlaget.

Departementsserie (Ds.1994:24) *Den Offentliga Sektorns Produktivitetsutveckling 1980–1992.* Stockholm: Fritzes.

Departementsserie (Ds.1995:73) *Fortsatt Reformering av Budgetprocessen.* Stockholm: Fritzes.

Departementsserie (Ds.1996:35) *Studiefinansiering och Examina i Forskarutbildningen.* Stockholm: Allmänna Förlaget.

Department Series, see Departementsserie (Ds.)

Dill, D. (1998) 'Academic accountability and university adaptation: The architecture of an academic learning organization.' Paper presented at the CHER Conference, Kassel, Germany, 3–5 September 1998.

Dill, D. and Friedman, C. (1979) 'An analysis of frameworks for research on innovation and change in higher education.' *Review of Educational Research 49*, 3, 411–435.

Dill, D. and Sporn, B. (1995a) 'University 2001: What will the university of the 21st century look like?' In D. Dill and B. Sporn (eds) *Emerging Patterns of Social Demand and University Reform: Through a Glass Darkly.* New York: Pergamon.

Dill, D. and Sporn, B. (eds) (1995b) *Emerging Patterns of Social Demand and University Reform: Through a Glass Darkly.* New York: Pergamon.

Dowding, K. (1995) 'Model or metaphor? A critical review of the policy network approach.' *Political Science 42*, 1, 136–158.

Eklund, P. (1986) *Vem styr Förändringar? Lokala Lösningar på Centrala Problem.* UHÄ-rapport 1986:5. Stockholm: Universitets-och högskoleämbetet.

Ekonomifakta. See Näringslivets ekonomifakta.

El-Khawas, E. (1995) 'One professoriate, or many? Assessing aspects of differentiation among academics.' Paper presented at the 17th Annual EAIR Forum, Zürich, August 1995.

Elton, L. (1992) 'University teaching: A professional model for quality and excellence.' Paper presented at the 'Quality by Degrees' Conference at Aston University.

Elton, L. (1996) 'Task differentiation in universities: Towards a new collegiality.' *Tertiary Education and Management 2*, 2, 138–145.

Elzinga, A. (1993) 'Universities, research and the transformation of the state in Sweden.' In S. Rothblatt and B. Wittrock (eds) *The European and American University since 1800. Historical and Sociological Essays.* Cambridge: Cambridge University Press.

Elzinga, A. (1994) 'Disciplinary development and institutional change.' LOS-Centre Notat 9442. Bergen.

Enders, J. and Teichler, U. (1994) 'The academic profession: An international comparison.' Paper presented at CHER conference, Twente September 1994.

Eriksson, C. (1997) 'What does it take to lead a department?' Paper presented at the 10th Annual CHER Conference in Alicante, 19–20 September 1997.

Etzioni, A. (1968) *The Active Society.* New York: The Free Press.

Farnham, D. (ed) (1998) *Managing the Academic Profession.* London: Open University Press.

Frackmann, E. (1992) 'The German experience.' In A. Craft (ed) *Quality Assurance in Higher Education. Proceedings of an International Conference in Hong Kong, 1991.* London: Falmer Press.

Fulton, O. (1996) 'Which academic professions are you in?' In R. Cuthbert (ed) *Working in Higher Education.* London: Open University Press.

Geertz, C. (1983) 'The way we think now: Toward an ethnography of modern thought.' In C. Geertz (ed) *Local Knowledge: Further Essays in Interpretive Anthropology.* New York: Basic Books.

George, A. (1979) 'Case studies and theory development: The method of structured, focused comparison.' In P. Lauren (ed) *Diplomacy: New Approaches in History, Theory, and Policy.* New York: The Free Press.

Gerholm, L. and Gerholm, T. (1992) *Doktorshatten.* Stockholm: Carlssons Bokförlag.

Gibbons, M., Limoges, C., Nowotny, H., Schwartsman, S., Scott, P. and Trow, M. (1994) *The New Production of Knowledge. The Dynamics of Science and Research in Contemporary Societies.* London: Sage.

Government Proposition, see 'Regeringsproposition'.

Government Proposition (1986/87:100) *Budget.* Stockholm.

Government Proposition (1994/95:100) *Särskilda Utbildningssatsningar inom Högskolan.* Stockholm.

Government Proposition (1996/97:141) *Om Högskolans Ledning, Lärare och Organisation.* Stockholm.

Government Proposition (1997/98:1) *Budget.* Stockholm.

Gumport, P. (1997) 'Political economic challenges to autonomy: A case study of restructuring in American public research universities.' Paper presented at the conference 'What Kind of University?' London, 18–20 June 1997.

Gustavsson, C.G. (1995) *En ny Struktur för Statens Budget.* Stockholm: RRV.

Gustavsson, S. (1982) '1985 års forskningsproposition.' *Tiden 10,* 602–608.

Gustavsson, S. (1997) 'Varför inte lägga ned universiteten?' In S. Dahl (ed) *Kunskap så det Räcker? Arton Debattinlägg om Utbildning och Forskning.* Stockholm: SACO.

Harvey, L. (1997) 'Quality is not free! Quality monitoring alone will not improve quality.' *Tertiary Education and Management 3,* 2, 133–143.

Heclo, H. (1972) 'Review article: Policy analysis.' *British Journal of Political Science 2,* January, 83–108.

Heclo, H. and Madsen, M. (1987) *Policy and Politics in Sweden. Principled Pragmatism.* Philadelphia: Temple University Press.

Henkel, M. (1991) 'The new "evaluative state".' *Public Administration 69,* 1, 121–136.

Henkel, M. (1997a) 'The project and concept of academic identity.' Working paper for the Higher Education Studies Group, and book draft, Cowlinge, June 1997.

Henkel, M. (1997b) 'Academic values and the university as corporate enterprise.' *Higher Education Quarterly 51,* 2, 134–143.

Henkel, M. (1997c) 'Evaluation in higher education: Conceptual and epistemological foundations.' Paper presented at the CHER Conference, Alicante, 18–20 September 1997.

Henkel, M. (1998) Personal communication.

Higher Education Ordinance, See 'Svensk Författningssamling'.

Hogget, P. (1991) 'A new management in the public sector?' *Policy and Politics,* 19, 4.

Högskoleverket (1996a) *1993 Års Reform. Vad Blev det av Den? Sju Vittnesmål efter tre År.* Stockholm: Högskoleverkets skriftserie 1996:6S.

Högskoleverket (1996b) *Quality Audit of Uppsala University.* Stockholm: Högskoleverkets rapportserie 1996:28R.

Högskoleverket (1996c) *The National Quality Audit of Higher Education in Sweden.* Stockholm: Högskoleverkets rapportserie 1996:10R.

Högskoleverket (1996d) *Årsrapport för Universitet och Högskolor 1994/95.* Stockholm: Högskoleverkets rapportserie 1996:8R.

Högskoleverket (1997a) *Examinationen i Högskolan.* Slutrapport från Högskoleverkets examinationsprojekt. Stockholm: Högskoleverkets skriftserie 1997:39R.

Högskoleverket (1997b) *Granskning och Bedömning av Kvalitetsarbetet vid Lunds Universitet.* Stockholm: Högskoleverkets rapportserie 1997:23R.

Högskoleverket (1997c) *Grundläggande Högskoleutbildning: Politik och Planering eller Den Osynliga Handen i full Verksamhet?* Stockholm: Högskoleverkets skriftserie 1997:2S.

Högskoleverket (1997d) *Kvalitetsarbete – ett sätt att förbättra verksamhetens kvalitet vid universitet och högskolor?* Halvtidsrapport för granskningen av kvalitetsarbetet vid universitet och högskolor. Stockholm: Högskoleverkets rapportserie 1997:41R.

Högskoleverket (1998a) *Årsrapport för Universitet och Högskolor 1997*. Stockholm: Högskoleverkets rapportserie 1997:17 R.

Högskoleverket (1998b) *Swedish Universities and University Colleges 1997. Short version of Annual Report*. Stockholm: Högskoleverkets rapportserie 1998:24.

Högskoleverket (1998c) *Årsrapport för Universitet och Högskolor 1997*. Tabellbilaga. Stockholm: Högskoleverkets rapportserie 1998: 23R.

Högskoleverket (1998d) *Basic Statistics*. (Personal Communication). Stockholm: Högskoleverket.

Hölttä, S. (1995) *Towards the Self-Regulative University*. Juensuu: University of Juensuu, Publications in Social Sciences No 23.

Hölttä, S. and Karjalainen, K. (1997) 'Cybernetic institutional management theory and practice: A system of flexible workload for university teachers.' *Tertiary Education and Management 3*, 3, 229–236.

Hölttä, S. and Pulliainen, K. (1993) 'Model of an entrepreneurial university: A challenge.' Paper presented at the 15th Annual EAIR Forum, 16–18 August Turku, Finland.

Høstaker, R. (1997) *A Study of the Relations between Political Processes and Institutional Conditions in two University Faculties*. Bergen: LOS-Centre, Rapport 9707.

Husén, T. (1975) *Universiteten och Forskningen: En Studie av Forrskningens och Forskarutbilningens Villkor i Multiversitetens Samhälle*. Stockholm: Natur och Kultur.

Jenniskens, I. (1997) *Governmental Steering and Curriculum Innovations. A Comparative Study of the Relation Between Governmental Steering Instruments and Innovations in Higher Education Curricula*. Utrecht: Lemma.

John, P. and Cole, A. (1997) 'Networks or networking? The importance of power, position and values in local economic policy networks in Britain and France.' Paper presented at the Annual Meeting of the American Political Science Association. Washington, 28–31 August 1997.

Jordan, G. and Schubert, K. (1992) 'A preliminary ordering of policy network labels.' *European Journal of Political Research 21*, 7–27.

Kells, H. (1992) *Self-Regulation in Higher Education: A Multi-National Perspective on Collaborative Systems of Quality Assurance and Control*. London: Jessica Kingsley Publishers.

Kells, H. and van Vught, F. (eds) (1988) *Self-regulation, Self-study and Program Review in Higher Education*. Culemborg: Lemma.

Kerr, C. (1987) 'A critical age in the university world: Accumulated heritage versus modern imperatives.' *European Journal of Education 22*, 2, 183–193.

Kerr, C. (1994a) *Higher Education Cannot Escape History*. Albany: State University of New York Press.

Kerr, C. (1994b) *Troubled Times for American Higher Education. The 1990s and Beyond*. Albany: State University of New York Press.

Kim, L. (1997) 'Utvärdering av högre utbildning på nationell nivå – systemutvärdering eller kvalitetskontroll?' Paper presented at Högskoleverket and Uppsala University Quality Conference. Uppsala, 9–10 January 1997.

Kogan, M. (1984) 'The political view.' In B.R. Clark (ed) *Perspectives on Higher Education*. Berkeley: University of California Press.

Kogan, M. (1992) 'Political science.' In B.R. Clark and G. Neave (eds) *International Encyclopedia of Higher Education*. London: Pergamon Press.

Kogan, M. (1996a) 'Academic and administrative interface.' Paper presented at the IMHE seminar on staffing and institutional infrastructure, Budapest, Hungary, 29–30 August 1996.

Kogan, M. (1996b) 'Academics and administrators in higher education.' Paper presented at the CHER Conference, Turku, 27–29 June 1996.

Kogan, M. (1996c) 'Comparing higher education systems.' *Higher Education 21*, 4, 395–402.

Lane, J-E. (1989) 'Linkages of national and institutional decision-making processes in higher education.' Paper presented at the CHER Conference, Twente.

Lane, J-E. (1990) *Institutional Reform. A Public Policy Perspective.* Hampshire: Dartmouth.

Lane, J-E. (1991) 'Sweden in the aftermath of educational reform.' In G. Neave and F. van Vught (eds) *Prometheus Bound: The Changing Relationship Between Government and Higher Education in Western Europe.* Oxford: Pergamon Press.

Lane, J-E. (1992) 'Sweden.' In B. Clark and G. Neave (eds) *The Encyclopedia of Higher Education.* Oxford: Pergamon Press.

Lane, J-E. (1993) *The Public Sector: Concepts, Models and Approaches.* London, SAGE.

Lane, J-E. and Fredriksson, B (1983) *Higher Education and Public Administration.* Stockholm: Almqvist och Wiksell.

Lane, J-E. and Murray, M. (1985) 'The significance of decentralisation in Swedish education.' *European Journal of Education 20*, 2/3 163–170.

Larsson, T. (1993) *Det Svenska Statsskicket.* Lund: Studentlitteratur.

Levine, A. (1980) *Why Innovation Falls: The Institutionalization of Innovation in Higher Education.* Albany: State University of New York Press.

Lewin, L. (1994) 'The rise and decline of corporatism: The case of Sweden.' *European Journal of Political Research 26*, 2/3 59–79.

Liedman, S-E. (1992) *Swedish Unversities – Cumbersome but Dynamic.* Essay written for the OECD 1992 review of Swedish educational policies. Stockholm: Ministry of Education and Science.

Liedman, S-E. and Olausson, L. (eds) (1988) *Ideologi och institution. Om forskning och högre utbildning 1880–2000.* Stockholm: Carlssons Bokförlag.

Lindbeck, A. (1997) *The Swedish Experiment.* Stockholm: SNS.

Lindensjö, B. (1981) *Högskolereformen.* Stockholm: Stockholm University.

Lindensjö, B. and Lundgren, U. (1986) *Politisk styrning och utbildningsreformer.* Stockholm: Liber.

Lundgren, U. (1977) *Model Analysis of Pedagogical Processes.* Lund: Liber.

Lundgren, U. (1996) Utbildningspolitik och utbildningsplanering. Personliga reflektioner. In C. Gustafsson (ed) *Pedagogikforskarens Roll i Utbildningsplanering. Rapport från ett Minisymposium vid Pedagogiska Institutionen, Uppsala Universitet 3 Maj 1994 med Anledning av Urban Dahllöfs Pensionsavgång.* Uppsala University.

Lundqvist, L. (1984) 'Aktörer och strukturer.' *Statsvetenskapliga Tidskrift 87*, 1, 1–22.

Lundqvist, L. (1987) *Implementation Steering. An Actor-Structure Approach.* Lund: Studentlitteratur.

Maassen, P. (1996) *Governmental Steering and the Academic Culture.* Utrecht: Tijdstroom.

Maassen, P. and van Vught, F. (1994) 'Alternative models of governmental steering in higher education.' In L. Goedegebuure and F. van Vught (eds) *Comparative Policy Studies in Higher Education.* Utrecht: Lemma.

Maassen, P. and van Vught, F. (eds) (1996) *Inside Academia. New challenges for the Academic Profession.* Utrecht: Tijdstroom.

MacIntyre, A. (1981) *After Virtue: A Study in Moral Theory.* London: Duckworth.

March, J.M. and Olsen, J.P. (1989) *Discovering Institutions.* New York: The Free Press.

March, J.M. and Olsen, J.P. (1994) 'Institutional perspectives on governance'. In *Systemrationalität und Partialinteresse: Festschrift fur Renate Mayntz/ Hans Ulrich Derlien.* Baden-Baden: Nomos Verlagsgesellschaft.

Marklund, S. (1988) *Paradise Lost? The Nordic Welfare States and the Recession 1975–1985.* Lund: Arkiv.

Marshall, N. (1995) 'Policy communities, issue networks and the formulation of Australian higher education policy.' *Higher Education 30,* 3, 273–293.

Marton, F. (1998) 'Towards a theory of quality in higher education.' In B. Dart and G. Boulton-Lewis (eds) *In Teaching and Learning in Higher Edcuation: From Theory to Practice.* Melbourne: ACER.

Marton, F. and Booth, S. (1997) *Learning and Awareness.* Mahwah, NJ: Lawrence Erlbaum.

Marton, F. and Fazey, J. (1997) Understanding as the Space of Variation Experienced. (Manuscript).

Marton, S. (1997) *Changes in Swedish Higher Education Policy.* Bergen: LOS-Centre Notat 9702.

Marton, S. (forthcoming) *The Mind of the State: The Politics of University Autonomy in Sweden, 1968–1998.* Göteborg: Göteborg Studies in Politics.

Marton, S., Hanney, S., and Kogan, M. (1995) 'Interest groups and elites in higher education policy making: The cases of England and Sweden.' Paper presented at the European Consortium of Political Research, Bordeaux, 27 April–2 May 1995.

Massaro, V. (1997) 'Learning from audit? Preliminary impressions from a survey of OECD countries.' In Högskoleverket (ed) *Quality Assurance as Support for Processes of Innovation.* Stockholm: Högskoleverket Studies 1997:1.

Mayer, E. (1997) 'The future of the research university: German universities and the Humboldt mythos today.' Paper presented at the conference 'University, Idea and Identity,' Göteborg, 24–26 November 1997.

McNay, I. (1995) 'From the collegial academy to corporate enterprise: The changing cultures of universities.' In T. Schuller (ed) *The Changing University?* Buckingham: SRHE and Open Univeristy Press.

Mellbourn, A. (1986) *Bortom det Starka Samhället.* Stockholm: Carlsson.

Merton, R. (1973) *The Sociology of Science; Theoretical and Empirical Investigations.* Chicago: University Press.

Middlehurst, R. (1993) *Leading Academics.* London: Open University Press.

Middlehurst, R. (1997) 'Reinventing higher education: Leadership challenge.' *Quality in Higher Education 3,* 2, 183–198.

Ministry of Education and Science (1993) *Knowledge and Process: The Summary of the Swedish Government's Bills on Higher Education and Research.* Stockholm: Utbildningsdepartementet.

Mishra, R. (1990) *The Welfare State in Capitalist Society.* Toronto: University of Toronto Press.

Moderate Party Programs, 1969, 1979, 1984, 1993. Stockholm: Moderata Samlingspartiet.

Möller, T. (1996) *Brukare och Klienter i Välfärdsstaten.* Stockholm: Publica Norstedts.

Murray, R. (1996) *Productivity of the Public Sector in Sweden.* Stockholm: Finansdepartementet.

Myrdal, G. (1982) *Hur Styrs Landet?* Stockholm: Rabén and Sjögren.

Näringslivets ekonomifakta. *Ekonomifakta.* Stockholm: Näringslivets ekonomifakta AB, various years.

National Agency for Higher Education, see 'Högskoleverket'.

Neave, G. (1988) 'On the cultivation of quality, efficiency and enterprise: an overview of recent trends in higher education in Western Europe 1986–1988.' *European Journal of Education 23*, 2–3, 7–23.

Neave, G. (1994) 'The politics of quality: Developments in higher education in Western Europe 1992–1994.' *European Journal of Education 29*, 2, 115–134.

Neave, G. (1997b) 'The evaluative state: The moment of truth from an imagined Spanish perspective.' Paper presented at the CHER Conference, Alicante 18–20 September 1997.

Neave, G. and van Vught, F. (eds) (1991) *Prometheus Bound. The Changing Relationship Between Government and Higher Education in Western Europe.* Oxford: Pergamon Press.

Newby, H. (1997) 'Keynote speech' delivered at the 19th Aunnual EAIR-Forum at the University of Warwick, 26–29 August 1997.

Niklasson, L. (1996) *Reglering som spel – Universiteten som Förebild för Offentliga Sektorn.* Stockholm: Fritzes.

Nybom, T. (1985) 'Forskning och byråkratisering i Sverige efter 1945 som problem och historia.' Internal Manuscript. Uppsala: Historiska Institutionen.

Nybom, T. (1997) *Kunskap, Politik, Samhälle: Essäer om Kunskapssyn, Universitet och Forskningspolitik 1900–2000.* Hargshamn: Arete.

OECD. *Economic Outlook.* Paris: OECD, various years.

OECD. *Main Economic Indicators.* Paris: OECD, various years.

OECD. *National Accounts*, Vol. I and II, Main Aggregate. Paris: OECD, various years.

Olausson, L. (1995) 'Att blicka framåt i backspegeln.' In M. Bauer (ed) *Universitetet: Ett Framtidstema med Variationer – Röster om Göteborgs Universitet.* Göteborg: Göteborgs universitet, Informationsavdelningen.

Osborne, D. and Gaebler, T. (1992) *Reinventing Government: How the Entrepreneurial Spirit is Transforming the Public Sector.* New York: Penguin.

Pandolfi, A. (1996) 'Den hopplösa könskvoteringen.' In *Svenska Dagbladet.* February 24 1996. Stockholm.

Parliament Education Committee, see 'Utbildningsutskottet betänkande'.

Parsons, M. (1997) *Power and Politics: Federal Higher Education Policymaking in the 1990s.* Albany: State University of New York Press.

Pierre, J. (1995) 'Governing the welfare state: Public administration, the state and society in Sweden.' In J. Pierre (ed) *Bureaucracy in the Modern State: An Introduction to Comparative Public Administration.* Aldershot: Elgar.

Polanyi, M. (1958) *Personal Knowledge. Towards a Post-Critical Philosophy.* London: Routledge & Kegan Paul.

Polanyi, M. (1962) 'The republic of science. Its political and economic theory.' *Minerva 1*, 1, 54–73.

Premfors, R. (1980) *The Politics of Higher Education in a Comparative Perspective.* Stockholm: Stockholm University.

Public Investigative Committee, see 'Statens Offentliga Utredningar', (SOU).

Raab, C. (1992) 'Taking networks seriously: Education policy in Britain.' *European Journal of Political Research 21*, 69–90.

Raab, C. (1994) 'Theorising the governance of education.' *British Journal of Educational Studies 42*, 1. 6–22.

Ramsden, P. (1998) *Learning to Lead in Higher Education.* London: Routledge.

Rasmussen, J. (1998) 'The chief and the ordinary professor. Decentralized and informal relationships as preconditions for strategic management in universities.' *Tertiary Education and Management 4*, 1, 38–47.

Rau, E. (1993) 'Inertia and resistance to change of the Humboldtian university.' In C. Gellert (ed) *Higher Education in Europe*. London: Jessica Kingsley Publishers.

Regeringsproposition (1975:9) *Om Reformering av Högskoleutbildningen*. Stockholm: Allmänna Förlaget/Fritzes.

Regeringsproposition (1976/77:59) *Om Utbildning och Forskning inom Högskolan*. Stockholm: Allmänna Förlaget/Fritzes.

Regeringsproposition (1983/84:52) *Om vissa Högskoleorganisatoriska Frågor*. Stockholm: Allmänna Förlaget/Fritzes.

Regeringsproposition (1987/88:100) *Budget*. Stockholm: Allmänna Förlaget/Fritzes.

Regeringsproposition (1987/88:150) *Bilaga 1*. Stockholm: Allmänna Förlaget/Fritzes.

Regeringsproposition (1988/89:65) *Om Formerna för Högskolepolitiken*. Stockholm: Allmänna Förlaget/Fritzes.

Regeringsproposition (1990/91:150) *Anmälan till Proposition med Förslag till Slutlig Reglering av Statsbudgeten för Budgetåret 1991/92*. Stockholm: Allmänna Förlaget/Fritzes.

Regeringsproposition (1992/93:1) *Universitet & Högskolor – Frihet för Kvalitet*. Stockholm: Allmänna Förlaget/Fritzes.

Regeringsproposition (1992/93:169) *Högre Utbildning för Ökad Kompetens*. Stockholm: Allmänna Förlaget/Fritzes.

Regeringsproposition (1992/93:170) *Forskning för Kunskap och Framsteg*. Stockholm: Allmänna Förlaget/Fritzes.

Regeringsproposition (1993/94:177) *Utbildning och Forskning: Kvalitet och Konkurrenskraft*. Stockholm: Allmänna Förlaget/Fritzes.

Regeringsproposition (1994/95:100) *Särskilda Utbildningssatsningar inom Högskolan*. Stockholm: Allmänna Förlaget/Fritzes.

Regeringsproposition (1994/95:164) *Jämställdhet*. Stockholm: Allmänna Förlaget/Fritzes.

Regeringsproposition (1994/95:165) *Ett Högskoleverk*. Stockholm: Allmänna Förlaget/Fritzes.

Regeringsproposition (1995/96:150) *Ekonomiska Vårproposition*. Stockholm: Allmänna Förlaget/Fritzes.

Regeringsproposition (1995/96:184) *Tillträde till Högre Utbildning m.m.* Stockholm: Allmänna Förlaget/Fritzes.

Remiss: Chalmers University of Technology, 15 April 1992.

Remiss: FRN, 31 March 1992.

Remiss: Göteborg University, 16 April 1992.

Remiss: HFR, 24 January 1974.

Remiss: HSFR, 18 February 1992.

Remiss: Industriförbundet, 22 April 1992.

Remiss: IVA, 30 January 1974.

Remiss: IVA, 22 April 1992.

Remiss: KVA, 22 April 1992.

Remiss: LO, 1974.

Remiss: LO, 3 April 1992.

Remiss: Lund University, 13 April 1992.

Remiss: MFR, 6 December 1973.

Remiss: SACO, 23 November 1973.

Remiss: SACO, 21 April 1992.

Remiss: SAF/IF, 28 January 1974.

Remiss: SAF, 24 April 1992.

Remiss: SFR, 30 January 1974.

Remiss: SFS, 4 March 1974.

Remiss: Stockholm University, 28 November 1974.

Remiss: TCO, 5 February 1974.

Remiss: TCO, 21 April 1992.

Remiss: Umeå University, 25 November 1974.

Remiss: Uppsala University, 27 November 1974.

Rhodes, M. and Marsh, D. (1992) 'New directions in the study of policy networks.' *European Journal of Political Research 21*, 181–205.

Richardson, J. (1997) 'Interest groups, multi-arena politics and policy change.' Paper presented at the Annual Meeting of the American Political Science Association. Washington, 28–31 August 1997.

Ringqvist, M. (1996) *Om den Offentliga Sektorn: Vad Den Ger och Vad Den Tar.* Stockholm: Fritzes.

Rolf, B. (1993) 'Competence, professionality and quality maintenance in higher education.' *Nordisk Pedagogik*, 1, 13, 5–13.

Rolf, B. (1997) 'Kvalitet I högskolans utbildning.' In *Kvalitet och Förbättringsarbete vid Universitet och Högskolor.* Stockholm: Högskoleverkets Skiftserie 1997:4S.

Rolf, B., Ekstedt, E. and Barnett, R. (1993) *Kvalitet och Kunskapsprocess i Högre Utbildning.* Nora: Nya Doxa.

Rothblatt, S. (1994) 'Tesen om universitetets id och dess antites.' *Tvärsnitt 16*, 3–4, 2–9.

Rothblatt, S. (1995) 'An historical perspective on the university's role in social development.' In D. Dill and B. Sporn (eds) *Emerging Patterns of Social Demand and University Reform: Through a Glass Darkly.* New York: Pergamon.

Rothstein, B. (1998) *Just Institutions Matter: The Moral and Political Logic of the Universal Welfare State.* Cambridge: Cambridge University Press.

Rothstein, B. (1988) 'Aktör – strukturansatsen: Ett metodiskt dilemma.' *Statsvetenskapliga Tidskrift 1*, 91, 27–39.

Ruin, O. (1979) *Studentmakt och Statsmakt.* Stockholm: Publica.

Ruin, O. (1982) 'Sweden: External control and internal participation: Trends in Swedish higher education.' In H. Daalder and E. Shils (eds) *Universities, Politicians and Bureaucrats.* Cambridge: Cambridge University Press.

Ruin, O. (1991) 'Bending with the breeze. Political preferences and institutional reforms in the modern university system – a case study.' In M. Trow and T. Nybom (eds) *University and Society. Essays on the Social Role of Research and Higher Education.* Higher Education Policy Studies. London: Jessica Kingsley Publishers.

Sainsbury, D. (1993) 'The Swedish Social Democrats and the legacy of continuous reform: Asset or dilemma?' *West European Politics 16*, 1, 39–61.

Salter, B. and Tapper, T. (1994) *The State and Higher Education.* Ilford: The Woburn Press.

Sánchez-Ferrer, L. (1997) 'From bureaucratic centralism to self-regulation: The reform of higher education in Spain.' *West European Politics 20*, 3, 164–184.

Sannerstedt, A. (1989) *Riksdagen och Lagstiftningen.* Lund: Studentlitteratur.

Scott, P. (1995) *The Meanings of Mass Higher Education.* London: Open University Press.

Scott, P. (1996) 'University governance and management. An analysis of the system and institutional level changes in Western Europe.' In P. Maassen and F. van Vught (eds) *Inside Academia. New Challenges for the Academic Profession.* Utrecht: De Tijdstroom.

Scott, P. (1997) 'The changing role of the university in the production of new knowledge.' *Tertiary Education and Management 3*, 1, 5–14.

Segerstedt, T. (1974) *Hotet mot den Högre Utbildningen.* Stockholm: Askild and Kärnekull.

Selznick, P. (1966) *TVA and the Grass Roots.* New York: Harper and Row.

SFS, see 'Svensk Författingssamling'.

Social Democratic Party Documents: Program för aktiv näringspolitik (1968) *Towards Equality* (1971) and *Industrial Democracy* (1971). Stockholm: Socialdemokratiska Arbetarepartiet.

Social Democratic Party Programs 1975, 1991. Stockholm: Socialdemokratiska Arbetarepartiet.

Söderlind, D. and Petersson, O. (1992). *Svensk Förvaltningspolitik.* Stockholm: Fritzes.

SOU, see 'Statens Offentliga Utredningar'.

Statens Offentliga Utredningar (SOU 1957:24) *Den Akademiska Undervisningen. Forskarrekryteringen.* (U-55) Stockholm: Utbildningsdepartementet.

Statens Offentliga Utredningar (SOU 1959:45) *Universitet och Högskolor i 1960-talets Amhälle.* (U-55) Stockholm: Utbildningsdepartementet.

Statens Offentliga Utredningar (SOU 1963:9) *Universitetens och Högskolornas Organisation och Förvaltning.* (U-55) Stockholm: Utbildningsdepartementet.

Statens Offentliga Utredningar (SOU 1965:11–12) *Utbyggnaden av Universitet och Högskolor. Lokalisering och Kostnader.* (U63) Stockholm: Utbildningsdepartementet.

Statens Offentliga Utredningar (SOU 1973:2) *Högskolan* (U:68) (Högskoleutredningen) Stockholm: Utbildningsdepartementet.

Statens Offentliga Utredningar (SOU 1990:44) *Demokrati och Makt i Sverige.* Stockholm: Allmänna. Förlaget.

Statens Offentliga Utredningar (SOU 1992:1) *Frihet, Ansvar, Kompetens: Grundutbildningens Villkor i Högskolan.* Stockholm: Allmänna Förlaget.

Statens Offentliga Utredningar (1992:15) *Ledning och Ledarskap i Högskolan – Några Perspektiv och Möjligheter.* Stockholm: Utbildningsdepartementet.

Statens Offentliga Utredningar (SOU 1993:3) *Ersättning för Kvalitet och Effektivitet.* Stockholm: Allmänna Förlaget.

Statens Offentliga Utredningar (SOU 1993:16) *Nya Villkor för Ekonomi och Politik.* Stockholm: Fritzes.

Statens Offentliga Utredningar (SOU 1993:102) *Kvalitet och Dynamik.* Stockholm: Allmänna Förlaget.

Statens Offentliga Utredningar (SOU 1995:110) *Viljan att Veta och Viljan att Förstå.* Stockholm: Allmänna Förlaget.

Statens Offentliga Utredningar (SOU 1996:21) *Reform och Förändring. Organisation och Verksamhet vid Universitet och Högskolor efter 1993 Års Universitets-och Högskolereform.* Stockholm: Utbildningsdepartementet.

Statens Offentliga Utredningar (SOU 1996:29) *Forskning och Pengar.* Stockholm: Allmänna Förlaget.

Statens Offentliga Utredningar (SOU 1996:166) *Lärare för Högskola I Utveckling.* Stockholm: Allmänna Förlaget/Fritzes.

Statens Offentliga Utredningar (SOU 1997:7) *Byråkratin i backspegeln- Femtio år av förändring på sex förvaltningsområden.* Stockholm: Allmänna Förlaget.

Statistiska Centralbyrån (1982) *Politiska Resurser – Levnadsförhållanden Rapport 31.* Stockholm:SCB.

Statistiska Centralbyrån (1996a) *Politiska Resurser och Aktiviteter 1978–94 – Levnadsförhållanden Rapport 90.* Stockholm:SCB.

Statistiska Centralbyrån (1996b) *Universitet och Högskolor. Grundutbildning: Nybörjare, Registrerade och Examina 1994/95.* U 20 SM 9601. Stockholm: SCB.

Statistiska Centralbyrån (1996c) Universitet och högskolor. *Personal vid Universitet och Högskolor 1995.* U23 SM 9609. Stockholm: SCB.

Stenelo, L. (ed) (1988) *Makten Över den Decentraliserade Skolan.* Lund: Studentlitteratur. (SFS 1993:886). Stockholm.

Strömholm, S. (1972) *Sverige 1972: Försök till en Lidlesekri Betraktelse.* Stockholm: Norstedt.

Svensk Författningssamling. (SFS 1993:886). Stockholm: Allmänna Förlaget/Fritzes.

Svensk Författningssamling. (SFS 1995:945). Stockholm: Allmänna Förlaget/Fritzes.

Svensson, L. (1987) 'State Control and Academic Autonomy.' Stockholm: UHÄ 1987:4.

Tasker, M.E. and Packham, D.E. (1990) 'Freedom, funding and the future of the universities.' *Studies in Higher Education 15,* 2, 181–195.

TCO (1966) *Post High School (Secondary) Education. ('Den Postgymnasiala Utbildningen')* TCO's utbildningskommittés andra rapport. Stockholm: TCO.

Teichler, U. (1988) *Changing Patterns of the Higher Education System. The Experiences of Three Decades.* London: Jessica Kingsley Publishers.

Teichler, U. (1996a) 'Comparative higher education; potentials and limits.' *Higher Education 32,* 4, 431–465.

Teichler, U. (1996b) 'The conditions of the academic profession.' In P. Maassen and F. van Vught (eds) *Inside Academia. New Challenges for the Academic Profession.* Utrecht: Tijdstroom.

Tight, M. (1992) 'Institutional autonomy.' In B.R. Clark and G. Neave (eds) *International Encyclopedia of Higher Education.* London: Pergamon Press.

Toshach Gustafsson, I. (1996) 'Kursvärderingar vid Göteborgs universitet – beskrivning och analys.' *Skriftserie från Enheten för Kvalitetsutveckling och Kvalitetssäkring,* 15. Göteborg: Göteborg University.

Toulmin, S. (1972) *Human Understanding 1.* Oxford: Clarendon Press.

Trow, M. (1974) 'Problems in the transition from elite to mass higher education.' In *Policies for Higher Education.* General Report of the Conference on Future Structure and Post-Secondary Education. Paris: OECD.

Trow, M. (1993a) 'Reflections of the reform of Swedish higher education.' Paper presented at the Royal Institute of Technology, Stockholm. April 29, 1993.

Trow, M. (1993b) 'Reflections on higher education reform in the 1990s: The case of Sweden.' *Studies of Higher Education and Research 1993:4.* Stockholm: The Council for Studies of Higher Education.

Trow, M. (1994) *Academic Reviews and the Culture of Excellence.* Stockholm: Kanslersämbetet 1994:1.

Trow, M. (1995) *Two Essays on Quality in Higher Education.* Stockholm: Kanslersämbetet 1995:2.

Unckel, P. (1994) *Changing Relationships between the State and Universities.* Paper presented at the OECD/IMHE Conference, Paris, 5–7 September 1994.

Universitetskanslersämbetet (UKÄ) (1970): *Den Akademiska Undervisningen. Principbetänkande Avgivetav Universitetspedagogiska Utredningen (UPU) 1970.* Universitetskanslersämbetet skriftserie nr 10. Stockholm: Utbildningsförlaget.

Universitets och Högskoleämbetet (UHÄ) (1985) 'Arbetsrapport från utredningssektionen 8: Statens utgifter för högskola och forskning 1977–1983 av Lillemor Kim.' Stockholm: UHÄ.

Utbildningsdepartementet (1995) *Universitet och Högskolor i Förändring.* RUT-93, Arbetsrapport nr 1. Stockholm: Utbildningsdepartementet.

Utbildningsutskottet (1997) *Grundläggande Högskoleutbildning. Former för Politik och Planering.* Stockholm: Riksdagen. 1996/97:URD4.

Utbildningsutskottet betänkande (UbU91/92:18). 'Central myndighetsorganisation för högskolan, m.m' Stockholm: Riksdagen.

Utbildningsutskottet betänkande (UbU92/93:14). 'Grundläggande högskoleutbildning'. Stockholm: Riksdagen.

Utbildningsutskottet betänkande (UbU93/94:12). 'Utbildung och forskning'. Stockholm: Riksdagen.

Vabø, A. (1996) 'Instituttsammenslåing som styringsredskap.' In I. Bleiklie (ed) *Kunnskap og makt. Norsk Höyere Utdanning i Endring.* Bergen: Aschehoug.

van Vught, F. (1988) 'A new autonomy in European higher education? An exploration and analysis of the strategy of self-regulation in higher education governance.' *International Journal of Institutional Management in Higher Education 12*, 1, 16–26.

van Vught, F. (ed) (1989) *Governmental Strategies and Innovation in Higher Education.* London: Jessica Kingsley Publishers.

van Vught, F. (1995) 'The new context of academic quality.' In D. Dill and B. Sporn (eds) *Emerging Patterns of Social Demand and University Reform: Through a Glass Darkly.* New York: Pergamon.

van Vught, F. (1997) 'To innovate for quality.' In *Quality Assurance as Support for Processes of Innovation.* Stockholm: Högskoleverket 1997:1.

van Waarden, F. (1992) 'Dimensions and types of policy networks.' *European Journal of Political Research 21*, 29–52.

Verket för Högskoleämbetet (UHÄ) (1994) 'Årsrapport för Universitet och Högskolor 1992/93.' VHS Skriftserie 1994:2, p.60. Stockholm: VHS.

Walford, G. (1988) 'The privatisation of British higher education.' *European Journal of Education 23*, 2/3, 47–64.

Westerheijden, D., Brennan, J. and Maassen, P. (eds) (1994) *Changing Contexts of Quality Assessment. Recent Trends in West European Higher Education.* Utrecht: Lemma.

Westling, H., Angsmark, G. and Blomqvist, G. (1997) 'Universitet och högskolor.' In Statens Offentliga Utredningar (SOU:1997:7) *Byråkratin i Backspegeln. Femtio år av Förändring på sex Förvaltningsområden.* Stockholm: Allmänna Förlaget.

Wittrock, B. (1993) 'The modern university: The three transformations.' In S. Rothblatt and B. Wittrock (eds) *The European and American University since 1800. Historical and Sociological Essays.* Cambridge: Cambridge University Press.

Worcester College (1994) 'Peer review of a Master's programme in pedagogics at the University of Gothenburg.' Göteborg University: Internal Report.

Wyatt, J. (1990) *Commitment to Higher Education. Seven West European Thinkers on the Essence of the University.* Buckingham: SRHE and Open University Press.

Subject
Index

*Page references in italic
indicate figures or tables*

Author Index